ONE WEEK LOAN

Other titles available from Law Society Publishing:

Employment Law Handbook
Daniel Barnett and Henry Scrope

TUPE: A Practical Guide
Gill Sage

Wrongful Dismissal
Julian Yew

All books from Law Society Publishing can be ordered through good bookshops or direct from our distributors, Marston Book Services, by telephone 01235 465656 or e-mail law.society@marston.co.uk (please confirm prices including postage before ordering). For further information or a catalogue, call our editorial and marketing office on 020 7316 5878.

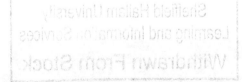

EQUAL PAY

A Practical Guide to the Law

Sara Leslie, Sue Hastings and Jo Morris

The Law Society

ISBN 1–85328–827–6

Published in 2003 by the Law Society
113 Chancery Lane, London WC2A 1PL

Typeset by Columns Design Ltd, Reading
Printed by Antony Rowe Ltd, Chippenham, Wilts

Contents

Acknowledgements

There have been many people over the last 20 years who have shared the authors' fascination with equal pay and have, unknowingly, contributed to the development of this book. A special mention to the Ford sewing machinists, who awakened the interest of many in the complexities of the value of work. We thank them all for their passion and commitment.

A number of individuals have generously given of their time to suggest improvements to the design of the book, comment on the text or give other assistance – Lord Lester of Herne Hill QC; Rita Donaghy, Chair of ACAS; Laura Cox QC; Alice Leonard and Sheila Wild. In particular we would like to thank Vivienne Gay for her painstaking and detailed comments and Janet Noble, Senior Commissioning Editor at Law Society Publishing. We are grateful to them all for their help, but of course the responsibility for any errors is ours alone.

Foreword from Lord Lester QC

The continuing inequality in the pay of men and women is a source of real injustice in the workplace. Equal pay law is notoriously opaque and its procedures are tortuous and open to abuse. This handbook is invaluable as a practical guide for employers, trade unions, lawyers and ordinary women and men seeking to find their way through the labyrinth of UK and EC equal pay law. It draws upon the great experience of three wise and principled individuals, dedicated to the use of law to combat unfair discrimination. It should be read not only by judges and lawyers but everyone who needs to unravel the complexities of the law, practice and procedure in this important area.

Introduction from Rita Donaghy, Chair, ACAS

Thirty years ago the Equal Pay Act outlawed pay discrimination. Since then the pay gap between men and women has narrowed from 31 per cent to 18 per cent. But a significant disparity between men's and women's earnings persists. At the current rate of progress equal pay will take another 42 years to achieve! We cannot afford this waste of human resources.

I had the privilege to be a member of the recent Equal Opportunities Commission (EOC) Equal Pay Task Force. Our report identified three main causes for the gender pay gap: occupational segregation, the unequal impact of women's family responsibilities and pay discrimination. Although the vast majority of employers who gave evidence to the Task Force did not believe they had a gender pay gap within their organisations, we found overwhelming evidence to the contrary. Indeed, we established that nearly half the gap was caused by pay discrimination.

Pay discrimination is of concern to employers, employees and trade unions. It means that employers are vulnerable to unpredictable equal pay claims with serious consequences for their businesses; employees have to undertake lengthy and costly legal proceedings to gain equal pay; and trade unions spend resources on legal challenges that could have been better resolved through normal employment relations channels.

The Advisory, Conciliation and Arbitration Service (ACAS) has a wealth of experience working with employers, employees, trade unions and other representatives. We know that working together in partnership is the best way forward for a lasting solution. ACAS believes that employers and trade unions should work together to resolve the difficult problem of institutional pay discrimination and avoid the need for costly litigation.

Equal Pay, written by experts in the field, is essential reading for anyone with an interest in pay. It explains the causes of unequal pay and demonstrates how to identify the extent of equal pay problems within an organisation. It sets out the practical steps involved in an equal pay audit and provides guidance to ensure that pay and reward systems remain within the law. This book offers practical help to employers, trade unions and lawyers on implementing equal pay.

There has never been a better time for us to take a long hard look at whether our pay systems are fair. I know all too well how easy it is for an organisation unintentionally to discriminate in pay. In 1999, ACAS had a successful equal pay case brought against it by some female staff. We did not intend to discriminate. We have now resolved the issue by joint agreement. If it can happen to ACAS, I believe it can happen to anyone!

I recommend this book to all employers and trade unions that want to ensure their pay systems are fair, as well as to lawyers who advise those involved in equal pay claims.

Table of cases

Table of statutes

Table of statutory instruments, European and international legislation

CHAPTER 1

The origins and causes of the gender pay gap

KEY POINTS

- The historical roots of unequal pay
- The impact of the Equal Pay Act 1970 (EqPA 1970)
- Institutional pay discrimination
- The role of part-time working and family responsibilities
- Race discrimination in pay

1.1 INTRODUCTION

Despite more than 30 years of equal pay legislation, women earn 82 pence for every pound earned by men, and part-time women workers earn 60 pence. The UK has the one of the widest overall gender pay gaps for hourly earnings in Europe.[1]

Recent reports by the government and the Equal Opportunities Commission (EOC) have highlighted the negative impact of the pay gap on women and the economy. The Cabinet Office calculated that the 'female forfeit' for a woman with GCSEs and no children was £241,000 over her lifetime and higher for mothers.[2] Unequal pay follows women into old age. Lower pensions and the long-term effects of divorce and career-breaks contribute to the poverty of older women.

The independent Equal Pay Task Force set up by the EOC in 2000 estimated in its report *Just Pay* that pay discrimination accounted for up to 50 per cent of the large and persistent gender pay gap, with occupational segregation and family responsibilities accounting for the remainder.[3]

While the EqPA 1970 formally made different rates for the same job unlawful, a highly segregated labour market and the perpetuation of de facto women-only grades and pay structures has meant that discrimination continues to exist to an extent almost unparalleled elsewhere in Europe.

The history of UK pay structures has contributed to the stark pay disparity between men and women. Through an understanding of the roots and causes of pay discrimination it is possible to identify hidden discrimination in pay structures that might lead to an equal pay claim.

1.2   ROOTS OF UNEQUAL PAY

Pre-1970

In the early nineteenth century Trade Boards, later Wages Councils, were established to set minimum rates for the sweated trades, notorious for low pay, long hours, and the exploitation of women workers. Trade union witnesses to the Fair Wages Committee of 1907 gave evidence on how men and women were paid different rates for doing exactly the same work. Male knitters were paid almost double the wage of their female colleagues. In the leather trades, the men's rate was 8d an hour, the women's rate was 3d an hour. Mary Macarthur, secretary of the Women's Trade Union League, argued in 1903 that employers made 'some simple adjustment to machinery – a twist drill, perhaps, was replaced by a flat cutter, an automatic stop was fitted to a lathe, and it was declared that the work was not the same'. Blatant wage discrimination continued through the Second World War, when female workers were paid less than the men whose jobs they had taken over. Employers, government and trade unions believed that male workers needed a higher income to support dependants – the so-called family wage. As late as 1971 the National Board for Prices and Incomes argued the 'social significance of the fact that men's earnings are normally the main source of family income'.[4]

In 1968 sewing machinists at Ford's Dagenham factory went on strike for the right to be included on a higher paid grade. Following a job evaluation exercise, the women were placed on the B grade (second lowest), but were paid only 85 per cent of the (male) grade B rate. The women claimed 'we have to pass a test on three machines. If we don't pass that test, then we don't get a job. So why shouldn't they recognise us as skilled workers?' The following year 200 women at Lucas's Acton factory went on strike for equal pay and grading rights. At a time of great social change, these strikes highlighted the radical idea that women's work was unfairly valued simply because it was performed by women. The Employment Minister, Barbara Castle, intervened in the Ford strike on behalf of the women and persuaded her cabinet colleagues to allow time for legislation.

Impact of the Equal Pay Act 1970

The Equal Pay Act became law in 1970, although it did not come into force for another five years. While the intention was to give employers a period of time in which to adapt to the new law, in practice it provoked adaptations to pay structures that often had the effect of institutionalising aspects of pay discrimination. Although specific rates of pay for women were eliminated, de facto women-only grades were created. Jobs were sometimes regraded in a discriminatory way, for example by valuing heavy work above repetitive light work, and negotiating different terms and conditions of employment for men and women doing equal work. Such structures perpetuated the gender segregation in the labour market and sometimes made it harder, not easier, for women to compare their work to men's. Where structures had been negotiated both the employer and the union had a vested interest in the new arrangements, the legacy of which continues to affect many current pay structures.

The question of value

One of the main difficulties of the original EqPA 1970 was its narrow definition of equal pay and the requirement that a woman compare her work to a man doing the 'same or broadly similar work or work rated as equivalent'. The problem was that in a gender-segregated labour market men and women did not do the same work and relatively few employers had carried out job evaluation studies. The EqPA 1970 made no provision for the concept of equal pay for work of equal value embodied in the equal pay provisions of the Treaty of Rome (now Article 141). Infringement proceedings brought by the European Commission against the UK government resulted in the implementation of the Equal Pay (Amendment) Regulations 1983, SI 1983/1794. These Regulations, brought in by an unwilling government, were described in the parliamentary debate as a 'statutory instrument of Byzantine complexity' and by Lord Denning as 'tortuous and complex beyond compare'.

The undervaluing of women's work, especially 'caring' jobs such as nursing, teaching, childcare and service jobs has resulted in systemic inequality. National cultural norms, influenced by a highly segregated labour market, continue to affect the way women's work is assessed and valued. For example, in the UK a full-time qualified female nurse earns 6 per cent less than the average earnings of all male full-time employees. But in contrast equivalent nurses in Australia earn 18 per cent more than average male earnings.[5]

3

A gender-segregated labour market

Women are employed within a very narrow range of occupations – more than 60 per cent of women work in just 10 out of 77 occupations. Many of these 'women's jobs' are low paid with poor employment prospects.[6] The relative low pay of many predominantly female occupations has resulted in pay structures vulnerable to equal value claims, particularly in the public sector and larger private sector companies where a significant number of women work. Equal value challenges have proved costly and unpredictable to employer and claimant alike – cases such as the speech therapists' claim (*Enderby* v. *Frenchay Health Authority and Secretary of State for Health* [1993] IRLR 591, ECJ) led to protracted legal proceedings, taking up scarce NHS resources.

In 1985 five domestic assistants at the Royal Victoria Hospital, Belfast compared their work with that of male porters and groundsmen at the same hospital. Eleven years after the claim was first lodged, the number of domestic assistants claiming equal pay had risen to 900. The Health Board eventually agreed a settlement with the women's union, UNISON, at an estimated cost of over a million pounds.

1.3   INSTITUTIONAL PAY DISCRIMINATION

EOC research has confirmed that a significant proportion of the pay gap is caused by institutional pay discrimination. This includes discriminatory pay and grading systems and a failure to apply equal pay principles to all workers, including part-time and contract workers.

In the service sector full-time female sales assistants earn 45 per cent of the average pay of all male employees.[7] Even in professions where formal equal pay predates the EqPA 1970, such as teaching, the areas where women predominate are lower paid than male preserves – primary school teachers earn less on average than secondary teachers and female secondary teachers earn less than male colleagues. In 2000 the union representing teachers in further and higher education found that women academics were being paid up to £8,000 pa less than men doing the same jobs in exactly the same subjects.[8]

UK pay structures

The particular nature of UK pay structures has compounded the problem of low paid women-only wage rates and grades. For instance, a report by

London local authorities in 1987 cautioned that 'the pay structures in local authorities for manual and craft employees have arisen with little regard to the idea of equal value and the knock-on effects of a successful claim could be enormous'. The authorities examined the gender distribution of bonus, overtime and plus payments and concluded that while there were relatively small differences between the basic rates of men and women, there were enormous differences between their actual earnings. An employee's sex was a better indicator of their earnings than their grade or basic rate – a crucial factor determining an employee's earning was access to bonus and productivity awards. Historically these had been negotiated for male-dominated jobs but not for women's work, where union organisation was weaker and because some managers believed that the women were already 'so productive that there was nothing to be gained from introducing an incentive scheme'.[9]

Evidence suggests that women face overwhelming difficulties establishing gender parity in access to bonuses, increments and fringe benefits.[10] Another potential barrier to equal pay is the secrecy surrounding pay structures and what people earn. Discrimination is most likely to occur where pay systems are not transparent. Additional payments are particularly vulnerable to discrimination where there is a discretionary element or if payments are given to single-sex job groups.

Part-time working

Part-time working, a key feature of a highly segregated labour market, further accentuates the pay gap. Eighty per cent of part-time workers are women and many earn wages under the National Insurance Lower Earnings Limit (LEL) – one in six female employees, many part-timers, aged 25–54 earn below the LEL, compared to one in a hundred male employees. The Low Pay Commission calculated that over two-thirds of the beneficiaries of the national minimum wage were women, of whom two-thirds worked part time. Around 44 per cent of all women work part time: women working part time earn only 74 per cent of the earnings of women working full time.[11]

As well as lower hourly pay, women working part time may have reduced entitlements to a range of pay benefits, including pension contributions, unsocial hours premiums, performance-related pay, additional holiday entitlement and discount schemes. Where work has been redesigned around part-time contracts, wage norms and job security standards may have been decreased. Part-time workers also frequently experience discrimination in recruitment, training and promotion. Part-time jobs tend to be low skilled, with limited opportunities available to work part time in higher grade occupations.

Some employers view high quality flexible work as crucial in their effort to recruit and retain employees and become an employer of choice. By 2011 nearly 80 per cent of workforce growth will be accounted for by women, who will make up over half the employed workforce by 2006.[12] Flexible working for women and men is an important strategy in assisting women combine work and family. Good employers have reorganised work to ensure that employees working flexible patterns are not disadvantaged and trapped in low paid, part-time jobs.

In spite of an increase in flexible work contracts and the new right of parents to request a variation in their working hours to fit in with childcare responsibilities, discrimination against part-time workers continues to be an important factor in pay inequality.

Atypical workers

Women are over-represented in 'non-standard' employment, working as homeworkers, temporary and agency workers, and as casuals. These workers are less likely to receive the pay and benefits of the full-time, permanent employees they work alongside. In some sectors this increases the gender pay gap significantly.

Compulsory competitive tendering

The move towards the privatisation of public services in an increasingly competitive market has had long-term implications for the equal pay principle, particularly in services dominated by women. Compulsory competitive tendering (CCT) resulted in many women across the public sector facing a reduction in hours of work and pay, and a general worsening of terms and conditions of employment. For example, CCT widened existing pay inequalities in local authorities because different approaches were adopted when authorities competed for contracts in services delivered predominantly by women, as compared to those adopted in services dominated by men. In refuse collection, a male-dominated service, pay levels increased and contractual hours remained the same, while women working in catering and cleaning had their hours cut by up to 25 per cent and wages fell in some authorities.[13] The disparity resulted in pay systems vulnerable to equal pay claims.

Costly failure to equality-proof pay arrangements

In 1994, the North Yorkshire Council made radical wage cuts when re-tendering for the school meals service. But other jobs in male-dominated management or traditional blue-collar areas did not have their hours or pay cut in this way. According to Teresa Higgins, who worked for the school meals service, 'Management said we had to take reductions in pay because of CCT. When we found that it was only the ladies in the kitchen who were being asked to take a wage cut, we got extremely angry and we went to the union. Personally I was going to lose £7.51 a week, and yet I was supposed to do more work. Taking the case was horrible for all the year. Not only were we working for less money but management kept telling us we wouldn't win, or we'd lose our jobs.'

The women won and gained not only full reinstatement of pre-CCT terms and conditions, but nearly £5 million in compensation. In 1997 the dinner ladies took further legal action, challenging the 40 per cent productivity bonus paid to male council workers since the early 1970s. The women won the right to the same bonus.[14]

1.4 IMPACT OF FAMILY RESPONSIBILITIES

Family responsibilities play an important part in the pay disparity between men and women. Comparing the UK with six other industrialised countries, the UK has the widest pay penalties for women with children, even those working full time.[15] Women with two children on average suffer an 18 per cent reduction in their lifetime earnings and women with three children lose 30 per cent when compared to childless women employees. The lack of family friendly employment practices, together with inadequate childcare provision are likely to be reasons why the UK fares worse than other countries. The level of a woman's educational achievement has the biggest impact on her likely earnings, but how many children she has, when she has them and the number of hours she works all have a significant impact on her lifetime income.[16]

In its evidence to the Equal Pay Task Force, the CBI highlighted how 'employers and the economy as a whole are losing out' because women who have relatively high skills are working in lower skilled jobs as a way of balancing work and caring responsibilities. Maternity and paternity provision as well as paid parental leave and flexible employment practices can be crucial factors in redressing the financial penalties of family responsibilities.

1.5 RACE

Black workers continue to face inequality in pay, despite nearly a generation of race relations legislation. While there is a wide variation between different ethnic groups, there is a concentration of black workers in low paid sectors, such as textiles and security. Within these sectors black workers tend to be concentrated in lower graded occupations. In 2001 the overall difference in average weekly earnings between black and white men was £97. Black women are likely to be faced with the double discrimination of race and gender. Hourly pay varies considerably according to ethnic group.

Research has shown that where subjective judgements are involved, such as the placing of a worker on a point on a pay scale, discrimination can affect the outcome. Performance-related pay schemes are particularly likely to discriminate. A major study into pay inequality commissioned by the Cabinet Office and the Council for Civil Service Unions found 'statistically significant differences in box markings' in relation to black workers as compared to white workers.[17] This is illustrative of how indirect race discrimination can take place even in an organisation committed to racial equality and despite the highly organised collective bargaining arrangements of the Civil Service.

The Race Relations Act 1976 (as amended) (RRA 1976) requires employers not to discriminate on grounds of race or ethnicity. This means that a black or ethnic minority worker could claim equal pay with a white colleague of either the same or opposite sex or vice versa. Some cases have been taken, for example, by Indian male nurses complaining that they were undergraded compared to their white colleagues, but these are rare. The new code of practice, linked to the Race Relations (Amendment) Act 2000 (RRA 2000), encourages employers to monitor their employees by ethnic origin. The revised EOC *Code of Practice on Equal Pay* advises that public sector organisations that are obliged by the RRA 2000 to adopt an equality plan should ensure that their equal pay review deals with any pay gaps between workers from different ethnic groups, as well as the gaps between men's and women's pay.

1.6 CONCLUSION

The causes of pay discrimination in the UK are rooted in the past. Ending institutional discrimination in pay systems can be challenging for employer and union alike because it disrupts established differentials and assumptions. Most pay discrimination is unintentional and arises because

8

employers and union negotiators have simply not thought about the impact of long-standing pay arrangements.

Despite the extent of gender pay disparity in the UK, the EOC Equal Pay Task Force reported in *Just Pay* that there was:

> ... a surprising and worryingly widespread lack of awareness of the existence and persistence of the gap between women's and men's pay ... evidence suggests that the vast majority of employers do not believe they have a gender pay gap and therefore do not believe an equal pay review is necessary ...

(Just Pay, 2001)

The subtlety and hidden nature of pay disparity means that an employer is unlikely to be sure that a pay structure is free from bias unless a pay review is undertaken that includes all elements of the pay package.

The following chapters outline the practical steps for employers and unions who wish to ensure that pay systems are free from discrimination and are not vulnerable to costly legal challenge.

ENDNOTES

1. *European Structure of Earnings Survey*, SES, 1995.
2. *Women's Incomes Over a Lifetime*, Cabinet Office Women's Unit, 2000.
3. *Just Pay: Report of the Equal Pay Task Force*, EOC, 2001.
4. *Campaigning to Close the Gap*, TUC, 2000.
5. Grimshaw, D. and Rubery, J., *The Gender Pay Gap: A Research Review*, EOC, 2001.
6. Ibid.
7. *New Earnings Survey*, Office for National Statistics, 2000.
8. NAFTHE Report, 2000.
9. *A Question of Earnings: A Study of the Earnings of Blue-Collar Employees in London Local Authorities*, London Equal Value Steering Group, 1987.
10. Lissenburgh, S., *Value for Money: The Costs and Benefits of Giving Part-time Workers Equal Rights*, (Report for the TUC), 1996.
11. *New Earnings Survey*, Office for National Statistics, 2000.
12. Institute for Employment Research, 2001.
13. Escott, K. and Whitfield, D., *The Gender Impact of CCT Local Government*, EOC, 1995.
14. *Campaigning to Close the Gap: Celebrating 30 Years of the Equal Pay Act*, TUC, 2000.
15. Harkness, S. and Waldfogel, J., *The Family Gap in Pay*, Centre for the Analysis of Social Exclusion, 1999.

16. *Women's Incomes Over a Lifetime*, Cabinet Office Women's Unit, 2000.
17. *Equality in Performance Review*, CAPITA/Institute of Employment Studies, 2001.

CHAPTER 2

Pay systems and discrimination in the UK

KEY POINTS

There is a great diversity of pay systems in the UK. This chapter examines:

- The impact of collective bargaining arrangements on pay structures
- The elements of pay structures
- Types of basic pay structures
- Additional payments to basic pay, for example, performance payments, payments for experience or seniority, working patterns, payments in kind
- How each of these elements of pay structures, while gender-neutral in theory, may in practice discriminate against female employees

---

2.1 IMPACT OF COLLECTIVE BARGAINING ARRANGEMENTS

There is a great diversity of pay systems in the UK, partly as a result of our decentralised collective bargaining arrangements (as compared to other European countries). Historically, pay structures have also been fragmented, in parallel with collective bargaining structures within organisations. So, for example, it has been common for large manufacturing companies, as in motor manufacturing for instance, to have up to four or five distinct pay structures matching their collective bargaining arrangements – for production workers, technical employees, administrative and clerical staff, senior managers and possibly a separate craft structure also. Manufacturing companies operating at different locations may also have different collective bargaining arrangements and pay structures at the different sites, especially where the current organisation is the product of past mergers.

In banking until the mid-1980s, there was a nationally agreed pay structure for cashiering and clerical staff, plus separate individual bank arrangements for what were known as the 'appointed grades', senior managers and for messengers and related support workers. Even in small companies, where structures are often less formalised, it is nevertheless common to have distinct arrangements for different groups, for instance, production workers on skill-related hourly rates of pay (or piece rates – see below), technical and clerical staff on annual salaries.

Public sector pay systems, although generally negotiated at national level, have been equally fragmented between different bargaining arrangements. Until the 'single status' agreement of 1997, local government had separate collective bargaining arrangements for manual workers, APT&C (administrative, professional, technical and clerical) employees, craft workers and chief officers, not to mention those covered by what are known as the Burgundy Book arrangements (on account of the cover colour of the agreement handbook). The 1997 agreement merged the first two of these groups but left all other arrangements and pay structures as they were. The NHS currently has more than 20 separate 'Whitley' sub-committees (named after the civil servant who started collective bargaining in the public sector) for pay bargaining purposes, each with its associated grading and pay structure, all of which are under review as part of the government's Health Service pay modernisation process.

Where such collective bargaining arrangements are associated with domination by one gender or the other, especially where some groups are regarded as more powerful than others, then the arrangements may constitute an integral part of institutionalised pay discrimination. For example, a male-dominated production group may have levered higher pay rates through the threat of industrial action, thus establishing an increased differential with the female-dominated administrative and clerical support group. Even if the increased differential cannot be justified by the relative demands of the jobs, it is nevertheless perpetuated over time and becomes part of the organisation's pay structure legacy.

2.2   ELEMENTS IN THE PAY STRUCTURE

Although not all pay structures neatly fit the framework and some systems combine two or more elements, it is helpful to use a building block analogy:

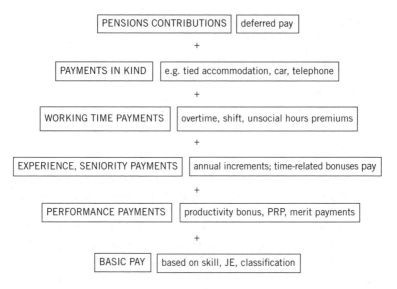

Figure 2.1 Elements in the pay structure

2.3 BASIC PAY SYSTEMS

Most basic pay systems fall into a limited number of forms, based on one of the following:

1. *Broad skill or competence levels*
   Traditionally, this type of system applied to production workers, who were categorised as skilled, semi-skilled or unskilled. The modern version is more likely to cover most employees and to be based on National Vocational Qualifications (NVQs), the Scottish equivalent (SVQs) or an in-house equivalent. For example, at Scottish Power's wholesale generation division, the six-grade structure for support workers to power station managers is based on SVQs modified to suit the particular skill 'pathways' required by the organisation.

2. *Market rates*
   Some organisations do not have formal internal grading structures, but pay their employees in accordance with 'the market rate' for the particular type of work. Such systems are often found in high technology companies and among senior managers in both private and public sector organisations.

3. *Classification system*
   Such systems take account of skill levels, but also levels of

responsibility and decision making, combined into grading definitions for groups such as:

- administrative assistant;
- administrative officer;
- executive officer;
- senior executive officer;
- higher executive officer.

4. *Job evaluation scheme*

Because the concepts and practices of job evaluation are relevant to several sections of this book and integral to an understanding of equal pay legislation, they are examined in more detail in **Chapter 3**. Here it is sufficient to say that under a job evaluation scheme, jobs to be graded are analysed under a set of factor headings (for example, knowledge and skills, responsibilities, effort) and then assessed against the scheme's levels of demand for each factor. The outcomes are total weighted scores for each job, giving a rank order, which forms the basis for a grading structure.

Discrimination occurs in basic pay structures if the grading scheme or system itself is discriminatory, perhaps by using criteria that are more appropriate to jobs carried out by men than to jobs undertaken by women, or if it is implemented in a discriminatory way.

2.4 PERFORMANCE PAYMENT SYSTEMS

The second pay structure element identified is payment for performance. As with basic pay structures, there are a limited number of main forms:

1. *Productivity bonus schemes*

Here employees can earn additional payments, or bonuses, on top of their basic pay, by achieving pre-set work rates (usually based on work study systems of measurement). Such systems are most commonly found in organisations where production or service levels are relatively easily quantified (for example, number of units produced, number of dustbins emptied).

2. *Piece rate payment systems*

These combine basic pay with the productivity bonus and have been the usual basis for pay in the textiles, clothing and footwear sectors and in some forms of metal manufacture. So, while there may be a weekly or hourly 'fall back' rate for those situations where there is no work to do or the employee is unable to achieve the pre-set rate, most of total earnings comes from undertaking duties at an above-standard rate.

3. *Performance-related payment (PRP) systems*
    PRP systems more usually apply to non-manual employees, who are appraised annually or more frequently against a predetermined set of performance criteria or agreed objectives.

4. *Merit payment systems*
    These are a form of performance-related pay, but usually less dependent on pre-set criteria or targets and more dependent on line managers' assessment of the performance of their subordinates.

5. *Target-based bonus schemes*
    These are the 'white-collar' version of productivity bonus schemes for manual workers. They are common in sales generally and in investment banking and finance, in particular. In such systems, individual employees are rewarded according to their level of 'sales', often called 'commission' in the retail sector. The target levels may be pre-advertised to employees, or in some cases, for example, in the investment banking sector, they are determined retrospectively, when overall sales are known.

6. *Profit-related pay systems*
    Such systems reward employees in accordance with the overall financial performance of the organisation or some part of it.

Again, discrimination can occur either in the design of the productivity or performance measurement system (for example, by setting more demanding work rates or targets for jobs carried out by women compared to those set for men) or, more commonly, through the way in which the performance system is implemented. In many textile and clothing firms, for instance, there were separate piece rate or productivity schemes covering the female machinists and the generally male cutters or weavers. The belief prevailed among employers and unions in the relevant sectors that there was no discrimination in such schemes, because some women could earn more than most men. The more appropriate comparison is between the average earnings of women and men, or pay for the standard measured work rates. The latter were often set, so that most men earned more than most women.

A further major cause of discrimination is that of assessment. Performance and merit (and in some cases, retrospectively determined targets and bonus levels) are inherently subjective concepts and therefore risk introducing scope for gender and race discrimination. Research has indicated that different criteria may be used in practice in assessing performance for employees of different genders and ethnic minorities (Grimshaw, D. and Rubery, J., *The Gender Pay Gap: A Research Review*, EOC, 2001).

Additional problems can arise in relation to performance payment systems, where women are excluded from them, for example, if their work is less readily subject to quantification, or on account of their working arrangements, for instance, if part-time employees are outside the scope of the pay system because it relates to productivity, performance or profit.

In the local government sector, for instance, where productivity bonus arrangements have been in place since the early 1970s, schemes were readily applied to refuse collectors, on the basis of the numbers of bins emptied, and to grounds maintenance workers, on the basis of areas mowed or pruned. They were not generally applied to home helps and school meals staff, partly because the work rates of these groups were seen as more difficult to measure. The other reason was that these jobs were usually carried out by part-time employees, who were specifically excluded from the scope of the productivity bonus schemes.

2.5 EXPERIENCE, SENIORITY PAYMENTS

There are only two main types:

1. Incremental pay scales, in which a job is allocated to a pay scale, up which the employee moves virtually automatically a step at a time, usually on the anniversary of starting the job or on a set date in the year (historically, on the employee's birthday). Such systems were common in most large white-collar organisations in both private and public sectors and remain so for some public sector groups, for example, school teachers, university lecturers. The length of the incremental scale can vary from two or three points up to nine or 10.
2. One-off payments or additions to basic pay when an employee has achieved a pre-set number of years' service with the organisation, for example, after 10, 15, 20 or 25 years' service. Such long service payments may be in money form and/or in terms of additional leave entitlements.

Experience and seniority payments have been common in organisations where employees have been expected to spend their whole career. They can discriminate against women, if they are less likely to follow traditional male career patterns. They may also cause discrimination where a part-time worker is required to work a longer number of years than a full-time worker in order to be promoted to another grade.

2.6 WORKING TIME PAYMENTS

It is common practice in the UK to pay additional premium payments over and above the basic rate for the job to those employees who work non-standard patterns. The aim is to compensate for the social inconvenience and possible adverse health effects of such practices, while also providing an incentive to people to work non-standard patterns. Examples are:

(a) shift premium payments for those who work rotating (early, late and night) or alternating (early and late, but no night) shifts, usually on a rostered system;
(b) unsocial hours payments to those who work outside whatever are considered to be 'normal' working hours, but generally to a less rigid pattern than rotating shifts;
(c) weekend premium payments (which may vary as to whether the working pattern covers Saturdays and/or Sundays) for those whose working pattern includes weekend work;
(d) overtime premium payments for those who work beyond the agreed normal weekly hours.

Discrimination may occur if women do not have access to such payments for the types of work they do outside normal hours (for example, when working 'twilight' evening shifts), or if their working patterns accrue disproportionately low compensation compared to the premium payments made for working patterns associated with men. Historically, women working part time have received lower shift premiums for unsocial hours working, such as the early morning or twilight shifts, while full-time male colleagues received overtime rates for working at these hours.

2.7 PAYMENTS IN KIND

The main forms are:

(a) accommodation at reduced rents or rent free for those whose work requires them to be available on site;
(b) cars, either in relation to mobile jobs (company salespersons, district nurses) or as an addition to basic pay, generally to senior managers;
(c) regular supplies of the company's product, for example, coal to miners, sugar to the employees of a sugar refinery.

Such payments in kind can be discriminatory, where male-dominated groups and female-dominated groups are treated differently, for example, reduced rent for resident wardens of sheltered accommodation for the elderly, while housing caretakers have rent free property; different models of car for male and female senior managers; or where access criteria are in practice more difficult for women to meet, for instance, an initial service or a minimum number of hours qualification.

2.8 TYPES OF PAY SYSTEM

The pay structure elements discussed above can be combined in different ways to give different types of pay structure, for example:

1. Manual, production, stores and warehouse employees have generally received flat or spot rates of pay for a job based either on its skill level, or on a job evaluated structure, as, for instance, at most of the major motor manufacturing companies in Britain.

2. Employees on spot or flat rates may receive an hourly rate, which is deemed to be 'the rate for the job', or alternatively they may be paid at a lower rate, but in either case with the opportunity to increase their earnings through a productivity bonus system. Such systems operate in many manufacturing industries and in some parts of the public sector, for instance, local government.

3. The jobs of non-manual employees have more often been graded according to a classification or job evaluation system, each grade being associated with an incremental pay scale through which individuals have moved with experience in post. In such systems there is no, or limited, overlap between the pay scales for different grades.

4. As automatic incremental pay scales went out of fashion in the 1980s, some, especially in the private sector, but also in government departments and some other parts of the public sector, were replaced by movement on the basis of performance, for instance, up to and above a scale mid-point, which reflected the evaluated rate for the job.

5. In some private and public sector organisations, discrete pay scales have been replaced by broad and usually overlapping pay bands or ranges, often with no published steps and within which movement is on a percentage increase basis. Jobs are placed in a pay band on the basis of a job evaluation system, or less frequently a competence level system. Movement within the pay range is usually dependent on assessment of performance or competence.

6. In all the above systems, the aim of the organisation is to position the

overall pay structure in relation to its general or local labour market, so that rates of pay or annual salaries are sufficient to recruit and retain suitable staff, but do not result in excessive pay bill costs. An organisation may purchase labour market survey data to assist in setting its pay structure at the desired level against the market. Where this results in difficulties in recruiting to some jobs, for example, information technology specialists, then some form of market supplement is often paid.

7. In a purely market-based pay system, all salaries are determined by reference to labour market surveys and are uprated according to market movements. Market-related salaries may be a fixed annual salary or be supplemented by some sort of performance payment system, for example, when organisational targets are met.

Discrimination can occur in either the design or the implementation of the payment system, or both, for example:

(a) in design, if job evaluation grade boundaries are drawn in such a way as to leave predominantly female groups just below the boundary and predominantly male groups just above;

(b) in implementation, if recruiters are given discretion over starting salaries within a broad salary range and their decisions result in lower average starting salaries for women than for men.

Problems may also occur as a result of the assimilation process by which existing employees are transferred from an old pay structure to a new one. For example, long-standing male employees may be assimilated from the top of an incremental pay scale into the top part of a broad banded structure, while women whose jobs have been upgraded as a result of a job evaluation exercise may be promoted into the bottom part of the same salary range, but can never in practice achieve the same salaries as their male colleagues on account of the performance system rules.

The identification of pay structure discrimination often only happens when an equal pay claim is taken to tribunal (see **Chapters 6–16**). A more constructive approach may be an equal pay review and action plan to rectify any pay discrimination identified (see **Chapter 5**).

2.9 'TRANSPARENCY'

Pay structures in the UK, especially in the private sector but in more recent years in parts of the public sector, have sometimes been quite secretive, in the sense that employees have not known or understood how their own pay was made up and have been unaware of the systems for determining pay generally within the organisation. In some organisations, employees are not allowed to disclose their salary to others. Such pay structures may give rise to suspicions of pay discrimination, whether justified or not, and are open to challenge under equal pay legislation. Where the pay structure is not 'transparent', and there is some indication of pay discrimination, the burden of proof switches to the employer to demonstrate that the pay system is fair and non-discriminatory (see **Chapter 11**).

CHAPTER 3

Job evaluation

KEY POINTS

Job evaluation is relevant to equal pay in a number of ways. This chapter looks at:

- What is job evaluation
- How to develop a job evaluation system
- How job evaluation systems can result in pay discrimination

(How job evaluation can be used to implement equal pay is considered in **Chapter 4**.)

3.1   WHAT IS JOB EVALUATION?

Job evaluation is a technique for comparing the demands of jobs within a population or organisation, in order to develop a rank order of jobs, usually as the basis for a grading and pay structure. There are a number of different types of job evaluation scheme, but what most have in common are:

(a)   an analysis of job demands under a selected set of criteria or headings (usually called factors, but sometimes characteristics or elements); and

(b)   a comparison of each job under each factor heading, either with other jobs or against a scale of demand.

3.2   TYPES OF JOB EVALUATION

The main types of job evaluation scheme are:

1.   *Non-analytical systems*, in which jobs are compared with each other on a whole job basis. In such systems, jobs may either be placed in

a rank order on the basis of an assessment of the overall job demands (whole job ranking), or each job can be compared in turn with every other job (whole job paired comparisons). These schemes are increasingly rare and do not meet the requirements of the equal pay legislation (see **Chapters 10 and 11**), so are not further considered in this chapter.

2. *Analytical paired comparison systems*, in which each job is compared with every other job under each of the selected factor headings. This approach is best suited to small numbers of jobs and can be used for making equal value assessments (see **Chapter 4**) but becomes unwieldy for large numbers of jobs, where the number of comparisons to be made increases geometrically.

3. *Factor points rating systems*, in which each job is compared against a common scale of demand under each factor heading and then checked against the other jobs evaluated to ensure consistency. These are the most common form of job evaluation in the UK.

3.3   ELEMENTS OF A JOB EVALUATION SCHEME

The elements of a points rating system are:

(a) a set of factors (which often fall into groups under main headings, such as knowledge and skills, responsibilities, effort and environment);

(b) defined levels of demand for each factor;

(c) a scoring system giving a number of points to each level on each factor scale;

(d) a weighting system, to reflect the relative contribution of each factor to the organisation.

3.4   DESIGNING A JOB EVALUATION SCHEME

The steps in designing a points rating system are:

1. Identify factor headings, which between them encompass all the significant features of all the jobs to be evaluated. Test that this is the case by analysing a benchmark sample of jobs against the selected factors. Revise if necessary in the light of the tests.

2. Define the scope of each selected factor to ensure that it measures a discrete job feature.

3. Using information about the benchmark sample of jobs from step 1 and any other available information about the job population (for example, organisational job descriptions, organisation charts, previous job evaluation documents) identify distinct demand levels for each of the selected factors.

4. Define each factor level. Test, through trial or pilot evaluations, that the levels are appropriate to the jobs and user friendly to those who will apply the scheme. Revise the level definitions, if necessary in the light of the pilot exercise, and develop any additional guidance considered necessary to enable evaluators to apply the system consistently across all jobs.

5. Develop a scoring system. The simplest system would be one point per level per factor, but scoring systems are usually larger than this, for example, 10 or more points per level.

6. Agree a weighting system that reflects the values of the organisation, for example, by reference to a mission statement. The weighting system may be applied as a multiplier to the factor scores (for example, multiply all knowledge scores by two) or built into the scoring system (knowledge scores to increase in steps of 20, while scores for effort factors increase in steps of 10). The effect is the same.

3.5 IMPLEMENTING A JOB EVALUATION SCHEME

The steps in implementing a points rating job evaluation system are then:

1. Collect information about each job in relation to the general job duties and responsibilities, and to the job demands under each factor heading – usually by means of a job questionnaire and/or interview with a trained job analyst, or from a detailed job description.

2. Evaluate each job separately against the factor plan, identifying which level definition for each factor best matches the information from the job questionnaire or description. In a paper-based job evaluation scheme, this stage is carried out by a small trained panel or committee.

3. At regular intervals during and again at the end of the evaluation process, undertake checks on a factor-by-factor basis to ensure that job evaluations are consistent. At the end of the process, it is also usual to identify any jobs that appear to stand out as unusual or out of place, in terms of the total weighted score, and to recheck all stages of the process for these jobs. This is often called 'sore-thumbing'.

4.   Apply the scoring and weighting systems to the job evaluations, to give a total weighted score for each job, which can then be put in rank order.

3.6   COMPUTERISED JOB EVALUATION

In large organisations, carrying out job evaluation is inevitably a major exercise, as all distinct jobs may need to have job questionnaires completed, analysed and evaluated. In order to speed up the process, computer software has been developed to:

(a)   apply the scoring and weighting systems to panel evaluations: this is sometimes called computer aided job evaluation;

(b)   combine the roles of job analyst and evaluation panel through completion by the analyst of a structured questionnaire, at or following the interview with the jobholder (this can be input direct to a computerised system, thus avoiding the need for evaluation panels to meet);

(c)   allow jobholders, with the assistance of a trained analyst or facilitator, to respond directly to an on-screen questionnaire (this avoids the need for both evaluation panel and completion of lengthy paper job questionnaires – these systems may be referred to as interactive computerised schemes).

3.7   HOW JOB EVALUATION SCHEMES CAN DISCRIMINATE

It can be seen from the above description that the technique of job evaluation is gender-neutral. Historically, however, job evaluation was often used to achieve specific purposes, for example, to replicate internally the external labour market; or to develop or maintain a desired organisational hierarchy. These aims could be achieved by, for instance:

(a)   selecting only those factors that reflected the external labour market or the pre-existing hierarchy;

(b)   defining the factors and levels to achieve the desired rank order;

(c)   developing the weighting system by reference to a 'felt-fair' rank order of jobs, often through a statistical technique called regression analysis, which calculates what factor weighting will most nearly achieve a predetermined 'felt-fair' rank order.

If the external labour market or the previous organisational hierarchy incorporated any elements of sex discrimination, then these are likely to be reproduced and perpetuated by such a job evaluation scheme.

There are relatively few legal cases on how job evaluation schemes can discriminate (see **Chapter 11**). In the absence of comprehensive legal guidance, both the European Commission and the Equal Opportunities Commission for Great Britain (EOC) have produced checklists to assist employers in reviewing their job evaluation schemes for bias. The most recent version of the EOC Checklist forms part of the Equal Pay Review Kit guidance notes (see **Chapter 5**) and is reproduced in **Annex 3A**.

In summary, the key sources of discrimination identified in these checklists are:

1. Omission or undervaluation of features of predominantly female jobs. Examples are caring and other interpersonal skills, responsibilities for clients, customers or members of the public generally, organisational skills and responsibilities (as in office management) and manual dexterity.
2. Double counting of features of predominantly male jobs. One scheme developed in the context of an equal pay claim had separate factors to measure decision making, problem solving, and analysis and judgement. As these concepts overlap and the male comparator job scored higher than the claimant job on all three factors, this is an example of discriminatory double counting.
3. Use of quantitative rather than qualitative measures of demand, for example, numbers of people supervised, rather than the nature of the supervision; size of budget, rather than the nature of the financial responsibility; formal qualifications, rather than the breadth and depth of knowledge required for the job.
4. Failure to 'capture' all the demands of jobs, particularly female-dominated jobs, in the job description or job description questionnaire.
5. Lack of training, particularly in the avoidance of bias, of analysts, evaluators and others involved in the process.

3.8 JOB EVALUATION AND THE EQUAL PAY ACT

Job evaluation features in the Equal Pay Act 1970 in a number of ways:

1. A claimant may argue that her job has been 'rated as equivalent' to that of a higher paid man under a fair and non-discriminatory job evaluation (see **Chapter 10**).
2. A claimant may argue that her job would have been rated as equivalent if the scheme had not been applied in a discriminatory way (also **Chapter 10**).

3. An employer may respond to an equal value claim by arguing that there is a fair and non-discriminatory job evaluation system covering both claimant and comparator jobs, which shows that the claimant job is of lower value than the comparator job(s) (see **Chapter 11**).

4. A job evaluation scheme may be used by experts on behalf of the parties, or occasionally by an independent expert, in an equal value claim to show that the jobs are or are not of equal value (see **Chapter 4**).

ANNEX 3A

The EOC Equal Pay Review Kit

Reproduced by kind permission of the Equal Opportunities Commission

[...]

GUIDANCE NOTE 4: JOB EVALUATION SCHEMES FREE OF SEX BIAS

The checklists

The aim of the checklists is to help you to ensure that the job evaluation scheme or schemes that you are using, or are intending to use, does not either directly or indirectly discriminate on grounds of sex. *You should complete the checklists for each job evaluation scheme used in your organisation. It is important to answer all of the questions in order to check each aspect of the scheme for sex bias.* If you do not know the answers to some of the questions, for example, about the background, or detailed design of, the scheme, you should seek the information from those who were involved, for instance, senior human resources staff, earlier generations of job evaluation panel members and longstanding trade union representatives. You may also need to contact the consultants who implemented the scheme or the external supplier.

Checklist 1: Background information

1.1   WHAT IS THE SCHEME CALLED?

1.2   WHICH GROUPS OF EMPLOYEES ARE COVERED BY THE SCHEME?

Excluding groups of jobs from a job evaluation scheme may perpetuate sex bias, especially if the groups excluded are composed predominantly of employees of one sex. Discrimination in the grading and pay of the jobs of female employees often occurs or is perpetuated by their separation into a different grading structure based on a different job evaluation scheme, or none at all. Incorporating female jobs within the same job evaluation scheme as the male jobs, provided that the job evaluation scheme is not discriminatory, will help you to achieve equal pay for equal work.

Clearly, you should only exclude groups of employees from a scheme for justifiable and non-discriminatory reasons. Employers and trade unions should appreciate that problems can be created if bargaining units are used as the sole basis for the scope of jobs to be covered, since this can often be discriminatory. Claims for equal pay for work of equal value can be brought where separate schemes or collective bargaining arrangements are used to justify differences in pay between the sexes, or where members of one sex are left out of a job evaluation scheme.

1.3 WHEN WAS THE JOB EVALUATION SCHEME INTRODUCED?

Older schemes are likely to have been developed without an understanding of the implicit or hidden forms of sex discrimination, if your scheme has been in use for several years you should review it to ensure that it does not discriminate on grounds of sex.

1.4 HAS THE SCHEME BEEN REVIEWED TO ENSURE THAT IT COMPLIES WITH GOOD EQUAL OPPORTUNITIES PRINCIPLES AND PRACTICES?

You should review your schemes regularly to check that they do not unwittingly discriminate against female employees.

1.5 IS THE JOB EVALUATION SCHEME TRANSPARENT?

If a pay system, or any part of it, is characterised by a total lack of transparency, the burden of proof is on the employer to show that the pay practice is not discriminatory. In respect of job evaluation, 'transparent' means that information about the design and implementation of the scheme should be available to employees in a readily understandable form.

1.6 WAS THE JOB EVALUATION SCHEME:

(a) developed in-house?
(b) modified from an external supplier's framework?
(c) bought 'off the shelf' from an external supplier?

If the scheme was either developed in-house or modified from the framework provided by an external supplier you should be able to use the checklists to test whether the scheme is non-discriminatory. If it was bought 'off the shelf' you will need to assure yourself that that supplier has reviewed the principles and practices of their scheme, in accordance with the guidance given here. You will also need to use the checklists to check out the way in which you are implementing the scheme.

1.7   IS THE JOB EVALUATION SCHEME COMPUTERISED?

Increasingly, the process of job evaluation is being computerised so that, for example, information on jobs is inputted onto computers in the form of answers to pre-formulated questions and a score for the job is then given. Schemes that are computerised are often quicker to implement and they are not inherently discriminatory. However, any computerised system will reflect the nature of the information it analyses. Therefore, it is important to ensure that your computerised scheme gathers comprehensive information about jobs and is based on factors that are non-discriminatory. At the benchmarking stage, an evaluation of the benchmark jobs should be made using both the computerised scheme and written job descriptions or completed job questionnaires. A comparison of the two exercises should then be undertaken to check for sex bias.

Checklist 2: The design of the scheme

2.1   IS THE SCHEME ANALYTICAL?

A job evaluation scheme must be analytical for it to be accepted by the courts as an appropriate method for determining whether jobs are, or are not, equivalent. You as the employer (rather than the supplier or consultant) must show that the scheme is analytical.

2.2   DOES THE SCHEME'S FACTOR PLAN FAIRLY MEASURE ALL SIGNIFICANT FEATURES OF ALL THE JOBS IT COVERS?

In particular, does the factor plan fairly measure all the significant features of jobs typically undertaken by women, for example, interpersonal skills, manual dexterity, responsibilities for customers, clients or members of the public?

A job evaluation scheme must be based on factors that fairly value all the main demands of the jobs covered by the scheme, irrespective of whether men or women perform them. Factors that tend to favour workers of one sex (e.g. physical effort) can be included, as long as the scheme also includes factors that tend to favour the other sex (e.g. manual dexterity).

To check whether a scheme factor plan fairly measures all significant demands of jobs *either*:

● Analyse job information (job descriptions, person specifications) from a sample of typically male and female jobs, listing the main job features and compare them with the scheme factors. If there are job features not covered by the factors, you should consider whether these factors are more common in jobs typically carried out by one gender or the other; *or*

- Check the scheme factors against a list of frequently overlooked factors and a list of factors that favour typically male or female jobs.

If the scheme factors favour predominantly one sex, then this may indicate that factors favouring the other sex have been omitted.

2.3   DO THE FACTOR LEVELS IN THE JOB EVALUATION SCHEME REFLECT MEASURABLE STEPS IN DEMAND WITHIN THE JOBS COVERED BY THE SCHEME?

Factor levels should reflect significant and measurable differences in levels of demand, which are appropriately reflected in the scoring/weighting systems.

2.4   IS THE RATIONALE FOR THE SCHEME'S SCORING AND WEIGHTING SYSTEM DOCUMENTED?

A weighting and scoring system should not introduce bias towards predominantly male or female jobs. You can check this by comparing the rank order resulting from simply adding up raw scores (one point per level per factor) with that resulting from applying the scheme's weighting and scoring systems. If the differences in position in the two rank orders affect jobs of predominantly one sex, then this indicates the introduction of bias through the weighting and/or scoring system. Any use of 'felt fair' ranking as a basis for generating weighting should be carefully checked for bias, as it may tend to perpetuate any discriminatory features in the existing hierarchy.

Checklist 3: Implementation of the scheme

3.1   WHEN JOBS ARE EVALUATED OR RE-EVALUATED, ARE JOBHOLDERS INVOLVED IN COMPLETION OF A JOB QUESTIONNAIRE OR EQUIVALENT JOB INFORMATION DOCUMENT?

Jobholders know more about the demands of their jobs than anyone else, although they may need help in explaining them.[1] Completion of Job Questionnaires by line managers or personnel staff, without jobholder involvement, can result in job demands being omitted or understated.

3.2   ARE JOB ANALYSTS USED TO ASSIST JOBHOLDERS TO COMPLETE JOB QUESTIONNAIRES OR EQUIVALENT JOB INFORMATION DOCUMENTS?

It is good job evaluation practice to use trained Job Analysts to assist jobholders to provide the information required by the scheme and to a consistently high standard, as this helps to prevent inconsistent and potentially biased evaluations.

3.3 HAVE THE JOB ANALYSTS BEEN TRAINED IN EQUALITY ISSUES AND THE AVOIDANCE OF SEX BIAS?

Job Analysts should understand how sex bias can occur in the information collection process and be trained to avoid it.

3.4 DOES THE JOB QUESTIONNAIRE OR EQUIVALENT JOB INFORMATION DOCUMENT FOLLOW THE JOB EVALUATION SCHEME FACTOR PLAN? THAT IS DOES IT USE ALL OF THE SAME HEADINGS?

Job information documents which follow the job evaluation scheme factors are easier to evaluate and help avoid evaluators making assumptions about job demands, which can result in them being omitted or undervalued in the evaluation process.

3.5 ARE JOBS EVALUATED OR RE-EVALUATED BY A JOB EVALUATION PANEL OR COMMITTEE?

Evaluation by only one or two people (e.g. line manager, personnel officer) can result in biased outcomes. This risk is reduced through evaluation by a panel with broad knowledge of jobs across the organisation.

3.6 ARE JOB EVALUATION PANEL MEMBERS REPRESENTATIVE OF THE MAIN AREAS OF WORK AND GENDER COMPOSITION OF THE WORKGROUPS BEING EVALUATED?

The more representative the evaluators the greater should be their combined understanding of job demands across the workgroup.

3.7 ARE PANEL MEMBERS TRAINED IN EQUALITY ISSUES AND THE AVOIDANCE OF SEX BIAS?

Training in the avoidance of sex bias in the evaluation process helps both to prevent it occurring and ensure that the exercise is seen as fair.

3.8 ARE EVALUATION RATIONALES OR RECORDS, INCLUDING THE REASON FOR EACH FACTOR ASSESSMENT, MAINTAINED FOR EACH JOB EVALUATED OR RE-EVALUATED?

It is good job evaluation practice to maintain detailed evaluation records, for a number of reasons:

- They allow evaluators to check back on their decision making process and thus help ensure consistent evaluations;

- They allow the reasons for evaluations to be explained to jobholders, for example, those considering appealing;
- They provide information to appeal panel members on what information was taken into account in the initial evaluation;
- They provide contemporary evidence for any evaluations subject to subsequent legal challenge.

3.9 HAS THE IMPACT OF EVALUATIONS, RE-EVALUATIONS AND APPEALS ON MALE AND FEMALE DOMINATED JOBS BEEN MONITORED?

You can do this by comparing the rank order implicit in the pre-evaluation pay structure with that resulting from the evaluation exercise (and any subsequent re-evaluations and appeals) and identifying the gender dominance, if any, of jobs which have moved up or down the rank order. If the pre-evaluation pay structure was biased against 'female' job characteristics, then upward moves would be disproportionately among female dominated jobs. Otherwise, one would expect moves to be roughly proportionate to the gender composition of the workforce.

3.10 HAVE ALL DISTINCT JOBS WITHIN THE RELEVANT EMPLOYEE GROUP BEEN ANALYSED AND EVALUATED?

In legal terms, jobs that have not been analysed and evaluated fall outside the scope of the 'job evaluation study'.[2] So the holder of a job which has not been analysed and evaluated (or whose job has changed to the extent that the original evaluation no longer applies) could make an equal pay claim. The job evaluation scheme would not provide you with a defence.

Checklist 4: For organisations with more than one job evaluation scheme

4.1 ARE ALL OF YOUR EMPLOYEES COVERED BY ONE OF THE JOB EVALUATION SCHEMES IN USE IN YOUR ORGANISATION?

It is possible for employees outside the scope of any job evaluation scheme to make an equal pay claim comparing their work with that of employees within the scope of the scheme. It is also possible for a jobholder in one scheme to claim equal pay with a jobholder in a different job evaluation scheme. In such cases, the job evaluation scheme(s) do not provide you with a defence.

4.2 HAVE YOU MADE ANY COMPARISONS BETWEEN THE DEMANDS (AND PAY) OF JOBS COVERED BY DIFFERENT JOB EVALUATION SCHEMES?

You can do this in either of two ways:

1. By evaluating a small number of jobs from scheme A, which are closest in nature to jobs in scheme B, using both schemes; and vice versa; then comparing the results and relative pay levels.
2. By undertaking 'equal value' checks on a sample of predominantly male and female jobs from each scheme, to test for vulnerability to equal pay claims.

If you have answered 'No' to any of the above Checklist questions, then your organisation's job evaluation system(s) could be vulnerable to challenge. The risk is increased, the larger your number of 'No' responses.

---

1   Working Time Analysts: How to Prepare a Job Evaluation Job Description: Lampeter, 1989.
2   The need for a scheme to be analytical was confirmed by the Court of Appeal in *Bromley et al v Quick* (1988 IRLR 249).

CHAPTER 4

The equal pay principle and what it means in practice

KEY POINTS

This chapter examines:

- Where the equal pay principle comes from
- The concept of equal value – comparing different types of jobs
- How independent experts (IEs) appointed under the Equal Pay Act 1970 (EqPA 1970), and parties' experts, have made comparative equal value assessments
- How to make a simple equal value assessment

4.1   THE EQUAL PAY PRINCIPLE

What has become known as the equal pay principle was first formally set down in Article 427 of the Treaty of Versailles in 1919. At the same time it was built in as the seventh principle in the constitution of the International Labour Organisation (ILO), also established under the Treaty. The principle has been re-authorised by the ILO on a number of occasions, ultimately as Equal Remuneration Convention (No. 100) of 1951, currently the second most highly ratified ILO convention.[1]

Article 119 of the Treaty of Rome 1957, which established the European Common Market, subsequently expanded in Article 141 of the Treaty of Maastricht, incorporated the principle that men and women should receive equal pay for equal work. This was further developed in the Equal Pay Directive of 1975, 75/117/EEC (see **Appendix C**) to state that:

- men and women should receive equal pay for work of equal value;
- job classification systems should not discriminate on grounds of sex; and
- member states should implement the equal pay principle.

UK legislation, initiated before and quite separately from the detailed EEC (now EU) provisions, identified two grounds for making an equal pay claim:

(a) like work, where claimant and comparator jobs are the same or broadly similar; and

(b) work rated as equivalent, where claimant and comparator jobs have been given equal rating (that is, the same, or similar, total points) under a job evaluation scheme.

The EqPA 1970 was amended in 1983 to add a third ground for a claim:

(c) work of equal value.

Collectively the three grounds are often termed 'equal work'. Between them they embody the equal pay principle.

This chapter looks at what the principle of equal pay for work of equal value means in practice, in terms of real jobs in real organisations, and how jobs of equal value can be identified.

4.2 THE CONCEPT OF EQUAL VALUE

The concept of equal value is not formally defined in either EU or domestic legislation. The EqPA 1970 says that, when a claimant claims equal pay on grounds of equal value, a comparison should be made between the claimant's work and that of the named comparator 'under such headings as effort, skill and decision'. What is clear is that this involves a weighing and balancing act between the features of claimant and comparator jobs and thus allows comparisons between quite different types of jobs. Examples of claims between different jobs, which have been successful at tribunal or settled in favour of the claimant(s) include:

(a) primary school classroom assistant – library service driver messenger;

(b) school nursery nurse – local government architectural technician;

(c) wholesale news distribution clerical assistant – warehouse operative;

(d) supermarket checkout operator – warehouse operative;

(e) head of speech and language therapy service – head of hospital pharmacy service;

(f) nursing home sewing room assistant – plumber;

(g) motor industry sewing machinist – upholsterer.

Whether jobs are of equal value is ultimately determined by an employment tribunal, either of its own accord or more frequently with the assistance of evidence from those accepted as being expert in the field of job assessment.

When the EqPA 1970 was originally amended to incorporate the concept of equal value, all equal value claims had to be referred to an independent expert (IE), from a panel appointed by ACAS. Since August 1996 determination of the question of equal value can be made by the tribunal, without an IE's report. In practice, in these circumstances tribunal members usually hear evidence from experts appointed by both parties.

The EqPA 1970 currently also says that where claimant and comparator jobs have already been evaluated under a 'job evaluation study', there will be 'no reasonable grounds' for consideration of the claim, unless the applicant can show that the 'study' was fundamentally flawed in design or implementation. The underlying assumption is that where both jobs have been evaluated, they will already have been compared 'under such headings as effort, skill and decision' (see **Chapter 3** for a description of job evaluation).

From this, it is generally understood that the comparison to be made in an equal value claim is similar to a mini-job evaluation exercise and that the phrase 'such ... as effort, skill and decision' is intended to give examples of the sort of criteria, commonly called 'factors', found in conventional job evaluation schemes. This is the approach adopted by both IEs and experts appointed by the parties in equal value claims.

4.3 INDEPENDENT EXPERTS AND EQUAL VALUE COMPARISONS

There are no constraints in the EqPA 1970 on how IEs should make an equal value comparison. As a result their approaches have varied, but they have invariably identified a set of criteria, or factors, that they consider to be suitable to the claimant and comparator jobs in question.

In the first equal value claim referred to an independent expert, *Hayward* v. *Cammell Laird* [1988] IRLR 257, HL, the expert used a limited set of criteria, or factors, to compare the work of the claimant cook with that of her named craft comparators, a shipboard painter, carpenter and heating technician:

- skill and knowledge demands;
- responsibility demands;
- planning and decision making demands;
- physical demands; and
- environmental demands.

For factors other than skills and knowledge the IE assessed the jobs against a simple low–moderate–high scale. For skills and knowledge he assessed them as equal, because both jobs required City & Guilds qualifications. With this relatively straightforward system, it was possible to see from the assessments that the jobs were of equal value. This assumed that all five factors were of equal importance or, in job evaluation jargon, weight.

Although superficially different, claimant and comparator jobs in the *Cammell Laird* case were similarly structured craft jobs and this allowed for a limited set of factors to be used. Where claimant and comparator jobs are differently structured, or where there are more jobs to be compared, IEs have sometimes used a larger number of criteria and/or more formal scoring systems.

For instance, in the case of *Beckett* v. *CR Barron (Meats) Ltd*, cited in an *Equal Opportunities Review* article on early equal value claims, where the claimant was a packer claiming equal pay with a labourer, the IE adopted a six factor system with defined factors and factor levels, and a weighted scoring scale (see **Table 4.1**).

Table 4.1 Example IE comparative assessment

Factor	Weighted maximum	Packer	Labourer
Physical effort	20	15	15
Mental effort	10	3	3
Responsibility for safety	10	7	7
Knowledge and skill	20	10	11
Training	10	3	3
Working conditions	10	7	8
Total	80	45	47

Source: *Equal Opportunities Review* 18, March/April 1988, p. 16

And, when comparing a large number of speech therapist claimant jobs with those from two comparator groups, clinical psychologists and hospital pharmacists, the team of IEs allocated to the work developed a relatively sophisticated assessment system, which looked similar to a conventional job evaluation scheme (see **Chapter 3**), with factors and sub-factors (see below):

1. Knowledge
    (a) Knowledge base

      (b) Development

      (c) Experience

2.   Responsibilities

      (a) Patients/clients and the provision of a service

      (b) Managing work of self and others

      (c) Plant/equipment/resources

      (d) Teaching/training/mentoring

3.   Mental demands

      (a) Concentration/accuracy

      (b) Stress/pressure

4.   Physical demands and environment

      (a) Physical effort

      (b) Working conditions

      (c) Hazards

5.   Decision making/initiative

      (a) Complexity/analysis

      (b) Freedom to act

6.   Communications/relationships (no sub-factors)

Each factor had five levels and each job was assessed against the factor scale, as in a conventional job evaluation scheme. However, each IE was free to determine their own scoring system and these could and did differ, but all involved one or more points per level.

In a small number of cases IEs have used pre-existing formal job evaluation schemes as the basis for their comparative assessments. For example, in a Health Service case, the IE made use of a revised version of the national job evaluation scheme for ancillary workers in the Health Service (which was never actually implemented, because overtaken by other events), although he modified the agreed scoring system. With the advent of more schemes designed specifically to incorporate equal pay principles and practices, this approach may become more common.

4.4   PARTIES' EXPERTS AND EQUAL VALUE COMPARISONS

Those making equal value comparisons on behalf of applicants and respondents have used more varied approaches than the IEs, who have regular opportunities to discuss their methods.

In the speech therapists' cases, for example, the claimants' expert selected a set of factors and then compared the jobs on a greater than, equal to, less than system, supported by a textual rationale (see **Table 4.2**).

Table 4.2 Example of parties' expert's comparative assessment

Factor	District speech therapist	Comparative assessment	District pharmaceutical officer
A. Skills, knowledge and experience	=		
B. Responsibilities for clients/patients	>		
C. Advisory/policy responsibilities	<		
D. Supervisory/managerial responsibilities	=		
E. Resource responsibilities	<		
F. Teaching responsibilities	>		
G. Research responsibilities	=		
H. Initiative/independence	=		
I. Mental effort	=		
J. Physical effort	=		
K. Working conditions	=		
Summary		= 7 factors	
		> 2 factors	
		< 2 factors	

The above approach could be converted into a more traditional paired comparisons exercise by scoring two points for greater than, one point to each job for equal and zero points for less than. In the above example this would have resulted in applicant and comparator jobs both scoring 11 points: $(7 \times 1) + (2 \times 2)$.

In contrast, the Hay consultants who acted as experts for the respondents in the same case used a version of their proprietary job evaluation system (see below):

1. Know-how
   (a) Depth and range of technical know-how (7 levels)
   (b) Planning and organising skills (5 levels)
   (c) Communicating and influencing skills (3 levels)
2. Problem solving
   (a) Thinking environment (7 levels)
   (b) Thinking challenge (4 levels)
3. Accountability
   (a) Decision making (6 levels)
   (b) Area and nature of impact (7 levels)
4. Additional work factors (4 defined levels for each, 2 other levels available)
   (a) Physical strain
   (b) Physical environment
   (c) Hazards

    (d) Concentration

    (e) Emotional and psychological strain

    (f) Verbal abuse

The first three factors each had a combined scoring matrix, while the additional work factor levels each scored from zero to five points.

In *William Ball Ltd* v. *Wood & Others* [EAT 89/01, decision of 21/02/02], where the tribunal had not appointed an IE and where the respondent's expert did not produce his own comparative assessment, but contented himself with criticising the approach adopted by the expert on behalf of the applicants, the Employment Appeals Tribunal (EAT) approved the use of *PayCheck*[2] (see **Appendix F**), a fairly simple comparative assessment system (see below):

1. Skill and knowledge factors
    - (a) Pre-appointment knowledge and skill
    - (b) In-post experience
    - (c) Interpersonal skills – internal and external
2. Responsibility factors
    - (a) Supervision
    - (b) Information
    - (c) Initiative and decision making
    - (d) Financial resources
    - (e) Physical resources
    - (f) Customers and clients
    - (g) Process and service
3. Effort factors
    - (a) Mental effort
    - (b) Strength
    - (c) Stamina
4. Environmental factors
    - (a) Working environment
    - (b) Emotional demands

Users of *PayCheck* are recommended to adopt either a greater than, equal to, less than comparative assessment system as above, or to apply a low–moderate–high scale of demand and convert this to scores on the basis of low = one, moderate = two, high = three.

4.5 MAKING EQUAL VALUE ASSESSMENTS

A simple approach can be adopted in the first instance to determine whether or not an equal value claim has merit. The approach is equally suitable for use by claimants, or those representing them, or by respondents. It is also appropriate for assessing equal value in the context of an equal pay review (see **Chapter 5**).

The approach is based on principles similar to those described above, but uses whatever information is readily available (organisational job descriptions and organisation charts, showing formal reporting relationships between jobs in relevant sections or departments) and a framework assessment, as illustrated below. It is sensible to write down the job information used and the reasons for the comparative assessment, as this aids objectivity and provides a rationale for the overall assessment.

Step 1: Identify the factors or sub-factors, which, between them, cover all the significant features of both claimant and comparator jobs (such as job knowledge, interpersonal skills).

Step 2: Analyse the available information about the claimant and comparator job demands under each of the selected factors or sub-factors (a factual statement about relevant job demands, for example, 'requires knowledge of clerical procedures and office management').

Step 3: Make a comparative assessment on a factor-by-factor basis and record the reasons for the factor assessments (for example, on a low–moderate–high scale, as in **Table 4.3**, or by some other means).

Step 4: Make an overall comparative assessment, either by inspection of the comparative assessments or by totalling points scores.

If an equal pay claim proceeds, then a more detailed assessment may be needed, based on job information by interview and, if appropriate, observation, of claimant, comparator and their line managers. In this case, it will be appropriate to record all the available job information in the form of a job description, consisting of a list of job duties and analysis under each of the selected factor or sub-factor headings. However, the same assessment format is applicable.

If the assessment is to be submitted to an IE or the tribunal, then it will usually be necessary to provide additional supporting information, for example, definitions of the factors selected, in order to delineate their scope; definitions for each level of a factor scale system; reasons for each factor assessment for each job. The principles, however, are the same as for the simple assessment.

Table 4.3 Making a preliminary comparative equal value assessment

Factors	Claimant job information (A)	Comparator job information (C)	Comparative assessment	Reasons
Knowledge and skills				
Job knowledge	Requires knowledge of clerical, office procedures	Requires knowledge of storekeeping procedures and records	M:M (2:2)	Both require procedural knowledge to NVQ3 level
Interpersonal skills	Skills for responding to colleague and client queries	Skills for exchanging information with stores users and delivery drivers	M:L (2:1)	A asks questions to identify needs
Physical skills	Keyboard skills for input, access and word processing	Keyboard skills for input, access to stores records; fork lift truck driving	H:M (3:2)	A requires speed and precision; C requires precision
Responsibilities				
For people (customers, clients)	Responsible for responding to client queries	Responsible for providing a stores service to users	L:M (1:2)	C has more direct contact and provides direct service
For other employees	Demonstrates own duties to new starters, temps	Demonstrates own duties to work experience trainees	L:L (1:1)	No specific responsibilities for either A or C
For resources	Careful use of office equipment	Careful handling of stores; use of FLT	L:M (1:2)	C has a positive responsibility of care for stores and equipment

For information	Responsible for processing, storing, retrieving client information	Responsible for inputting goods received to stores database	M:L (2:1)	A has a positive responsibility for information, less so for C
Initiative and decision				
Freedom to act	Organises office support function	Carries out day to day stores ops	M:L (2:1)	A works more independently than C
Problem solving	Answers queries, resolves office problems	Answers queries, resolves stores problems	M:M (2:2)	Equivalent level of problem solving
Effort				
Mental effort	Concentration for word processing	Concentration for stores input	M:L (2:1)	Longer periods for A
Physical effort	Sits in constrained position	Moves stores using FLT	L:M (1:2)	C lifts, carries, manoeuvres goods
Emotional effort	Angry, upset clients	Angry stores users	M:M (2:2)	Both deal with clients
Environment				
Working conditions	Office conditions	Stores conditions	L:M (1:2)	Dust from packing materials
Unavoidable hazards	Use of VDU	Use of VDU	L:L (1:1)	
Summary			23:22	

4.6 USING JOB EVALUATION TO IMPLEMENT THE EQUAL PAY PRINCIPLE

The technique of job evaluation is described in **Chapter 3**. Traditionally, job evaluation has often been used to rationalise and reinforce previous job hierarchies. Over the last 20 years, however, as equal opportunities policies and the concepts of pay equity have begun to impact, consideration has been given to what would make a job evaluation scheme less discriminatory and more gender-neutral, so that job evaluation might be used as a tool for moving towards equal pay for work of equal value. The principles emerging include:

(a) selecting factors to measure all significant job features and taking care to include factors measuring significant features of jobs typically undertaken by women, for example, interpersonal skills; responsibilities for patients, clients, customers, service users; emotional demands;

(b) defining factors and levels only by reference to the demands of the actual jobs to be evaluated;

(c) developing weighting systems by reference to agreed principles and organisational values.

The other major difference between modern job evaluation schemes and older ones is that historical schemes generally reflected contemporary collective bargaining arrangements, so a large organisation might operate four or five schemes, one for each of its collective bargaining groups. Because of the impact of changing technology and work organisation, such schemes are often unsuitable for present day needs. Modern job evaluation schemes often cover all, or most, jobs within an organisation.

The result of these changes is that modern job evaluation systems (JES) often look rather different from their predecessors. **Table 4.4** summarises the local government national joint council (NJC) 'single status' job evaluation scheme of 1997, which was developed to cover all previous manual and non-manual jobs in the sector and to meet with equal value principles and practices.

Equal value features of the design of the NJC JES include:

(a) a larger number of factors (13) than might historically have been the case, to ensure that no job features are omitted or undervalued;

(b) fewer levels per factor (between 5 and 8) than in some schemes, to avoid awarding points for insignificant differences in demand;

(c) equal points steps between factor levels, to reflect the aim of making the actual steps in defined levels equal;

Table 4.4 The NJC JES in summary

Factor/Level	1	2	3	4	5	6	7	8	Total	% of total
1. Knowledge	20	40	60	80	100	121	142	163	163	16.3
2. Mental skills	13	26	39	52	65	78			78	7.8
3. Interpersonal skills	13	26	39	52	65	78			78	7.8
4. Physical skills	13	26	39	52	65				65	6.5
Knowledge and skills total									**384**	**38.4**
5. Initiative and independence	13	26	39	52	65	78	91	104	104	10.4
6. Physical demands	10	20	30	40	50				50	5.0
7. Mental demands	10	20	30	40	50				50	5.0
8. Emotional demands	10	20	30	40	50				50	5.0
Effort totals									**254**	**25.4**
9. Responsibility for people	13	26	39	52	65	78			78	7.8
10. Responsibility for supervision	13	26	39	52	65	78			78	7.8
11. Responsibility for financial resources	13	26	39	52	65	78			78	7.8
12. Responsibility for physical resources	13	26	39	52	65	78			78	7.8
Responsibility totals									**312**	**31.2**
13. Working conditions	10	20	30	40	50				50	5.0
Environment totals									**50**	**5.0**
Overall total									**1000**	**100.0**

(d) a weighting system that treats groups of factors the same, so, for example, gives equal weighting to each of the responsibility factors.

In terms of process:

(a) the scheme was developed and tested by a joint management–union technical working group and is intended to be jointly implemented at local authority level;

(b) it is transparent (published in the collective agreement);

(c) job information is collected by means of a detailed factual (paper-based or computerised) questionnaire, with assistance from trained analysts;

(d) the user manual recommends training of analysts and evaluators in the principles of job evaluation, the scheme itself and the avoidance of bias.

ENDNOTES

1. Report of Committee of Experts (2001) ILO Conference – 50th Anniversary of the Equal Remuneration Convention of 1951, pp. 18–22.
2. TMS Equality and Diversity Consultants (1998) *PayCheck: Auditing Pay Systems for Sex Bias*, Appendix 2, pp. 87–103.

CHAPTER 5

Equal pay reviews

KEY POINTS

This chapter aims to answer the following questions:

- What is an equal pay review?
- Why do an equal pay review?
- Where to start?
- What are the points to remember?

The chapter is illustrated by an example using a small, imaginary company, Business Advice Company Ltd (BACL), but the principles and practices of carrying out an equal pay review are the same for any size or type of organisation.

5.1 WHAT IS AN EQUAL PAY REVIEW, OR AUDIT?

The idea of reviewing a whole organisation, in order to identify gender (and other forms of) pay inequalities probably came to the UK from the 1987 pay equity legislation of Ontario, Canada. This required organisations with more than 100 employees to conduct a pay equity review of all male- and female-dominated groups and to rectify any inequalities identified. Most such reviews have been carried out by means of job evaluation exercises, but statistical analyses are used to check the 'before and after' results.

The Equal Opportunities Commission (EOC) *Code of Practice on Equal Pay* (EOC, 1997) (being revised at the time of writing) included a simple eight-step model for an equal pay audit. The principles of this were developed as a manual for employers, *PayCheck*, published by TMS Consultants in 1998 (see **Appendix F**). *PayCheck* took a checklist approach to auditing the different elements of pay structures, but also recommended an initial statistical analysis to identify areas for investigation.

The report of the EOC Equal Pay Task Force, *Just Pay*, recommended that equal pay reviews be made mandatory and included as an appendix a framework equal pay review model (EPRM). The government declined to make equal pay reviews mandatory, but did say that all government departments and agencies would be required to carry out reviews by April 2003. It also provided funding to the EOC to commission work to develop a user friendly, tried and tested equal pay review model.

The resulting EPR Toolkit, together with a series of guidance notes, is published on the EOC website (see **Appendix F**). The EPRM is also at **Appendix D**; and the job evaluation checklist, which forms part of one of the EPRM guidance notes, can be found at **Annex 3A**.

An equal pay review starts with a statistical analysis of basic pay and total earnings by gender (and other features likely to have resulted in pay inequalities) for jobs where there is equal work (see **Chapter 4**). The initial analysis is supplemented by further investigations, analyses and checks, in order to identify the source of any apparent pay inequalities and possible justifications for the differences.

5.2   WHY DO AN EQUAL PAY REVIEW?

The obvious answer is that an equal pay review is a better way of identifying and resolving any pay inequalities than taking an equal pay claim to tribunal. A tribunal claim can be disruptive to management time and business objectives; expensive in terms of costs and, if the applicant is successful, compensation (including up to six years' back pay – see **Chapter 16**). A tribunal award is also disruptive in that it only determines the past and future pay of the claimant(s); it does not deal with any consequential effects, such as the relative positions of the claimants' supervisor(s) and colleagues. An equal pay review, on the other hand, allows a planned approach to rectifying any pay inequalities, the possibility of phasing in costs over a reasonable timescale, and usually no back payments or compensation. It provides an agreed, consensual approach to the rectification of pay inequalities, rather than an enforced, adversarial route.

Other positive reasons for undertaking an equal pay review include:

(a)   advantages in terms of recruitment and retention of female staff;

(b)   broadening the organisation's equal opportunities policy and practices to encompass equal pay; and

(c)   an opportunity to review and, if necessary, harmonise pay structures, creating a more flexible pay system to facilitate organisational flexibility.

5.3 WHERE TO START?

The recommended starting point for an EPR is to bring together a team with the necessary expertise – probably including representatives from HR or personnel, payroll, equal opportunities and, if necessary, an IT specialist to assist in organising the data. The credibility of the exercise will be improved if the team includes trade union or other employee representation, but it may be necessary to agree in advance issues, such as confidentiality of pay data and whether there should be a moratorium on union support for equal pay claims for the agreed duration of the review.

The first step is to collate the data required for initial analyses. This includes, for each employee:

(a) basic pay and total earnings (per hour, week, month or year, whichever is most convenient, but preferably on the same basis for all employees);
(b) gender (and, if possible, information on ethnicity and disability);
(c) job titles, grade and, if relevant, job evaluation scores; and
(d) age, time in post or in service.

A modern combined payroll and personnel system will usually include all of this information. Those without such a system may need to download or assemble data from different sources in spreadsheet or database form. Once all the information is assembled, it is possible to delete or 'hide' the names of individual employees, so that there is no scope for challenge under data protection legislation. All outputs of the review will be in terms of average pay and earnings of men and women in particular groupings.

In order to make comparisons across the organisations, it is necessary to bring all the data to common units of hours and salaries. So, if one group works different normal hours, then it is necessary to convert all salaries to a common hours base, for example, by multiplying basic salaries by 37/39 for employees on 39-hour contracts. It is also necessary to bring full-time and part-time employees on to a common salary basis. Where most employees work full time, then it is probably sensible to gross up the salaries of part-timers to their full-time equivalents. For an organisation employing many part-time staff, on varying weekly hours, it may be easier to convert all salaries to hourly rates of pay instead.

5.4   IDENTIFYING EQUAL WORK

Steps two and three of the EPRM are to identify equal work (like work; work rated as equivalent; work of equal value) carried out by males and females (see **Chapter 4**); to calculate average male and female basic pay and total earnings where there is equal work; and to record any significant differences.

Checking like work

The straightforward way of checking like work is by job title. In an organisation that applies job titles systematically, it will be possible to sort the spreadsheet or database by job title and to calculate average basic pay and average total earnings for males and females separately. In very large organisations with hundreds of job titles, it may be sensible to sample first those job titles with a clear gender mix. In organisations where job titles are not used systematically, it may first be necessary to conduct further investigations in order to be able to introduce a new 'common job title' column to the spreadsheet. In organisations where job titles occur in more than one grade, then the job title column could be amended to include the grade reference.

All gender pay differences identified through the like work check should be recorded for further investigation.

Checking work rated as equivalent

Where an organisation has a job evaluation scheme covering some or all of its employees, the next step is to ascertain, by inspection or calculation, the average basic pay and total earnings for all male and female employees separately in each evaluated grade. Any gender pay differences should be recorded.

An organisation with a single job evaluation scheme covering all employees (including senior managers and any ancillary groups) will not need to undertake the equal value checks described in the following paragraphs, but will need to check that its job evaluation scheme is fair and non-discriminatory in design and implementation. This can be done using the EOC checklist from **Annex 3A**.

Checking work of equal value

The third step is checking work of equal value. The most reliable way of checking equal value is by means of a fair and non-discriminatory job evaluation scheme covering all jobs. In the absence of such a scheme, it is necessary to make estimates of what is work of equal value. A possible first estimate is to assume for the purpose of the exercise that the current organisational grading structure is based on equal value principles and to calculate average basic pay and total earnings of males and females in each grade (the grading structure will need to be checked later).

This analysis does not allow for equal value comparisons across collective bargaining groups, a key check, as a number of equal value claims have arisen across occupational groups (see **Chapter 4**). One means of doing this is by applying a job evaluation scheme already in use within the organisation, or elsewhere, to those jobs suspected to be of equal value.

Other estimates of equal value recommended in the EPRM guidance notes are:

1. Use of a common qualification system, such as National Vocational Qualifications (NVQs), the Scottish equivalent (SVQs), or an in-house equivalent. For example, it would be possible to calculate average male and female basic pay and total earnings for jobs at each NVQ level.

2. Common hierarchical positions, such as heads of department, section managers, first line supervisors, production operatives, calculating average basic salary and total earnings for males and females in each group.

If none of the above is applicable, the remaining option is to undertake some equal value checks, as described in **Chapter 4**, to compare jobs across different pay structures, which could be of equal value.

5.5 FURTHER INVESTIGATIONS

Step four of the model requires further investigations of the significant differences identified, either by additional statistical analyses or by alternative checks. The actual investigations necessary will vary from organisation to organisation. Some commonly occurring explanations for gender differences in pay are listed below, together with appropriate analyses.

For each identified gender pay difference, the questions to be asked are: What is the explanation for the difference? Is it justified in terms of the business or service needs of the organisation and without reference to the gender of the relevant jobholders?

Table 5.1   Common explanations for pay differences

Possible reason for gender pay difference	Appropriate analysis
Experience	Compare basic pay/total earnings with experience in post (or length of service) for men and women doing equal work (e.g. same job title, same grade). Plot on a scattergram.
Starting salaries	Compare average starting salaries for men and women doing equal work over a suitable recent period (e.g. last 3 years).
Labour market factors	Compare average labour market supplements or premium payments for men and women doing equal work.
Performance	Compare performance assessments and payments, or bonus levels and payments, for men and women doing equal work.
Competence	Compare competence assessments and payments, or skills levels and payments, for men and women doing equal work.
Working patterns	Compare shift, unsocial hours or other working pattern premium payments for men and women doing equal work.
Pay structure history	Investigate how men and women doing equal work were assimilated into the current pay structure.

5.6   IMPLEMENTING THE RESULTS OF THE EQUAL PAY REVIEW

The final stage of an EPR is to draw up an action plan and timescale to rectify any gender pay differences that cannot be justified. This is obviously the crucial stage. If gender pay inequities are identified but not rectified, they become obvious sources for equal pay claims and the potential advantages of carrying out the review are lost.

5.7   A CASE STUDY – BACL

Data gathering

For the example company, Business Advice Company Ltd, names, starting dates, grades, basic salaries, additional allowances of various sorts, and total remuneration were available from the payroll system. The organisation has two structures, one for support staff (S) and a separate one for advisers and related employees (A), for each of which there are separate contractual arrangements, so information had to be brought together on to a single spreadsheet by combining the relevant data from two original payroll spreadsheets. Gender and job title information was added manually from personnel files and job descriptions (see **Annex 5A**). The analysis completed on this data comprises **Annexes 5A–5D** at the end of this chapter.

BACL does not currently hold data on ethnicity and disability centrally, but is taking steps to obtain the information and will repeat the review on these characteristics at a later date. Although senior managers are sure that the company does pay men and women equally, it appears that some female employees are considering equal pay claims, so the HR manager has decided not to delay the review until all data is available.

All BACL employees are contracted to work a 37-hour week, so no adjustments were required to bring the data on to a common basis. Nearly all employees work full time; the salaries of part-timers have been grossed up to their full-time equivalents.

The like work check

A like work check at BACL, in terms of job titles, shows that in most cases all staff with the same job title have the same basic salary (see **Annexe 5B**), so without any calculation it is possible to say that the average basic salary for both male and female administrative assistants is £13,738.77. Similarly, all senior business advisers have the same basic salary, so the average for both males and females is £27,444.44.

Note that **Annexe 5B** contains the same data as **Annexe 5A** but is sorted first by job title, second by sex, third by name. BACL is a relatively new firm established 30 years ago and has applied job titles consistently as it has grown. In larger or older organisations, this is not always the case, so it may be necessary to introduce an additional column of rationalised job titles.

There is one exception at BACL to basic salaries being the same for each job title. Closer inspection shows that there are two jobs with the title of health and safety adviser, one performed by a woman in the support structure with a basic salary of £16,404.44, and one carried out by a man in the advisers' structure with a basic salary of £20,333.33. This is recorded as a difference for further investigation (see **Table 5.2**) – first, to check whether the jobs are really the same or broadly similar; and, if they are, to identify the reason for the different treatment in relation to basic pay.

Repeating the checks on total remuneration shows more differences (average total earnings figures for mixed gender jobs, calculated using the 'average' function in a Microsoft Excel spreadsheet, are shown at the right of **Annexe 5B**). The total earnings of the female accounts assistant are lower than those of the male accounts assistant; the total earnings of the female health and safety adviser are lower than those of her male colleague, although by a smaller amount than the basic pay difference; and the average total earnings of the female senior business advisers are lower than the average total earnings of the male senior business advisers, although the difference is small. On the other hand, the average total earnings of the female administrative assistants are higher than those of their male colleagues, while the averages for male and female business advisers are equal. All the gender differences are recorded for further investigation (see **Table 5.2**).

The work rated as equivalent check

BACL has separate grading structures for support staff and advisers, but neither is based on job evaluation, so it is not possible to make any work rated as equivalent checks.

The equal value check

In the absence of a job evaluation exercise, it is possible to use the grades of each structure at BACL as the basis for a first estimate of equal value within each structure. It will later be necessary to check that the criteria for each grade are free from sex discrimination in both design and implementation.

For BACL, it is apparent from inspection that when the data is sorted by grade and gender, the company does have the same basic salary for all those in the same grade, for both the support staff and adviser groups. However, there are variations in total earnings and some significant gender differences when averages are calculated. For example, while the average total earnings of females in grade E is £20,231, the single male in this grade has total earnings of £22,814. For those in adviser grade Y, the difference in total earnings is around £1,500. These differences are also recorded for further investigation (see **Annexe 5C** sorted first by grade, second by gender, third by name. Average total earnings for males and females in each mixed gender grade shown to the right of the data).

This still leaves the question of equal value across the current structures. None of the further checks suggested above appears applicable to BACL, as the company does not use NVQs for its own employees and it is too small to have departmental or equivalent hierarchies.

For BACL, the areas of potential vulnerability are the female-dominated jobs towards the top of the support staff structure and the male-dominated business adviser group in grade Y and possibly the equally male dominated senior business adviser group and related jobs in grade Z. Instead of carrying out ad hoc equal value checks, BACL decided to undertake a partial job evaluation exercise, utilising a scheme developed within another advisory company known to the managing director. The results for those jobs evaluated are shown in the JE (job evaluation) column in **Annexe 5D**. These provide the basis for ascertaining male and female basic salaries and total earnings for the jobs with similar job evaluation points. While the job evaluation scores broadly confirm the relativities embodied in the current grading and basic pay structures, there are some significant exceptions and further gender differences to be recorded in the table. For example, although none of the support group jobs evaluated score as highly as the senior business adviser jobs, the two jobs in support grade F, both occupied by women, score as highly as the business adviser jobs evaluated, which have higher basic pay. The evaluation also confirms that, even if the two health and safety adviser jobs are not exactly the same, they are nevertheless of equal value, so the differences in basic pay and total earnings do require explanation.

The evaluations reveal other anomalies, which could give rise to equal pay claims. For example, the deputy head of administration job appears to be relatively overgraded in support grade E, as it scores similar points to jobs in support grade D. On the other hand, all of the business adviser jobholders have lower total earnings than the support grade F jobs.

Further investigations

At BACL, some of the significant differences relate to basic pay, with the obvious explanation being the fact that jobs are in different structures. The best solution to these anomalies would be to extend the job evaluation exercise to cover all jobs and to develop a single grading and pay structure to cover all employees.

However, most of the significant differences at BACL relate to total earnings, rather than basic salaries, so further investigations will concentrate on the various allowances paid.

BACL pays long service allowances to staff, so a scattergram analysis, showing earnings on the x axis and length of service on the y axis, plotted for males and females separately, may be a useful check. Observation indicates that, while there is a clear relationship between length of service and long service allowance, there are some exceptions

Table 5.2 Record of Step 2 gender differences identified for further investigation

Jobs	Nos.	Pay difference	Explanation
Health and safety advisers	1F 1M	Basic pay difference of around £4000	Different jobs? Different structures?
Health and safety advisers	1F 1M	Total earnings difference of around £1500	Different jobs? Different structures?
Accounts assistants	1F 1M	Total earnings difference of around £1250	Different regional payments?
Administrative assistants	3F 2M	Total earnings difference of around £750 (in favour of F)	Different long service allowances?
Senior business advisers	2F 7M	Total earnings difference of £400+	Different allowances?
D grade support jobs	9F 1M	Total earnings difference of around £700	Different long service allowances?
E grade support jobs	3F 1M	Total earnings difference of £2600	Different long service allowances?
Jobs with JE points 500, 515	2F 3M	Basic pay difference of £800	Different structures?
Jobs with JE points 500, 515	2F 3M	Total earnings difference (in favour of 2F) of £2–400	Different long service allowances?

and male employees appear to have benefited more from these than female employees. For example, the only employees with less than five years' service receiving a long service allowance are men – two in the support group and two in the adviser group. The rate of long service allowance is also lower for the female-dominated support group than for the male-dominated adviser group. This difference may be difficult to justify objectively. If a new single grading and pay structure were developed, then it would be appropriate to review the long service allowance system.

The other obvious contributory factor at BACL to differences in total earnings are the regional allowances paid to London-based staff and to those based in provincial centres. The predominantly female support staff receive slightly lower allowances, both London and provincial, than the predominantly male adviser group. This is the product of the historically separate pay settlements for the two groups. History thus provides the explanation for the difference, but is unlikely to provide objective justification for it. The first action of the post-review plan might, therefore, be to harmonise London and provincial allowances, either immediately, if finances allow, or as part of the next annual pay settlement.

Investigations also need to be made of any other allowances paid to individuals. In BACL's case, these seem to relate to specific job responsibilities and might be better consolidated into basic pay. Other organisations might have different sorts of payment – for example, bonus or performance payments or working pattern payments. Each such payment should be further investigated, if it results in significant differences in the average payments to men and women doing equal work. What is the explanation for the payment? And then: Is the payment justified?

Annexe 5A

EQUAL PAY REVIEW: BUSINESS ADVICE COMPANY LTD (BACL)

NO.	NAME	SEX	JOB TITLE	TYPE	START
1	Bowen A	F	Secretary	S	01-Aug-94
2	Brown S	F	Finance Officer	S	03-Dec-91
3	Cave P	F	MD's PA	S	18-Mar-84
4	Daly S	F	Health and Safety Adviser	S	18-Apr-92
5	Dawes J	F	Administrative Assistant	S	02-Jul-89
6	Denny G	F	Receptionist	S	24-Jul-88
7	Ford J	M	Deputy Head, Administration	S	05-Aug-77
8	Gale D	F	Senior Secretary	S	02-Jan-00
9	George H	M	Administrative Assistant	S	10-Jan-99
10	Glamis B	F	Accounts Assistant	S	27-Feb-94
11	Green L	F	Secretary	S	10-May-92
12	Howes M	F	Secretary	S	01-Apr-91
13	Howson R	F	Secretary	S	31-Jan-85
14	Jones S	M	Accounts Assistant	S	14-Feb-01
15	Jones T	F	Chief Executive's PA	S	07-Jun-81
16	Leigh D	F	Secretary	S	14-Oct-90
17	Lovatt F	F	Secretary	S	06-Dec-98
18	McCleary J	F	Administrative Assistant	S	04-Aug-85
19	Neill S	F	Senior Secretary	S	01-Jan-98
20	Parrott J	F	Administrative Assistant	S	01-Dec-97
21	Pears H	F	Secretary	S	15-Feb-98
22	Sands B	F	Head of Administration	S	08-May-72
23	Smith A	F	Receptionist/Mail Room Clerk	S	01-Oct-92
24	Sweetman J	M	Administrative Assistant	S	01-Sep-99
25	Wilson P	F	Secretary	S	24-Nov-98
26	Avery F	M	Health and Safety Adviser	A	04-Jan-98
27	Bennett P	M	Senior Business Adviser	A	01-Jan-91
28	Boreham W	F	Business Adviser	A	01-Oct-98
29	Chips C	M	Business Adviser	A	04-Jan-98
30	Clark K	M	Senior Business Adviser	A	01-Sep-91
31	Davis G	M	Senior IT Adviser	A	06-Apr-98
32	Evans R	M	Senior Business Adviser	A	01-Feb-97
33	Hyther M	M	Business Adviser	A	04-Jan-98
34	Kerry N	M	Senior Business Adviser	A	12-Feb-91
35	McCram V	M	Senior Business Adviser	A	02-Aug-98
36	Lawrence P	M	Business Adviser	A	06-Apr-98
37	Rogers G	F	Senior Business Adviser	A	01-Aug-97
38	Smith K	M	Senior Business Adviser	A	20-Dec-92
39	Storey C	F	Senior Business Adviser	A	28-Mar-87
40	Truman F	M	Company Law Adviser	A	01-Aug-91
41	Westman J	M	Senior Business Adviser	A	21-Jan-90

YRS	GRADE	BASIC £	L/P	OTHER	LSA	TOTAL
8.1	D	15209.19	2660.22		750	18619.41
10.7	H	23058.02	2660.22		3000	28718.24
18.5	F	19505.25	2660.22		3250	25415.47
10.4	E	16404.44	2660.22	1250	2250	22564.66
13.2	C	13738.77	2660.22		1500	17898.99
14.1	B	12601.09	2660.22		1500	16761.31
25.1	E	16404.44	2660.22		3750	22814.66
2.7	E	16404.44	2660.22			19064.66
3.6	C	13738.77	2660.22		750	17148.99
8.5	D	15209.19	1330.11		750	17289.3
10.3	D	15209.19	2660.22		750	18619.41
11.4	D	15209.19	1330.11		750	17289.3
17.6	D	15209.19	1330.11		2250	18789.3
1.5	D	15209.19	2660.22		750	18619.41
21.2	H	23058.02	2660.22		3000	28718.24
11.9	D	15209.19	2660.22		750	18619.41
3.7	D	15209.19	2660.22			17869.41
17.1	C	13738.77	2660.22		1500	17898.99
4.7	E	16404.44	2660.22			19064.66
4.8	C	13738.77	2660.22			16398.99
4.5	D	15209.19	2660.22			17869.41
30.3	F	19505.25	2660.22		4900	27065.47
9.9	B	12601.09	2660.22		600	15861.31
3.0	C	13738.77	2660.22			16398.99
3.8	D	15209.19	1330.11			16539.3
4.7	Z	20333.33	2900.9		800	24034.23
11.7	Y	27444.44	1450.45		2400	31294.89
3.9	Z	20333.33	2900.9			23234.23
4.7	Z	20333.33	2900.9			23234.23
11.0	Y	27444.44	2900.9	1450.45	1600	33395.79
4.4	Y	27444.44	2900.9	8500		38845.34
5.6	Y	27444.44	2900.9		800	31145.34
4.7	Z	20333.33	2900.9			23234.23
11.6	Y	27444.44	1450.45		2400	31294.89
4.1	Y	27444.44	2900.9		800	31145.34
4.4	Z	20333.33	2900.9			23234.23
5.1	Y	27444.44	1450.45			28894.89
9.7	Y	27444.44	1450.45		1600	30494.89
15.4	Y	27444.44	2900.9		3200	33545.34
11.1	Y	27444.44	2900.9	3250	2400	35995.34
12.6	Y	27444.44	1450.45		2400	31294.89

Annexe 5B

EQUAL PAY REVIEW: BUSINESS ADVICE COMPANY LTD (BACL): LIKE WORK CHECK

NO.	NAME	SEX	JOB TITLE	TYPE	START	YRS
10	Glamis B	F	Accounts Assistant	S	27-Feb-94	8.5
14	Jones S	M	Accounts Assistant	S	14-Feb-01	1.5
5	Dawes J	F	Administrative Assistant	S	02-Jul-89	13.2
18	McCleary J	F	Administrative Assistant	S	04-Aug-85	17.1
20	Parrott J	F	Administrative Assistant	S	01-Dec-97	4.8
9	George H	M	Administrative Assistant	S	10-Jan-99	3.6
24	Sweetman J	M	Administrative Assistant	S	01-Sep-99	3.0
28	Boreham W	F	Business Adviser	A	01-Oct-98	3.9
29	Chips C	M	Business Adviser	A	04-Jan-98	4.7
33	Hyther M	M	Business Adviser	A	04-Jan-98	4.7
36	Lawrence P	M	Business Adviser	A	06-Apr-98	4.4
15	Jones T	F	Chief Executive's PA	S	07-Jun-81	21.2
40	Truman F	M	Company Law Adviser	A	01-Aug-91	11.1
7	Ford J	M	Deputy Head, Administration	S	05-Aug-77	25.1
2	Brown S	F	Finance Officer	S	03-Dec-91	10.7
22	Sands B	F	Head of Administration	S	08-May-72	30.3
4	Daly S	F	Health and Safety Adviser	S	18-Apr-92	10.4
26	Avery F	M	Health and Safety Adviser	A	04-Jan-98	4.7
3	Cave P	F	MD's PA	S	18-Mar-84	18.5
6	Denny G	F	Receptionist	S	24-Jul-88	14.1
23	Smith A	F	Receptionist/Mail Room Clerk	S	01-Oct-92	9.9
1	Bowen A	F	Secretary	S	01-Aug-94	8.1
11	Green L	F	Secretary	S	10-May-92	10.3
12	Howes M	F	Secretary	S	01-Apr-91	11.4
13	Howson R	F	Secretary	S	31-Jan-85	17.6
16	Leigh D	F	Secretary	S	14-Oct-90	11.9
17	Lovatt F	F	Secretary	S	06-Dec-98	3.7
21	Pears H	F	Secretary	S	15-Feb-98	4.5
25	Wilson P	F	Secretary	S	24-Nov-98	3.8
37	Rogers G	F	Senior Business Adviser	A	01-Aug-97	5.1
39	Storey C	F	Senior Business Adviser	A	28-Mar-87	15.4
27	Bennett P	M	Senior Business Adviser	A	01-Jan-91	11.7
30	Clark K	M	Senior Business Adviser	A	01-Sep-91	11.0
32	Evans R	M	Senior Business Adviser	A	01-Feb-97	5.6
34	Kerry N	M	Senior Business Adviser	A	12-Feb-91	11.6
35	McCram V	M	Senior Business Adviser	A	02-Aug-98	4.1
38	Smith K	M	Senior Business Adviser	A	20-Dec-92	9.7
41	Westman J	M	Senior Business Adviser	A	21-Jan-90	12.6
31	Davis G	M	Senior IT Adviser	A	06-Apr-98	4.4
8	Gale D	F	Senior Secretary	S	02-Jan-00	2.7
19	Neill S	F	Senior Secretary	S	01-Jan-98	4.7

GRADE	BASIC £	L/P	OTHER	LSA	TOTAL		AVE. TOT.
D	15209.19	1330.11		750	17289.3	F	17289.3
D	15209.19	2660.22		750	18619.41	M	18619.41
C	13738.77	2660.22		1500	17898.99		
C	13738.77	2660.22		1500	17898.99	F	17398.99
C	13738.77	2660.22			16398.99		
C	13738.77	2660.22		750	17148.99	M	16773.99
C	13738.77	2660.22			16398.99		
Z	20333.33	2900.9			23234.23	F	23234.23
Z	20333.33	2900.9			23234.23		
Z	20333.33	2900.9			23234.23	M	23234.23
Z	20333.33	2900.9			23234.23		
H	23058.02	2660.22		3000	28718.24		
Y	27444.44	2900.9	3250	2400	35995.34		
E	16404.44	2660.22		3750	22814.66		
H	23058.02	2660.22		3000	28718.24		
F	19505.25	2660.22		4900	27065.47		
E	16404.44	2660.22	1250	2250	22564.66	F	22564.66
Z	20333.33	2900.9		800	24034.23	M	24034.23
F	19505.25	2660.22		3250	25415.47		
B	12601.09	2660.22		1500	16761.31		
B	12601.09	2660.22		600	15861.31		
D	15209.19	2660.22		750	18619.41		
D	15209.19	2660.22		750	18619.41		
D	15209.19	1330.11		750	17289.3		
D	15209.19	1330.11		2250	18789.3		
D	15209.19	2660.22		750	18619.41		
D	15209.19	2660.22			17869.41		
D	15209.19	2660.22			17869.41		
D	15209.19	1330.11			16539.3		
Y	27444.44	1450.45			28894.89	F	31220.11
Y	27444.44	2900.9		3200	33545.34		
Y	27444.44	1450.45		2400	31294.89		
Y	27444.44	2900.9	2900.9	1600	34846.24		
Y	27444.44	2900.9		800	31145.34	M	31645.21
Y	27444.44	1450.45		2400	31294.89		
Y	27444.44	2900.9		800	31145.34		
Y	27444.44	1450.45		1600	30494.89		
Y	27444.44	1450.45		2400	31294.89		
Y	27444.44	2900.9	8500		38845.34		
E	16404.44	2660.22			19064.66		
E	16404.44	2660.22			19064.66		

Annexe 5C

EQUAL PAY REVIEW: BUSINESS ADVICE COMPANY LTD (BACL): EQUAL VALUE CHECK 1

NO.	NAME	SEX	JOB TITLE	TYPE	START	YRS
6	Denny G	F	Receptionist	S	24-Jul-88	14.1
23	Smith A	F	Receptionist/Mail Room Clerk	S	01-Oct-92	9.9
5	Dawes J	F	Administrative Assistant	S	02-Jul-89	13.2
18	McCleary J	F	Administrative Assistant	S	04-Aug-85	17.1
20	Parrott J	F	Administrative Assistant	S	01-Dec-97	4.8
9	George H	M	Administrative Assistant	S	10-Jan-99	3.6
24	Sweetman J	M	Administrative Assistant	S	01-Sep-99	3.0
1	Bowen A	F	Secretary	S	01-Aug-94	8.1
10	Glamis B	F	Accounts Assistant	S	27-Feb-94	8.5
11	Green L	F	Secretary	S	10-May-92	10.3
12	Howes M	F	Secretary	S	01-Apr-91	11.4
13	Howson R	F	Secretary	S	31-Jan-85	17.6
16	Leigh D	F	Secretary	S	14-Oct-90	11.9
17	Lovatt F	F	Secretary	S	06-Dec-98	3.7
21	Pears H	F	Secretary	S	15-Feb-98	4.5
25	Wilson P	F	Secretary	S	24-Nov-98	3.8
14	Jones S	M	Accounts Assistant	S	14-Feb-01	1.5
4	Daly S	F	Health and Safety Adviser	S	18-Apr-92	10.4
8	Gale D	F	Senior Secretary	S	02-Jan-00	2.7
19	Neill S	F	Senior Secretary	S	01-Jan-98	4.7
7	Ford J	M	Deputy Head, Administration	S	05-Aug-77	25.1
3	Cave P	F	MD's PA	S	18-Mar-84	18.5
22	Sands B	F	Head of Administration	S	08-May-72	30.3
2	Brown S	F	Finance Officer	S	03-Dec-91	10.7
15	Jones T	F	Chief Executive's PA	S	07-Jun-81	21.2
37	Rogers G	F	Senior Business Adviser	A	01-Aug-97	5.1
39	Storey C	F	Senior Business Adviser	A	28-Mar-87	15.4
27	Bennett P	M	Senior Business Adviser	A	01-Jan-91	11.7
30	Clark K	M	Senior Business Adviser	A	01-Sep-91	11.0
31	Davis G	M	Senior IT Adviser	A	06-Apr-98	4.4
32	Evans R	M	Senior Business Adviser	A	01-Feb-97	5.6
34	Kerry N	M	Senior Business Adviser	A	12-Feb-91	11.6
35	McCram V	M	Senior Business Adviser	A	02-Aug-98	4.1
38	Smith K	M	Senior Business Adviser	A	20-Dec-92	9.7
40	Truman F	M	Company Law Adviser	A	01-Aug-91	11.1
41	Westman J	M	Senior Business Adviser	A	21-Jan-90	12.6
28	Boreham W	F	Business Adviser	A	01-Oct-98	3.9
26	Avery F	M	Health and Safety Adviser	A	04-Jan-98	4.7
29	Chips C	M	Business Adviser	A	04-Jan-98	4.7
33	Hyther M	M	Business Adviser	A	04-Jan-98	4.7
36	Lawrence P	M	Business Adviser	A	06-Apr-98	4.4

GRADE	BASIC £	L/P	OTHER	LSA	TOTAL		AVE. TOT.
B	12601.09	2660.22		1500	16761.31		
B	12601.09	2660.22		600	15861.31		
C	13738.77	2660.22		1500	17898.99		
C	13738.77	2660.22		1500	17898.99	F	17398.99
C	13738.77	2660.22			16398.99		
C	13738.77	2660.22		750	17148.99	M	16773.99
C	13738.77	2660.22			16398.99		
D	15209.19	2660.22		750	18619.41		
D	15209.19	1330.11		750	17289.3		
D	15209.19	2660.22		750	18619.41		
D	15209.19	1330.11		750	17289.3		
D	15209.19	1330.11		2250	18789.3	F	17944.92
D	15209.19	2660.22		750	18619.41		
D	15209.19	2660.22			17869.41		
D	15209.19	2660.22			17869.41		
D	15209.19	1330.11			16539.3		
D	15209.19	2660.22		750	18619.41	M	18619.41
E	16404.44	2660.22	1250	2250	22564.66		
E	16404.44	2660.22			19064.66	F	20231.33
E	16404.44	2660.22			19064.66		
E	16404.44	2660.22		3750	22814.66	M	22814.66
F	19505.25	2660.22		3250	25415.47		
F	19505.25	2660.22		4900	27065.47		
H	23058.02	2660.22		3000	28718.24		
H	23058.02	2660.22		3000	28718.24		
Y	27444.44	1450.45			28894.89	F	31220.12
Y	27444.44	1450.45		3200	33545.34		
Y	27444.44	1450.45		2400	31294.89		
Y	27444.44	2900.9	1450.45	1600	33395.79		
Y	27444.44	2900.9	8500		38845.34		
Y	27444.44	2900.9		800	31145.34		
Y	27444.44	1450.45		2400	31294.89	M	32767.41
Y	27444.44	2900.9		800	31145.34		
Y	27444.44	1450.45		1600	30494.89		
Y	27444.44	2900.9	3250	2400	35995.34		
Y	27444.44	1450.45		2400	31294.89		
Z	20333.33	2900.9			23234.23	F	23234.23
Z	20333.33	2900.9		800	24034.23		
Z	20333.33	2900.9			23234.23	M	23434.23
Z	20333.33	2900.9			23234.23		
Z	20333.33	2900.9			23234.23		

Annexe 5D

EQUAL PAY REVIEW: BUSINESS ADVICE COMPANY LTD (BACL): EQUAL VALUE CHECK 2

NO.	NAME	SEX	JOB TITLE	TYPE	START	YRS
6	Denny G	F	Receptionist	S	24-Jul-88	14.1
23	Smith A	F	Receptionist/Mail Room Clerk	S	01-Oct-92	9.9
5	Dawes J	F	Administrative Assistant	S	02-Jul-89	13.2
18	McCleary J	F	Administrative Assistant	S	04-Aug-85	17.1
20	Parrott J	F	Administrative Assistant	S	01-Dec-97	4.8
9	George H	M	Administrative Assistant	S	10-Jan-99	3.6
24	Sweetman J	M	Administrative Assistant	S	01-Sep-99	3.0
1	Bowen A	F	Secretary	S	01-Aug-94	8.1
10	Glamis B	F	Accounts Assistant	S	27-Feb-94	8.5
11	Green L	F	Secretary	S	10-May-92	10.3
12	Howes M	F	Secretary	S	01-Apr-91	11.4
13	Howson R	F	Secretary	S	31-Jan-85	17.6
16	Leigh D	F	Secretary	S	14-Oct-90	11.9
17	Lovatt F	F	Secretary	S	06-Dec-98	3.7
21	Pears H	F	Secretary	S	15-Feb-98	4.5
25	Wilson P	F	Secretary	S	24-Nov-98	3.8
14	Jones S	M	Accounts Assistant	S	14-Feb-01	1.5
4	Daly S	F	Health and Safety Adviser	S	18-Apr-92	10.4
8	Gale D	F	Senior Secretary	S	02-Jan-00	2.7
19	Neill S	F	Senior Secretary	S	01-Jan-98	4.7
7	Ford J	M	Deputy Head, Administration	S	05-Aug-77	25.1
3	Cave P	F	MD's PA	S	18-Mar-84	18.5
22	Sands B	F	Head of Administration	S	08-May-72	30.3
2	Brown S	F	Finance Officer	S	03-Dec-91	10.7
15	Jones T	F	Chief Executive's PA	S	07-Jun-81	21.2
37	Rogers G	F	Senior Business Adviser	A	01-Aug-97	5.1
39	Storey C	F	Senior Business Adviser	A	28-Mar-87	15.4
27	Bennett P	M	Senior Business Adviser	A	01-Jan-91	11.7
30	Clark K	M	Senior Business Adviser	A	01-Sep-91	11.0
31	Davis G	M	Senior IT Adviser	A	06-Apr-98	4.4
32	Evans R	M	Senior Business Adviser	A	01-Feb-97	5.6
34	Kerry N	M	Senior Business Adviser	A	12-Feb-91	11.6
35	McCram V	M	Senior Business Adviser	A	02-Aug-98	4.1
38	Smith K	M	Senior Business Adviser	A	20-Dec-92	9.7
40	Truman F	M	Company Law Adviser	A	01-Aug-91	11.1
41	Westman J	M	Senior Business Adviser	A	21-Jan-90	12.6
28	Boreham W	F	Business Adviser	A	01-Oct-98	3.9
26	Avery F	M	Health and Safety Adviser	A	04-Jan-98	4.7
29	Chips C	M	Business Adviser	A	04-Jan-98	4.7
33	Hyther M	M	Business Adviser	A	04-Jan-98	4.7
36	Lawrence P	M	Business Adviser	A	06-Apr-98	4.4

GRADE	JE PTS	BASIC £	L/P	OTHER	LSA	TOTAL
B		12601.09	2660.22		1500	16761.31
B		12601.09	2660.22		600	15861.31
C		13738.77	2660.22		1500	17898.99
C		13738.77	2660.22		1500	17898.99
C		13738.77	2660.22			16398.99
C		13738.77	2660.22		750	17148.99
C		13738.77	2660.22			16398.99
D		15209.19	2660.22		750	18619.41
D		15209.19	1330.11		750	17289.3
D	430	15209.19	2660.22		750	18619.41
D		15209.19	1330.11		750	17289.3
D		15209.19	1330.11		2250	18789.3
D	430	15209.19	2660.22		750	18619.41
D		15209.19	2660.22			17869.41
D		15209.19	2660.22			17869.41
D		15209.19	1330.11			16539.3
D		15209.19	2660.22		750	18619.41
E	550	16404.44	2660.22	1250	2250	22564.66
E	470	16404.44	2660.22			19064.66
E	470	16404.44	2660.22			19064.66
E	430	16404.44	2660.22		3750	22814.66
F	515	19505.25	2660.22		3250	25415.47
F	500	19505.25	2660.22		4900	27065.47
H	530	23058.02	2660.22		3000	28718.24
H	530	23058.02	2660.22		3000	28718.24
Y		27444.44	1450.45			28894.89
Y		27444.44	2900.9		3200	33545.34
Y		27444.44	1450.45		2400	31294.89
Y		27444.44	2900.9	1450.45	1600	33395.79
Y		27444.44	2900.9	8500		38845.34
Y		27444.44	2900.9		800	31145.34
Y		27444.44	1450.45		2400	31294.89
Y		27444.44	2900.9		800	31145.34
Y	570	27444.44	1450.45		1600	30494.89
Y		27444.44	2900.9	3250	2400	35995.34
Y	570	27444.44	1450.45		2400	31294.89
Z	500	20333.33	2900.9			23234.23
Z	550	20333.33	2900.9		800	24034.23
Z	500	20333.33	2900.9			23234.23
Z		20333.33	2900.9			23234.23
Z		20333.33	2900.9			23234.23

CHAPTER 6

The legal framework

KEY POINTS

The key UK and EU provisions relevant to equal pay are the Equal Pay Act 1970 (EqPA 1970) and Article 141 of the Treaty of Rome. Depending on the particular circumstances, a number of other provisions may be relevant, including:

- The Sex Discrimination Act 1975 (SDA 1975), which covers discrimination in the provision of non-contractual benefits
- The Pensions Act 1995 (PA 1995), which covers equal treatment in occupational pension schemes
- The Race Relations Act 1976 (RRA 1976), which covers discrimination in terms and conditions of employment and the provision of contractual and non-contractual benefits on grounds of race
- The Part-time Workers (Prevention of Less Favourable Treatment) Regulations 2000, SI 2000/1551 (PTW Regs), which prohibit discrimination against part-time workers unless the treatment is justified on objective grounds
- The Fixed-term Employees (Prevention of Less Favourable Treatment) Regulations 2002, SI 2002/2034 (FTE Regs), which prohibit discrimination against fixed-term employees unless the treatment is justified on objective grounds

Codes of Practice supplement the EqPA 1970 and Article 141 with important practical guidance.

6.1 USING THE LEGAL SECTIONS OF THE BOOK

This chapter summarises the UK and EU provisions relevant to equal pay and explains how they relate to one another in practice. For example:

- **Chapters 7 to 13** examine the right to equal pay under the EqPA 1970 and Article 141 of the Treaty of Rome.

- **Chapter 14** considers the relevant provisions of the SDA 1975, RRA 1976, the PTW Regs, and the FTE Regs.
- **Chapter 15** sets out the time limits and procedures for bringing a claim.
- **Chapter 16** considers the question of remedies.

Although the EqPA 1970 applies to both men and women, it is assumed throughout that the claimant is a woman.

6.2 EQUAL PAY ACT 1970

Operation of the equality clause

The device used by the EqPA 1970 to achieve equality in pay and terms and conditions is the equality clause. Under s.1(1) every contract of employment at an establishment in Great Britain is deemed to contain one. If a contract of employment does not have an express equality clause, one is implied into the contract by EqPA 1970, s.1(1).

The equality clause is defined in EqPA 1970, s.1(2). It is a clause whereby a woman (or a man) is contractually entitled to equal pay with any man (or woman) in the same employment who is doing:

- like work;
- work rated as equivalent; or
- work of equal value;

to a member of the opposite sex in the same employment, unless the difference in pay is genuinely explained by something that has nothing to do with sex.

Who is protected?

All workers at any establishment in the UK are covered, including employees, the self-employed, and contract workers. This includes employees in Crown employment and members of the armed services.

A comparable employee

A claimant must choose one or more comparators of the opposite sex who are in the 'same employment'. This means the comparator must work at the same establishment as her or at one where 'common terms and conditions' apply. In either case, under domestic law, the woman and the man must be employed by the same employer or by an associated employer. There is some scope for cross-employer comparisons under Article 141.

What is pay?

Under the EqPA 1970 the definition of pay includes not only wages and salary but other contractual benefits: for example, allowances, fringe benefits, pay progression and pension benefits.

Proving equal work

Like work claims are the simplest. Two people will be regarded as doing like work if they do the same work or broadly similar work provided there are no differences or no important differences in the tasks they actually perform. The tribunal will analyse the nature and extent of any differences, the frequency with which they occur and whether they are of practical importance.

Work rated as equivalent claims depend on the woman's and the man's jobs having been measured and rated as equivalent under a job evaluation scheme that meets the requirements of the EqPA 1970. This means the scheme in question must be analytical, objective and non-discriminatory.

Equal value claims are the most complicated. In an equal value claim, the tribunal has to make an objective assessment as to whether the woman's and the man's jobs are of equal value. This involves analysing the demands of the two jobs (for instance under such headings as effort, skill and decision) to see if they are the same.

Unless the tribunal is satisfied that the claimant's claim has no reasonable prospect of success, it may refer the assessment to an independent expert for a report. Alternatively, the tribunal can determine the matter itself. Either party may put forward expert evidence in support of their case.

Equal Pay Act 1970, s.1(3): genuine material factor defence

Once a claimant establishes that she is doing equal work to that of a comparable man, a presumption arises that the difference in pay and other contractual terms is because of sex discrimination. The burden is then on the employer to show that the explanation for the difference in treatment is genuinely due to a 'material factor' that is not tainted by sex discrimination.

In practice, an employer may identify several factors to account for the difference in treatment between the man and the claimant. Examples include:

- recruitment and retention difficulties;
- different skills, qualifications and experience; and
- red circling (protected pay).

The factor will be 'material' if it is the significant and relevant cause of the difference in pay.

The requirement of 'genuineness' will be satisfied if the reason put forward for the difference in pay is the actual reason and not a sham or a pretence.

Each case will fall into one of three categories:

1. The difference in pay involves direct discrimination. This means the employer's defence cannot succeed.
2. The difference in pay involves indirect discrimination. This means the employer is under a burden to justify objectively the difference in pay or other benefits. This involves showing that the difference corresponds to a 'real need', and is necessary, appropriate and pro-portionate to that need.
3. There is no evidence of direct or indirect discrimination, in which case objective justification may still be required.

What can a claim achieve?

When an equal pay claim is successful, a claimant is entitled to:

(a) an order from the tribunal declaring her rights;
(b) equalisation of contractual terms for the future (if the claimant is still in the relevant employment); and/or
(c) compensation consisting of arrears of pay (if the claim is about pay) and/or damages (if the complaint is about some other contractual term) usually up to a maximum of six years.

In addition, the tribunal may award interest on an award of compensation.

How equalisation is achieved

The equality clause operates so as to vary the claimant's pay and con-tractual terms so that they are no less favourable than the man's. In prac-tice, this means:

1. Equalisation applies to all elements of contractual pay. The concept of pay under the EqPA 1970 includes not only wages and salary but

also other contractual benefits such as allowances and fringe benefits, pay progression and pension benefits.

2. Equalisation takes place on a term-by-term basis. Particular terms that are unfavourable may not be counterbalanced by others that are in the claimant's favour.

3. The equality clause operates to bring the lower standard up to the higher and cannot be used to bring the higher down to the lower.

6.3 PENSIONS ACT 1995 AND THE OCCUPATIONAL PENSION SCHEMES (EQUAL TREATMENT) REGULATIONS 1995

The PA 1995 makes detailed provision for the operation of equal treatment in occupational pension schemes. Sections 62–66 of the PA 1995 mirror the provisions contained in the EqPA 1970 by incorporating an equal treatment rule into every occupational pension scheme. These provisions are supplemented by the Occupational Pension Schemes (Equal Treatment) Regulations 1995, SI 1995/3183, which set out the procedural rules for enforcing any rights under the equal treatment rule. The Regulations adopt the procedural structures contained in the EqPA 1970.

It is important to note that the equal treatment provisions in the PA 1995 only relate to claims based on sex discrimination. Claims based on race discrimination continue to be governed by the RRA 1976.

6.4 ARTICLE 141 OF THE TREATY OF ROME AND THE EQUAL PAY DIRECTIVE

The Treaty of Rome was one of the three treaties that founded the European Union. Article 141 (previously Article 119) requires member states to ensure that the principle of equal pay for male and female employees for equal work or work of equal value is applied. The concept of pay is broadly defined to include 'the ordinary basic or minimum wage or salary and any other consideration, whether in cash or in kind, which the worker receives directly or indirectly, in respect of his employment, from his employer'. Article 141 is directly enforceable by individuals against their employers in national courts and tribunals: *Defrenne* v. *Sabena (No.2)* [1976] ECR 455, ECJ. Note also that the principle of equal pay under Article 141 gives a right to complain of pay discrimination that is either direct or indirect in nature: *Stadt Lengerich* v. *Helmig* [1995] IRLR 216, ECJ.

The Equal Pay Directive (EPD), 75/117/EEC is designed to facilitate the practical application of the principle of equal pay outlined in Article 141. It is not intended to alter the scope of Article 141 and does not create an alternative cause of action to Article 141.

Among other things the EPD requires that:

1. The principle of equal pay for men and women outlined in Article 141 applies to the same work or work of equal value.
2. There must be the elimination of all discrimination on grounds of sex with regard to all aspects and conditions of remuneration.
3. A job classification system used for determining pay must be based on the same criteria for both men and women and drawn up as to exclude any discrimination on the grounds of sex (Article 1).
4. There must be no provisions that are contrary to the principle of equal pay in legislation, administrative rules, collective agreements, wage scales or individual contracts of employment (Articles 3 and 4).
5. Employees must be protected against victimisation for taking steps aimed at enforcing compliance with the principle of equal pay (Article 5).

Relationship between Article 141 and UK law

The following principles apply to the relationship between Article 141 and UK law:

1. The House of Lords has held that the EqPA 1970, the SDA 1975 and Article 141 should be regarded as part of a single code requiring, so far as possible, consistent interpretation: *Strathclyde Regional Council* v. *Wallace & Ors* [1998] IRLR 146, HL.
2. Where domestic law is less favourable than the position would be under Article 141, the community law standard may be relied upon and must prevail: *Barber* v. *Staffordshire County Council* [1996] IRLR 209, CA.
3. UK domestic time limits and procedures apply to a claim relying on Article 141, unless it can be shown that they are less favourable than those relating to similar actions of a domestic nature or are such as to make it impossible in practice to exercise the rights under Article 141: *Biggs* v. *Somerset County Council* [1996] IRLR 203, CA.
4. Any claim under Article 141 must be brought through a UK statute, most commonly the EqPA 1970 but occasionally the SDA 1975.
5. Unlike the EqPA 1970, Article 141 is not restricted to contractual entitlements. Pay for the purposes of Article 141 also includes indirect and non-contractual benefits.

6. Where a benefit is pay under Article 141 but not under the EqPA 1970, the claim should be brought under the SDA 1975 (and the time limits and procedures under the SDA will apply – see **Chapter 16**).

7. Article 141 does not apply to non-pay terms such as contractual holiday entitlement that in domestic law would be included within the remit of the EqPA 1970. The relevant EU provision for non-pay terms is the Equal Treatment Directive, 76/207/EEC.

8. The scope for comparison under Article 141 is also wider than under the EqPA 1970. Under Article 141, a claimant may compare her work with a successor or a predecessor (although not a hypothetical comparator). Cross-employer comparisons are also permitted in certain circumstances.

6.5 SEX DISCRIMINATION ACT 1975

The SDA 1975 provides protection, in defined circumstances, against direct and indirect discrimination on the ground of sex and marital status. The SDA 1975 applies to non-contractual terms such as recruitment, promotion, access to benefits, transfer, training, dismissal and any other detriment.

Relationship between the Equal Pay Act 1970 and the Sex Discrimination Act 1975

In principle, there is no overlap between the EqPA 1970 and the SDA 1975. The inter-relationship between the two statutes may be summarised as follows:

1. If the less favourable treatment relates to the payment of money that is regulated by the contract of employment, only the EqPA 1970 can apply: SDA 1975, s.6(6).

2. If the less favourable treatment relates to a matter that is not regulated by the contract (such as a discretionary payment not regulated by the contract of employment) only the SDA 1975 can apply.

3. If the complaint is that a person has been victimised for bringing proceedings, giving evidence or information, or doing anything else under the EqPA 1970, or making an allegation in good faith under the EqPA 1970, the claim must be brought under the SDA 1975: SDA 1975, s.4.

'Regulated by' means more than merely mentioned in the contract of employment. For example, the contract might provide that an employee was eligible for a discretionary allowance when moving house. If that is all that exists in the contract, it would be a benefit provided for in the contract of employment but not one regulated by the contract. If there is any doubt about which provision applies, the claim should be brought under both statutory provisions.

The Court of Appeal has held that so far as possible the two Acts should be construed together so as to produce a harmonious result: *Shields* v. *Coomes (Holdings) Ltd* [1978] ICR 1159.

There is no cap on arrears of pay under the SDA 1975. The tribunal also has the power to make awards for injury to feelings, aggravated and exemplary damages.

6.6 RACE RELATIONS ACT 1976

Part II of the RRA 1976 deals with unlawful discrimination in employment on the grounds of race. The scheme of the RRA 1976 closely mirrors that of the SDA 1975. In particular, under RRA 1976, s.4(2), employers must not discriminate against employees in the terms of employment that they afford them, or by denying them benefits that they might otherwise expect, or by subjecting them to 'any other detriment'. These provisions are broad enough to cover pay and other benefits (contractual and non-contractual) as well as pay practices that indirectly discriminate against a particular racial group.

There is, however, one qualification where the employee is denied, or given restricted access to, benefits that the employer also offers to the public at large. In those circumstances the issue is whether the employee suffered discrimination as an employee or as a member of the public. The test by which the issue is judged is laid down in RRA 1976, s.4(4). In particular, the claimant must show that the benefits are regulated by the contract of employment or that there is a material difference between the benefits provided to the public and those provided to the employee. Otherwise, the claim should be brought under RRA 1976, s.20.

It is important to note that it is possible to make same sex comparisons under the RRA 1976. The provisions for compensation are also more generous in that there is no cap on arrears of pay and the tribunal also has the power to make awards for injury to feelings, aggravated and exemplary damages.

Race discrimination and the Equal Pay Act 1970

If the claimant is a black woman and her comparator is a white man, or vice versa, it may be appropriate to bring the claim under the RRA 1976 as well as the EqPA 1970. If the claimant and the comparator are the same sex, the claim can be brought under the RRA 1976 only.

6.7 PART-TIME WORKERS (PREVENTION OF LESS FAVOURABLE TREATMENT) REGULATIONS 2000

The Part-time Workers (Prevention of Less Favourable Treatment) Regulations 2000, SI 2000/1551 (PTW Regs) give part-time male and female workers a right to the same pay and terms and conditions of employment on a pro rata basis as full-time workers, with a similar contract, doing broadly similar work, unless any difference in treatment can be objectively justified. In addition, where full-time workers become part-time, they are entitled to retain pro rata terms and conditions.

The PTW Regs apply to all aspects of pay and occupational pensions. It is not necessary to show that the discriminatory pay practice has a disparate impact. A comparison can be made with same sex workers.

The Part-time Workers Regulations and the Equal Pay Act

The range of comparators is more restrictive under the PTW Regs than under the EqPA 1970, even though the comparator under the EqPA 1970 must be of the opposite sex. For example, under the PTW Regs, there is no scope for part-time workers to use a comparator employed by an associated employer. Furthermore, a comparison cannot be made between persons on different types of contract (there are four types in the PTW Regs) or workers not engaged on broadly similar work.

Depending on the circumstances, a claimant who has a claim under the PTW Regs may also have a claim under the EqPA 1970 and Article 141.

6.8 THE FIXED-TERM EMPLOYEES (PREVENTION OF LESS FAVOURABLE TREATMENT) REGULATIONS 2002

The Fixed-term Employees (Prevention of Less Favourable Treatment) Regulations 2002, SI 2002/2034 (FTE Regs) give fixed-term employees, male and female, the right to the same pay and terms and conditions of employment as permanent employees on broadly similar work, unless the different treatment can be objectively justified. It is important to note that comparisons can be made between same sex workers.

The Fixed-term Employees Regulations and the Equal Pay Act

There are several important differences between the FTE Regs and the EqPA 1970:

1. The classes of employees protected by the FTE Regs are narrower than under the EqPA 1970. For example, the FTE Regs do not apply to agency workers or apprentices.
2. The range of comparators is more restrictive under the FTE Regs than under the EqPA 1970, even though the comparator under the EqPA 1970 must be of the opposite sex. For example, a fixed-term employee cannot select a predecessor as a comparator or someone employed by an associated employer.
3. The FTE Regs also adopt a 'package' approach. This means the employer can justify the difference in treatment by showing that the value of the fixed-term employee's total package of terms and conditions is at least equal to the value of a permanent employee's total package of terms and conditions. The 'package' approach is not permitted under the EqPA 1970: *Hayward* v. *Cammell Laird Shipbuilders Ltd (No.2)* [1988] IRLR 257, HL.

Depending on the circumstances, an employee who has a claim under the FTE Regs may also have a claim under the EqPA 1970 and Article 141.

6.9   CODES OF PRACTICE ON PAY

There are two Codes of Practice on pay: one issued by the European Commission in 1996 and the other issued by the EOC in March 1997. Both Codes assist employers to identify sex discrimination in pay practices and recommend that employers undertake pay reviews of their pay systems in order to eliminate discrimination. Codes of Practice are not binding under EU or domestic law. Thus, while a failure to conduct reviews, or otherwise monitor pay systems against discrimination is not unlawful, it is a factor that a tribunal may take into account if it is invited to draw inferences about the employer's conduct.

Pay review model

The Equal Pay Review Toolkit (see **Chapter 5** on what it is and how to use it) was developed as part of the work on a revised version of the EOC *Code of Practice on Equal Pay*, due to be published in spring 2003. The EPR Toolkit should thus have the same legal status as the current Code.

CHAPTER 7

What is pay?

KEY POINTS

- Under the Equal Pay Act 1970 (EqPA 1970) pay includes wages and other contractual benefits
- Under Article 141 pay includes not only contractual wages and benefits but also indirect and non-contractual benefits
- A claim for non-contractual benefits should be brought under the Sex Discrimination Act 1975 (SDA 1975)
- An equal pay review should cover all elements of the pay and benefits package
- If the claimant is successful, she is entitled to have each of her terms and conditions 'levelled up' to those of her comparator

---

7.1   EQUAL PAY ACT 1970

Despite its name, the EqPA 1970 applies to all contractual terms 'whether concerned with pay or not': s.1(2). Thus the EqPA 1970 applies not only to wages and salary but also to other contractual benefits such as:

- overtime;
- holiday pay/leave entitlements;
- profit-related pay;
- profit sharing;
- contractual bonuses;
- share options;
- subsidised loans and mortgages;
- company car and car/petrol allowances;
- telephone allowances;
- private medical insurance;
- life assurance;

- free or subsidised accommodation;
- staff discounts and other subsidies;
- nursery or childcare facilities;
- sports and social facilities.

For further details on pensions, see paragraph **7.3** below.

Although most equal pay claims concern 'pay' terms, some claims may involve 'non-pay' terms such as holiday pay.

7.2 ARTICLE 141

For the purposes of Article 141 pay is defined as 'the ordinary basic or minimum wage or salary and any other consideration, whether in cash or in kind, which the worker receives directly or indirectly, in respect of his employment, from his employer'.

Although there is a significant degree of overlap between the EqPA 1970 and Article 141, there is one important difference: Article 141 is not restricted to contractual entitlements. It applies to indirect and non-contractual benefits as well. Where a benefit is pay under Article 141 but not under the EqPA 1970, the claim should be brought under the SDA 1975. The distinction is important for the question of time limits and remedies (see **Chapters 15 and 16**).

The ECJ has consistently defined pay widely. For example, Article 141 has been held to cover:

(a) discretionary bonuses: *Lewen* v. *Denda* [2000] IRLR 67, ECJ;
(b) discretionary travel facilities (in this case to retired employees): *Garland* v. *British Rail Engineering Ltd* [1982] IRLR 111, ECJ;
(c) severance pay provisions: *Kowalska* v. *Freie und Hansestadt Hamburg* [1990] IRLR 447, ECJ;
(d) redundancy payments (contractual and statutory): *Hammersmith and Queen Charlottes Special Health Authority* v. *Cato* [1987] IRLR 483, EAT and *Barber* v. *Guardian Royal Exchange Assurance Group* [1990] IRLR 240, ECJ;
(e) notice pay (including payments made by the Secretary of State if the employer is insolvent): *Clark* v. *Secretary of State for Employment* [1995] IRLR 421, EAT;
(f) sick pay (contractual and statutory): *Rinner-Kuhn* v. *FWW Spezial-Gebaudereinigung GmbH & Co KG* [1989] IRLR 493, ECJ;
(g) unfair dismissal compensation: *R* v. *Secretary of State for Employment, ex p. Seymour-Smith and Perez* [1999] IRLR 253, ECJ;

(h) paid time off for attendance at external courses and conferences, such as trade union and training conferences (whether made under statutory regulation or otherwise): *Arbeiterwohlfahrt der Stadt Berlin EV* v. *Botel* [1992] IRLR 423, ECJ and *Davies* v. *Neath Port Talbot County Borough Council* [1999] IRLR 769, EAT.

(i) a system or set of rules used to determine pay progression: *Hill and Stapleton* v. *Revenue Commission and Department of Finance* [1998] IRLR 466, ECJ.

Hill concerned a system of pay progression that was less favourable to job sharers than full-timers. Job sharers advanced up the pay scales to a lower point than if they had not been job sharing.

Note that Article 141 does not apply to non-pay terms such as contractual holiday entitlement that in domestic law would be included within the remit of the EqPA 1970. The relevant EU provision for non-pay terms is the Equal Treatment Directive, 76/207/EEC.

7.3 PENSION RIGHTS

Domestic provisions

Sections 62–66 of the Pensions Act 1995 mirror the provisions contained in the EqPA 1970 by incorporating an equal treatment rule into every occupational pension scheme. The procedural rules for enforcing rights under the equal treatment rule are set out in the Occupational Pension Schemes (Equal Treatment) Regulations 1995, SI 1995/3183. The Regulations adopt the procedural structures contained in the EqPA 1970.

Thus it is necessary for a claimant to establish that there has actually been a breach of the equal treatment rule. In practice, domestic provisions operate so as to apply the principles laid down by the ECJ referred to below.

Article 141

It has long been established that contributions to an occupational pension scheme and the benefits derived from such schemes count as 'pay' for the purposes of Article 141. All types of schemes are covered, whether contracted in or out or whether contributory or non-contributory. The decisive criterion is whether the pension is paid to the worker by reason of the employment relationship: *Bestuur van Algemeed Burgerlijk Pensioenfonds* v. *Beune* [1995] IRLR 103, ECJ.

Article 141 may be relied upon against both the employer and trustees of the scheme and has been held to apply to many aspects of pension schemes. For example:

(a) how members are treated by the pension scheme including, in particular, the right to join a pension scheme: *Bilka-Kaufhaus GmbH* v. *Weber von Hartz* [1986] IRLR 317, ECJ;

(b) the provision of retirement ages for pension purposes: *Barber* v. *Guardian Royal Exchange Assurance Group* [1990] IRLR 240, ECJ;

(c) the provision of survivors' pensions: *Ten Oever* v. *Stichting Bedrijfspensioenfonds voor het Glazenwassers-en Schoonmaakbedrijf* [1993] IRLR 601, ECJ.

However, not all aspects of pension practice are covered by Article 141. The following schemes and practices have been excluded:

(a) statutory social security schemes or benefits that do not involve any element of agreement within the undertaking or trade concerned and are compulsory for general categories of workers: *Bilka-Kaufhaus*;

(b) the use of actuarial factors that result in an employer making higher pension contributions on behalf of female employees: *Neath* v. *Hugh Steeper Ltd* [1994] IRLR 91, ECJ;

(c) the use of actuarial factors in determining the value of transfer benefits and capital sum benefits: *Coloroll Pension Trustees Ltd* v. *Russell* [1994] IRLR 586, ECJ;

(d) voluntary additional benefits (on the basis that they are a distinct fund made up of employee contributions only): *Coloroll*;

(e) in the case of a bridging pension, it is not unlawful for an employer to reduce the amount of a bridging pension to take account of the full state pension even though the result is that a female ex-employee between the age of 60 and 65 will receive a smaller bridging pension than that paid to a male counterpart (this is so even if the woman opted to pay reduced NI contributions and is thus not entitled to a full state pension) and an employer may also take account of any widow's pension the employee is receiving: *Birds Eye Walls Ltd* v. *Roberts* [1994] IRLR 29, ECJ.

7.4 EQUAL PAY AND MATERNITY

Special treatment afforded to women in connection with pregnancy or childbirth is excluded from the EqPA 1970: s.6(1). This means a man cannot complain about special treatment a woman receives in connection with pregnancy or childbirth. Precisely what falls within the exclusion is debatable. For example, it is arguable that a bonus to a returning mother falls outside the exclusion as the benefit is provided after the woman has returned to work.

The rights of women on maternity leave are complex and beyond the subject matter of this book. So far as the EqPA 1970 and Article 141 are concerned, the basic principle is that a woman on maternity leave is in a specially protected position and is not entitled to claim equal pay in respect of wages and salary: *Gillespie* v. *Northern Health and Social Services Board* [1996] IRLR 214, ECJ. Neither is she entitled to compare herself with a man on sick leave: *Todd* v. *Eastern Health and Social Services Board and Another (No.2)* [1997] IRLR 410, CA (NI). Thus a woman cannot use either the EqPA 1970 or Article 141 as a vehicle to claim full pay and benefits while she is on maternity leave.

Nevertheless, it has been held that a woman is entitled to the benefit of any pay increase awarded before or during her maternity leave (*Gillespie*) and where a pay review is due to be carried out during maternity leave, failure to carry it out may be a breach of contract and/or discrimination. If the review is based on productivity, this should be assessed on the basis of an average over the period, which does not include the maternity leave period: *CNAVTS* v. *Thibault* [1998] IRLR 399, ECJ.

It should be noted that during ordinary maternity leave contractual benefits other than remuneration are maintained by Employment Rights Act 1996, s.71. A challenge concerning the denial of contractual benefits during additional maternity leave should be brought under ERA 1996, s.23 as an unlawful deduction from wages.

7.5 TERM-BY-TERM COMPARISON

If the claimant wins her claim, she is entitled to have each of her terms and conditions 'levelled up' to those of her comparator – see **Chapter 16** on remedies.

7.6 PRACTICAL IMPLICATIONS

It is important to remember that an equal pay review should cover all elements of the pay and benefits package.

CHAPTER 8

Claimants and comparators

KEY POINTS

- The right to bring a claim under the Equal Pay Act 1970 (EqPA 1970) is available to any person employed under a 'contract for personal services': EqPA 1970, s.1(6)
- The comparator must be a person of the opposite sex
- The comparator must be employed at the same time as the claimant, or may be a predecessor or a successor (there is no scope for using a hypothetical comparator)
- Under the EqPA 1970, the comparator must be in the 'same employment'
- Under Article 141, there is scope for selecting a comparator from a different employment
- An equal pay review should cover all categories of workers entitled to bring an equal pay claim

---

8.1   WHO IS PROTECTED?

The right to claim equal pay is not confined to an 'employee' as defined in other statutes. It is available to any person employed under a 'contract of service or of apprenticeship or a contract personally to execute any work or labour': EqPA 1970, s.1(6). This includes:

- employees;
- ex-employees (up to six months after the termination of employment);
- contract workers;
- self-employed;
- partners;
- trainees and apprentices;
- home workers.

There is no length of service or hours of work requirement to bring a claim and it is important to note that any equal pay review should cover all categories of workers entitled to bring an equal pay claim.

Crown employees and office holders

Employment in the civil and public service is treated as private employment for the purposes of the EqPA 1970. So, a civil servant may take an equal pay claim in the same way as other employees.

Although those holding a statutory office (that is, an office set up by or in pursuance of any enactment) are specifically excluded from the EqPA 1970 by s.1(8), they are protected by Article 141. In *Perceval-Price* v. *Department of Economic Development* [2000] IRLR 380, CA (NI), the court held that tribunal chairmen are 'workers' who are in 'employment' in the context of EU law and therefore entitled to bring a complaint for equal pay under Article 141. This means that others in a comparable situation such as the police, judges and members of boards of government agencies have the same right.

Self-employed

The EqPA 1970 also covers the self-employed. In *Quinnen* v. *Hovells* [1984] IRLR 227, the respondent, who operated concessions in department stores, hired self-employed assistants on a commission basis. The claimant complained that two female assistants received a higher rate of commission. The EAT confirmed that he could bring a complaint under the EqPA 1970 as well as the Sex Discrimination Act 1975 (SDA 1975).

Agency workers

Individuals placed by an employment agency to work for another person are protected by the EqPA 1970. A current issue for agency workers is whether they can claim equal pay with employees employed by the principal. In *Allonby* v. *Accrington and Rossendale College* [2001] IRLR 364, the Court of Appeal has asked for guidance from the European Court of Justice on whether a self-employed lecturer working at a college through an employment agency can claim equal pay with a lecturer working at the same college but as the college's employee.

Trainees

Most trainees will fall within the definition of employed under EqPA 1970, s.1(6). If there is any doubt, a claim could also be brought under the SDA 1975 (or Race Relations Act 1976 (RRA 1976) as appropriate), which prohibits discrimination in the terms on which the individual was offered training and protects the trainee from suffering 'detriment': SDA 1975, s.6(2) and RRA 1976, s.4(2).

Armed service personnel

There are special procedures in relation to armed service personnel. A complaint cannot be presented to the tribunal unless the claimant has first made a complaint under the Service Redress Procedures: EqPA 1970, s.7A.

Overseas employment

The EqPA 1970 only applies to individuals employed at establishments in Great Britain: s.1(1) (see paragraph **8.4** for meaning of 'establishment'). Great Britain includes the continental shelf but excludes Northern Ireland, the Channel Islands and the Isle of Man. It also includes British territorial waters: EqPA 1970, s.1(12).

In *Banks* v. *Service Children's Education* (2302867/99), the claimant was employed at all times in a member state of the EC. The tribunal disapplied the words 'at an establishment in Great Britain' in EqPA 1970, s.1(1) and SDA 1975, s.62 since they were incompatible with Article 39 (ex Article 48) of the Treaty of Rome concerning the Freedom of Movement.

Special provisions apply to employment on board ships, aircraft and hovercraft: SDA 1975, s.10. Employment in these circumstances will be covered by the EqPA 1970 if the vessel is registered in the UK and, in the case of aircraft and hovercraft, operated by a party who has his principal place of business or is ordinarily resident in Great Britain, unless the employee works wholly overseas. For example, it was held that a tribunal did not have jurisdiction to hear the claim of an employee who worked on a German registered ship mainly outside territorial waters: *Haughton* v. *Olau Line (UK)* [1986] IRLR 465, CA.

Illegal contracts

An individual who has an illegal contract of employment may be excluded from claiming under the EqPA 1970. In *Hall* v. *Woolston Hall Leisure Ltd* [2000] IRLR 578, the Court of Appeal said it is necessary in the first instance to have regard to the degree to which the employee actively participated in the illegal performance of the contract. The correct approach is to consider whether the claimant's claim arises out of or is so inextricably bound up with her illegal contract that the court cannot permit her to recover compensation without appearing to condone her conduct. In *Hall*, the claimant knowingly acquiesced in a fraud on the Inland Revenue but the Court of Appeal held it was not fatal to her claim of sex discrimination. It is uncertain whether a similar result might be expected under the EqPA 1970 where the contract of employment is central to a claim.

8.2 MULTIPLE APPLICATIONS

While some cases involve just one claimant, frequently a group of cases arises out of the same facts. Equal value claims in the public sector, in particular, but also in large private sector organisations, commonly involve many claimants and several employers. In group cases and multi-party actions, it is usually necessary for the parties to agree to use representative cases simply because of the time and costs involved in trying numerous individual cases.

Legal considerations

All those directly affected by the claim must submit individual applications, although they can now do this by 'signing up' to a single application form (see **Chapter 15**). While the tribunal does not have the power to order a test case that will bind other parties without their agreement, it can try sample or representative cases where all the parties involved in the other cases agree. Although the tribunal rules do not contain a specific provision relating to representative cases, the EAT confirmed in *Bristol Channel Repairers Ltd* v. *O'Keefe* [1978] ICR 691 that the hearing of representative cases is within the tribunal's power to regulate its own procedure. The EAT has stressed, however, that tribunals must take great care to ensure that where representative cases are used all the cases are truly identical.

For example, in *Ashmore* v. *British Coal Corporation* [1990] IRLR 283, CA, 1,500 canteen assistants lodged equal pay claims. Out of the 1,500, 14 were selected as sample cases on the basis that they represented the common issues in the cases. The sample claims were unsuccessful but Mrs Ashmore, one of the 1,500 but not one of the 14 sample cases, sought to pursue her claim. The Court of Appeal held that in the absence of fresh evidence, namely evidence that 'should entirely change the aspect of the case', the claim should be struck out on the basis that it was an abuse of process. Notwithstanding that the sample cases were not formally binding in the sense of being test cases, the Court of Appeal held that it was contrary to the interests of justice to re-litigate the same factual issues.

Practical considerations for claimants

The first question for the claimants' representatives is whether all group members should submit applications or only a representative small number. The best approach is a matter for local judgement. The advantages of all submitting applications are that:

1. All of the claimants, if successful, will be entitled to up to six years' back pay (plus interest), as well as equal pay for the future, whereas if only representative claims are submitted, the wider group may benefit for the future, but only actual claimants will receive any back pay.
2. If some or all of the sample or representative cases from the group are successful, it should be possible to negotiate settlements for any similar cases. This may be important if the proceedings are likely to be protracted, when compensation figures may be large.
3. The majority will provide support for the minority whose claims are considered in detail and avoid the employer undermining the claim of a small number as unrepresentative.

The disadvantages are that:

1. Administration and co-ordination of a large number of claims, including updating records of changes in address, employment, etc., is a major undertaking for the claimants' representatives.
2. Even where representative cases are selected for trial, the proceedings are likely to take longer than with sample claims.
3. Any of the claimants may be proposed for selection by the employer as representative test cases (see below). Those selected may need to be interviewed by one or more experts and possibly give evidence to the tribunal. If they are unwilling to do this, their claims will have to be withdrawn (except in exceptional circumstances, such as the death or serious illness of the claimant).

Where all group members have submitted applications, the next step is to select a group of cases that represent all the factual and legal issues involved in the cases. This may involve lengthy negotiations between the parties. If agreement cannot be reached, one option is for the tribunal to order each party to choose an equal number of cases that they both consider to be representative of all the issues to be resolved (or the parties may agree to do this without the direction of the tribunal). The practice is then for the balance of the cases to be left in abeyance pending the outcome of the proceedings with the intention of settling them by negotiation thereafter.

8.3   IDENTIFYING A SUITABLE COMPARATOR

From the claimant's perspective, the selection of a comparator(s) involves a number of practical and legal considerations. So far as an employer is concerned, the choice of comparator will often impact on its ability to explain and justify any difference in pay under EqPA 1970, s.1(3).

Comparator must be of the opposite sex

The claimant must be able to point to a comparator of the opposite sex. In *Collins* v. *Wilkin Chaoman Ltd* (945/93), EAT, a question arose whether a claimant could claim equal pay with a comparator who physically appeared to be of the opposite sex but who biologically was of the same sex. The EAT upheld the tribunal's decision to dismiss the claim on the ground that the comparator was not a person of the opposite sex. However, this decision is unlikely to be followed, at least in the case of post-operative transsexuals, following the decision of the European Court of Human Rights that it is a breach of Articles 8 and 12 of the European Convention on Human Rights not to recognise the new gender of a post-operative transsexual: *Goodwin* v. *United Kingdom* [2002] IRLR 664.

A claimant's right to choose

The EAT has said that it is for the claimant to select the man with whom she wishes to be compared. In *Ainsworth* v. *Glass Tubes and Components Ltd* [1977] IRLR 74, EAT, a tribunal decided to substitute its own choice of comparator for that of the comparator selected by the claimant. The EAT held that the tribunal was wrong to do so. It is equally inappropriate for the employer to try to influence the choice of comparator.

Comparisons with predecessors or successors

The comparator may be:

- someone with whom the claimant works at the present time; or
- a predecessor: *Macarthy's Ltd* v. *Smith* [1980] ICR 672, ECJ; or

- a successor: *Diocese of Hallam Trustee* v. *Connaughton* [1996] IRLR 505, EAT.

In *Macarthy's Ltd* v. *Smith* [1979] IRLR 316, CA, Mrs Smith was claiming like work with her predecessor as manager of the stockroom. A majority of the Court of Appeal held that the EqPA 1970 requires the man and the woman to be employed at the same time but referred the case to the ECJ for guidance on the scope of Article 141. The ECJ held that under Article 141 a comparison could be made with Mrs Smith's predecessor: [1980] ICR 672, ECJ. In practice, the EqPA 1970 is now construed in conformity with Article 141 as not requiring contemporaneous employment. In the recent case of *Kells* v. *Pilkington plc* (1435/00), the EAT held that an employee was entitled to choose a predecessor who had been employed over six years previously. The EAT suggested that this would be permissible even where the claimant is paid more than her male predecessor was over six years ago.

While there is no legal impediment to a predecessor or a successor being a comparator, it may avoid potential evidential difficulties if the comparator is in post for the duration of the claim. A comparator who is no longer in post may not have the best recollection of his duties and responsibilities and, having left the workplace, he may also be reluctant to cooperate. Note that the tribunal's powers to compel the cooperation of a comparator in these circumstances are limited (see **Chapter 15**). Moreover, as the EAT noted in *Kells*, evidential problems may arise in cases where there has been a long passage of time between the employment of the claimant and the comparator. If the nature of the work, pay scales and working and economic conditions change over the years, it may be difficult to prove that the difference in pay is due to gender.

Choosing a successor for a comparator could potentially cause difficulties as well. For example, the longer the period of time between the two contracts of employment, the more likely it is that the employer will be able to explain and justify the difference in pay under EqPA 1970, s.1(3). The most obvious factor in such circumstances will be that market forces may have determined the successor's higher rate of pay.

Hypothetical comparisons

If there is no predecessor, successor or contemporaneous man with whom a claimant can make a comparison, it seems it is not open to her to construct a hypothetical comparator and to compare her treatment with how a man would be treated if he existed. In *Macarthy's Ltd* v. *Smith,* the ECJ rejected the Advocate General's opinion that the scope for comparison under Article 141 includes a hypothetical comparison.

In *Wallis* v. *Prudential Portfolio Managers Ltd* (35372/91) a tribunal took a different stance. The claimants alleged that they had been denied access to pension benefits because they worked part time. The tribunal took the view that the question whether a comparable man would have received the same or better benefits was irrelevant because any difference in the claimants' entitlement arose solely as a result of their part-time status. In the circumstances, the tribunal decided that the claimants did not need to name individual comparators since the necessary comparison was simply with a group of workers eligible for pension benefits under the scheme. In *Allonby* v. *Accrington & Rossendale College* [2001] IRLR 364, the Court of Appeal has asked for guidance from the European Court of Justice on whether, in the context of a statutory pension scheme covering a whole occupational group, a woman must have a comparator in the same employment.

Despite the ECJ's decision in *Macarthy's Ltd* v. *Smith*, there have been several cases where the ECJ has found that statutory provisions have been found to discriminate without any comparator being identified, for example, the case of *Rinner-Kuhn* v. *FWW Spezial-Gebaudereinigung GmbH* [1989] IRLR 493, ECJ, concerning statutory sick pay.

Does the comparator have to be representative?

Although the EAT held in *Thomas* v. *National Coal Board* [1978] IRLR 451 that it is not necessary for the comparator to be representative of the men in the group from which he has been selected, the EAT in *British Coal Corporation* v. *Smith* [1993] IRLR 308 took a different view. This makes good, practical sense because if the chosen male comparator is not representative of his group, the employer will have a defence under EqPA 1970, s.1(3) (see **Chapter 12**). For example, it would not usually be appropriate to choose a comparator whose pay has been red-circled.

It is sometimes tempting to a claimant to select a union steward as comparator, as he is more likely to be sympathetic, but this may be inappropriate, for example, where the steward's time off for union duties has resulted in adjustments being made to the job (for instance only undertaking the shorter and/or easier tasks).

How many comparators?

Many claimants select more than one comparator. This avoids the claim collapsing if the comparator turns out to be inappropriate for any reason (for example, atypical of his group, subject to personal protection). It also allows the claimant to select comparators from different grades or pay rates, or occupational groups (in the case of an equal value claim) if she is not sure which one will turn out to be of equal value.

Although, in theory, there is nothing to prevent a claimant choosing a range of comparators with whom to compare her work, in practice it could be unwise. A large number of comparators could extend considerably the time taken by the independent expert to produce a report. Moreover, the House of Lords has warned against the abuse of equal value procedures by claimants who cast their net too widely across a range of comparators: *Leverton* v. *Clwyd County Council* [1989] IRLR 28, HL. If faced with such a claim, an employer may use the procedure in EqPA 1970, s.2A to establish that there are no reasonable grounds in respect of certain of the comparators (see **Chapter 11**).

Comparator who is paid less but has more favourable conditions overall

There is no reason why a claimant cannot choose a comparator who is paid the same or less but has more favourable conditions overall. This is because, if the claimant wins her claim, she is entitled to have each of her terms and conditions 'levelled up' to those of her comparator (see **Chapter 16**).

Incremental pay scales

Where both claimant and comparator are on incremental pay scales, depending on the circumstances, it may be appropriate to select more than one comparator at different points on the scale. The Court of Appeal has held that a claimant can only be awarded equal pay with the comparator's point on the scale, not a point higher on the scale commensurate with her own experience in post: *Evesham* v. *North Hertfordshire Health Authority* [2000] IRLR 257, CA.

Does the comparator have to give his permission?

The comparator does not have to give his permission to be named in the proceedings or even be sympathetic to the claim. Nevertheless, a comparator who is cooperative and supportive will ease the preparation and conduct of the claim.

Male undertaking like work

A woman is not debarred from choosing a comparator from a different occupational group just because there is a man undertaking like work to her: *Pickstone* v. *Freemans* [1988] IRLR 357, HL. In *Pickstone*, the claimant and four other warehouse operatives pursued an equal value claim with checker warehouse operatives. The House of Lords rejected the employer's argument that as there were men employed as warehouse operatives the women were precluded from pursuing a claim.

Overseas comparator

By virtue of EqPA 1970, s.1(6) a claimant is limited in her choice of comparator to men employed at establishments in Great Britain. In *Harding* v. *Scandia Asset Management Ltd* (3204139/99) the claimant, a portfolio manager, sought to compare herself with two comparators based in another EU country. The case has been referred to the ECJ to determine whether the provision should be disapplied to enable the claimant to proceed with her claim.

Position of a woman on maternity leave

The ECJ has held that a woman on maternity leave is in a special position. In particular, a claimant is not entitled to compare herself with a man on sick leave, or a man actually at work, in order to claim full pay and benefits during maternity leave (see paragraph **7.4**). In *Alabaster* v. *Woolwich Building Society* [2002] IRLR 420, CA the claimant argued that no comparator is necessary under the EqPA 1970 because she was claiming to have suffered inequality of pay by reason of pregnancy. The case has been referred to the ECJ on other points but, in due course, the Court of Appeal will have to decide whether EU law requires that she has a remedy under the EqPA 1970 notwithstanding that she has no comparator.

8.4   SCOPE OF COMPARISONS

The precise scope for comparison is one of the unresolved issue in equal pay law.

Selecting a comparator from the same employment

Under EqPA 1970, s.1(6) the claimant must be able to point to a comparable man 'in the same employment'. This means the comparator must work at the same establishment as her or at one where 'common terms and conditions' apply. In either case, the claimant and the comparator must be employed by the same employer or by associated employers.

Associated employers

Employers are 'associated' where one company is controlled by another, or where both employers are companies controlled by a third person. Thus it is possible for an equal pay claim to be brought between employees of different companies in the same corporate group.

The Northern Ireland Court of Appeal has held that a statutory body corporate is not a 'company' within the meaning of the statutory definition of associated employer. Thus a female office administrator employed by the Fair Employment Agency was unable to claim equal pay with a male administrator in the Equal Opportunities Commission for Northern Ireland: *Hasley* v. *Fair Employment Agency* [1989] IRLR 106, CA (NI).

Establishment

The EqPA 1970 does not define what is an 'establishment' but there is case law on the meaning of the word in redundancy legislation. In *Secretary of State for Employment and Productivity* v. *Vic Hallam Ltd* [1969] 5 ITR 108, the Divisional Court held that there is no comprehensive test and that it is a question of fact and degree to be determined in each case. Relevant factors include:

(a)   some degree of permanence;
(b)   some organisation of people working there;
(c)   whether it is a place in which or from which people are employed; and
(d)   whether there is exclusive occupation of premises.

In *Rockfon A/S* v. *Specialarbejderforbundet i Danmark* [1996] IRLR 168, the ECJ defined establishment as meaning simply the local employment unit.

If the employee is not employed actually at an establishment, she is deemed to be employed at the establishment from which she works. If she does not work from an establishment, then she is deemed to be employed at the establishment with which her work has the closest connection: SDA 1975, s.10(4). This provision is designed to address the situation, for example, of freelance workers working from home. (SDA 1975, s.10 is deemed to apply to the EqPA 1970 by virtue of SDA 1975, s.10(1).)

Selection of a comparator from a different establishment

Where the claimant selects a comparator from a different establishment it must be shown that the comparator's terms and conditions of employment are sufficiently similar to those that apply to a similar male at the claimant's establishment. If there is no such man at the claimant's establishment then it has to be shown that like terms and conditions would apply if a man were employed in the particular job concerned. It is important to note that it is not necessary for the claimant to show that she shares common terms and conditions with her comparator.

Whether the terms and conditions are 'common' involves an enquiry into the extent to which each establishment acts autonomously in fixing terms. For example:

1. In *British Coal Corporation* v. *Smith* [1996] IRLR 404, HL, a question arose whether women canteen workers and cleaners could compare their work with surface mineworkers employed at different pits. The House of Lords held that terms and conditions of employment are 'common' if they are substantially comparable on a broad basis. They rejected the contention that they must be identical. In this case, the existence of nationally agreed terms for overtime, holidays and sick pay was a sufficient basis for establishing common terms and conditions.

2. In *Leverton* v. *Clwyd County Council* [1989] IRLR 28, HL, a nursery nurse chose a comparator who worked for the same local authority but at a different establishment. Although there were differences between their hours of work and holiday entitlement, their terms and conditions of employment were derived from the same collective agreement. The House of Lords held that terms and conditions of employment governed by the same collective agreement represent the paradigm, though not necessarily the only example, of common terms and conditions contemplated under EqPA 1970, s.1(6).

3. In *Thomas* v. *National Coal Board* [1987] IRLR 451, EAT, bonus payments and concessionary entitlements formed a substantial part of the comparators' remuneration. The amounts of the bonus and concessionary payments were negotiated locally, whereas the entitlement to the payments was negotiated nationally. The EAT held that the basic similarity of terms and conditions was not affected by the existence of the locally negotiated agreements.

Selecting a comparator from a different employment

In contrast to the position under the EqPA 1970, where a claimant's choice of comparator is defined by reference to the comparator's employer and his workplace, the scope for comparison under Article 141 is much broader. Sedley LJ has described it as 'a large terrain which is still being mapped': *Allonby* v. *Accrington and Rossendale College* [2001] IRLR 364, CA.

The scope for comparison under Article 141 extends to the 'same establishment or service': *Defrenne* v. *Sabena (No.2)* [1976] ECR 455, ECJ. The ECJ has not defined what is meant by a 'service' but it has been taken to mean that, in certain circumstances, cross-employer comparisons are permitted. The essential ingredients of a 'service' would seem to be:

(a) the existence of a public service with prescribed duties;
(b) a common pursuit of the same (statutory) objectives;
(c) underpinned by common control, via a Secretary of State.

So, for example, in *Scullard* v. *Knowles and Southern Regional Council for Education and Training* [1996] IRLR 344, EAT, Mrs Scullard, who worked for a regional advisory council, claimed equal pay with male employees employed by other regional councils. The EAT decided that the scope of comparison permitted under Article 141 is wider than the comparison permitted under EqPA 1970, s.1(6) and remitted the case to the tribunal to make relevant findings for the purpose of deciding whether workers employed by regional advisory councils were within the same 'service'. The EAT regarded the extent of common control of the regional councils by a third party (the Training and Education Directorate of the Department for Education, as it was) and the commonality or otherwise of the terms and conditions of employment observed in regional councils as relevant matters. Likewise, in *Hayes and Quinn* v. *Mancunian Community Health NHS Trust and South Manchester Health Authority* (16977/93) and (16981/93), a tribunal held that comparisons could be made between employees working in different NHS Trusts on the basis that all NHS Trusts are, to a sufficient degree, under the control of the Secretary of State for Health.

The case of *South Ayrshire Council* v. *Morton* [2002] IRLR 256, CS takes the principles of cross-employer comparisons one stage further. In *Morton,* a female primary school head teacher employed by one local authority claimed equal pay with a male secondary school head teacher employed by another education authority. The Court of Session held that not only does an equal pay claim not have to be confined to the claimant's own employer, it does not even have to be limited to a comparison with someone in the same 'service'. According to the Court of Session, the criteria of same establishment and service referred to in *Defrenne* are merely specific examples of cases that fall within Article 141. Citing another passage from the judgment in *Defrenne* as authority (paragraph 21), the Court of Session held that, if the discrimination originates from legislative provisions or collective agreements, a cross-employer comparison is permissible without deciding whether the work is carried out in the same establishment or service. In *Morton*, the pay settlement was negotiated under statutory authority and under overall governmental control.

Further guidance on the scope for comparison has been provided by the ECJ in *Lawrence* v. *Regent Office Care Ltd and Others* [2002] IRLR 822. The claimants in *Lawrence* were originally employed by a local council but were transferred to private companies as a result of compulsory competitive tendering. The issue to be determined was whether, for the purposes of an equal pay claim, the claimants could choose male comparators who were still employed by the local council. The ECJ confirmed that the scope for comparison under Article 141 is not necessarily limited to situations in which men and women work for the same employer. However, the Court held that the principle of cross-employer comparisons is limited to circumstances where the discrimination can be attributed to a single source and there is a body that is responsible for the inequality and could restore equal treatment. *Morton* is a good example of this principle.

The Advocate General identified three categories to which the principle would apply, that is, where:

- statutory regulations lay down pay terms and conditions for more than one undertaking, establishment or service, such as the NHS;
- several undertakings or establishments are covered by a common collective agreement, for example as in *Morton*;
- terms and conditions are laid down centrally for more than one business within a holding company or group.

In *Allonby* v. *Accrington and Rossendale College* [2001] IRLR 364, the Court of Appeal has asked for guidance from the European Court of Justice on whether a self-employed lecturer working at a college through an employment agency can claim equal pay with a lecturer working at the same college but as the college's employee. Although the claimant and her comparator are working for different employers, the college effectively controls what each is paid.

8.5 PRACTICALITIES OF IDENTIFYING A SUITABLE COMPARATOR

There are four procedures available to the claimant to gather information for a claim. They are not mutually exclusive and so, depending on the circumstances, more than one procedure may be used at a time.

Questionnaire procedure

The Employment Act 2002 introduced a questionnaire procedure designed to assist an individual who believes she has been the subject of sex discrimination in pay to ask the employer for information that will help her to decide whether she has a claim, and to frame her claim in the most effective way. The procedure will be included as an amendment at EqPA 1970, s.7B and is almost identical to the procedures available in disputes over matters of race, sex and disability. Regulations implementing the provision are expected in early 2003.

If a claimant has difficulty identifying a suitable comparator or establishing historical differences in pay, the employer could be asked in a questionnaire to:

(a) identify the individuals in certain posts or on certain grades by name and gender;
(b) provide details of their remuneration packages from the date of recruitment (for a full list of possible payments and benefits see the checklist in **Chapter 7**);
(c) provide details of relevant salary scales during the relevant period; and
(d) provide information about their jobs.

Guidance on how to use the questionnaire procedure is set out in **Chapter 15**.

Grievance procedure

By bringing an internal grievance before commencing tribunal proceedings, a claimant may glean information on which to base her claim. Note that, in due course, it will be compulsory for a claimant to take steps to resolve the matter through the employer's internal machinery before commencing proceedings: Employment Act 2002, s.32. It is expected this provision will be introduced in late 2003 – see paragraph **15.2** for further details.

Discovery

Once proceedings have been commenced, the claimant may apply for discovery of the relevant information. In *Leverton* v. *Clwyd County Council* [1985] IRLR 197, the EAT held that so long as there is a prima facie case that the claimant's contractual terms are less favourable than those of comparable male employees, the claimant can use the discovery process to obtain disclosure of documents that will enable her to identify appropriate comparators. The EAT cautioned against making orders merely to facilitate 'fishing expeditions'.

Disclosure of information to recognised trade union

Employers have a duty to disclose information to a recognised trade union:

(a) without which the trade union representatives would be to a material extent impeded in carrying on collective bargaining; and

(b) which it would be in accordance with good industrial relations practice to disclose for collective bargaining purposes: Trade Union and Labour Relations (Consolidation) Act 1992, s.181.

This may include earnings analysed by sex and where appropriate the distribution of pay among groups of employees. Note that the employer does not have to disclose information which relates specifically to individuals and that the union is restricted to claiming information about the workers in respect of whom the union is recognised. Nevertheless, the procedure could be used to obtain general information about the make-up and average rates of pay of different groups of workers in the organisation. See the ACAS *Code of Practice 2: Disclosure of information to trade unions for collective bargaining purposes* (for further information see **www.acas.org.uk**).

8.6 PRACTICAL IMPLICATIONS FOR EMPLOYERS

From an employer's perspective, the current uncertainties about the scope of comparisons in an equal pay claim mean it is difficult to know how broadly an equal pay review should draw its terms of reference. What is clear is that private sector employers within the same corporate group, and public sector employers operating within the same 'service', should be alive to the possibility of claims between companies and organisations, particularly where there are joint collective bargaining arrangements covering several employers.

CHAPTER 9

Like work

KEY POINTS

- The test for like work is defined in Equal Pay Act 1970 (EqPA 1970), s.1(4). The claimant and comparator will be regarded as doing like work if:
  - they do work of a broadly similar nature; and
  - there is no difference or no important difference in the tasks they actually perform
- The two stages of the test must be considered separately
- Even if the claimant can show that she and her male comparator do like work, it is still open to the employer to establish a defence under EqPA 1970, s.1(3)

9.1 BURDEN OF PROOF

Under domestic and EU law, it is for the claimant to prove that she does like work to her chosen comparator and that she receives less pay than him. In *Brunnhofer* v. *Bank der Osterreichischen Postsparkasse AG* [2001] IRLR 571, the ECJ held that if the pay system lacks transparency, so that it is not possible to determine the exact difference in pay between the claimant and her comparator, the burden of establishing that she receives less pay will be discharged if the claimant establishes, in relation to a relatively large number of employees, that the average pay for women is less than for men undertaking equal work.

Note that the evidential burden of showing 'differences of practical importance' rests on the employer: *E Coomes (Holdings) Ltd* v. *Shields* [1978] IRLR 263, CA.

9.2 SAME OR BROADLY SIMILAR

The question of the same or broadly similar work is one of fact for the tribunal to determine. In contrast to equal value claims, where expert evidence from the parties is common, tribunals in like work cases generally reject expert evidence on the grounds that the point of issue is a matter of fact within their own competence. The tribunal makes its decision on the question of like work in accordance with the following principles:

1. The focus is on the nature of the work done by the claimant and the comparator.
2. It is not necessary that the work is identical; it is enough if it is of a broadly similar nature.
3. The correct approach involves a general consideration of the similarity of the type of work involved and the skill and knowledge required to do it. In particular, it is not necessary or appropriate to undertake a minute examination of the work undertaken by the man and the woman: *Capper Pass* v. *Lawton* [1976] IRLR 366, EAT.
4. The comparison of the jobs must take into account the whole of the comparator's job. Duties that the claimant and comparator do not have in common cannot be excluded from consideration.
5. What is relevant is the work on which the man and woman *are* employed (namely, what they actually do) not the work for which they *were* employed: *Redland Roof Tiles Ltd* v. *Harper* [1977] ICR 349, EAT.

Examples of jobs found to be broadly similar work are:

(a) male and female shop assistants in different sections of the same department store;
(b) a female cook who prepares lunches for directors and a male chef who cooks breakfast lunch and tea for employees;
(c) a female teacher, head of business studies department and a male teacher, head of business studies department with additional vocational duties. (Note: in some other cases, teachers of different subjects have not been considered to be doing like work and have been dealt with instead as equal value cases.)

9.3 SIGNIFICANT DIFFERENCES

Once the claimant has shown that the work is of a broadly similar nature, it is for the employer to establish that there are differences between the claimant and comparator jobs that are of practical importance in relation to terms and conditions of employment. At this stage the differences in the tasks and duties performed by the claimant and the comparator become significant.

The tribunal will conduct a detailed examination of what the man and woman actually do to determine:

(a) What are the nature and extent of the differences?
(b) With what frequency do they occur in practice?
(c) Are the differences of practical importance in relation to terms and conditions of employment?

Differences in practice

In establishing what differences there are between the claimant and comparator jobs, what the contract of employment and job description require a person to do is irrelevant except to the extent that the duties are performed in practice. Thus the tribunal will concentrate on the work that is actually done rather than the work the claimant and the comparator can be required to do under their respective job descriptions or contracts of employment. For instance, in *Electrolux Ltd* v. *Hutchinson* [1976] IRLR 410, the comparators could be required to do night work or to transfer to other departments. The EAT held that that it was irrelevant what the comparators could be required to do unless they were in fact required to do so in practice.

Trivial differences

The correct approach, according to the EAT, is to disregard any trivial differences: *Capper Pass*. For example, in *British Leyland (UK) Ltd* v. *Powell* [1978] IRLR 57, a female driver in a catering department drove vans within the factory premises to and from the kitchen and a male driver in the transport section drove vans on the public highway. It was held that the differences were not of practical importance.

Do the differences justify the differences in pay and conditions?

It is not open to the employer to allege a partial justification of the different terms and conditions. The issue is whether the differences in the things that they do justify the whole of the differential. In *British Leyland (UK) Ltd* v. *Powell* [1978] IRLR 57, the EAT suggested that a practical guide is to ask whether the differences are such as to put the man and the woman into different categories or grades in a job evaluation scheme.

Examples of differences of practical importance

Skill levels

Skill levels may be important when differences of practical importance are considered. For example, in *Brodie* v. *Startrite Engineering Co Ltd* [1976] IRLR 101, EAT, male and female drill operators were held not to be employed on like work because the man was able to set his own machine, sharpen the drills and carry out minor repairs without the assistance of the charge hand.

Additional or differing duties

The amount of time the comparator spends on different or additional tasks may be highly relevant. In *Redland Roof Tiles Ltd* v. *Harper* [1977] ICR 349, EAT, the man and the woman were employed as clerks and the only difference between their jobs was that, for two periods of five weeks, the man had deputised for a transport supervisor. The EAT held that the infrequency with which the task arose meant that it was not of practical importance.

Note that it is only if the comparator actually carries out the additional duties that a tribunal should consider whether they contribute to differences of practical importance between the two jobs.

Greater responsibility

Whether and to what extent the man and the woman exercise responsibility may in practice amount to a difference of substance. In particular, the tribunal should take into account the degree and level of responsibility exercised by each party. For example, in *Eaton* v. *Nuttall* [1977] IRLR 71, EAT, a male production scheduler handling items worth between £5 and £1,000 each was held not to be doing like work to a female production scheduler handling 2,400 items worth no more than £2.50 each because the consequences of error on the part of the man were much greater than for the woman.

The time when the work is carried out

The EAT has held that the mere time at which the work is performed should be disregarded when considering the differences between the things that the man does for the purposes of EqPA 1970, s.1(4), provided it is the only difference: *Dugdale* v. *Kraft Foods Ltd* [1977] IRLR 368,

EAT. So, for example, where the man does the same work but at night, this may be classified as like work if it is the only difference. Payments for night and unsocial hours may either be disregarded in the equalisation process or they may amount to a defence under EqPA 1970, s.1(3) (see **Chapter 12**).

In contrast, in *Thomas* v. *National Coal Board* [1987] IRLR 451, EAT, 1,500 female canteen assistants compared their work with a male canteen assistant on permanent night work at a higher rate of pay. It was found that this was not a difference in mere time at which the work was performed that could be recognised by a separate allowance, but a difference in personal risk and responsibility that justified the different pay and conditions.

Flexibility

Flexibility may amount to a difference of practical importance, provided the claimant has not been denied the opportunity of being flexible. For example, in *Hatch* v. *Wadham Stringer Commercials (Ashford) Ltd* (40171/77), a female driver claimed like work with male drivers. The male drivers were required to change their routes and to work at different times, whereas the claimant worked on a fixed route at a set time. Although the claimant was prepared to undertake the same tasks as the men, management had decided not to require her to do the same things. In the circumstances, the tribunal held that the employer could not rely on flexibility as a difference of practical importance.

Training and professional qualifications

The ECJ has held that training and qualifications may be factors that are relevant to the question of 'same work': *Brunnhofer* v. *Bank der Osterreichischen Postsparkasse AG* [2001] IRLR 571, ECJ and *Angestelltenbetriebsrat der Weiner Gebietskrankenkasse* v. *Wiener Gebietskrankenkasse* [1999] IRLR 804, ECJ respectively.

Wiener involved graduate psychologists and specialist medical doctors employed as psychotherapists. The doctors were on a higher scale and earned 50 per cent more than the psychologists, most of whom were women. The ECJ noted that professional training may either be a factor that objectively justifies the difference in pay, or it may be one of the possible criteria for determining whether the same work is being performed. In this case, even though the two groups had been performing the same activities over a considerable period of time, the ECJ held that they could not be regarded as employed on the same work. The ECJ considered that they drew on different skills and qualifications acquired in different disciplines and that this affected the nature of the work and how it was done. Furthermore, the doctors were required to perform other medical tasks in an emergency that the psychologists were not qualified to perform.

Physical effort

A difference in physical strength needed for the job may be of practical importance but is now recognised as having the potential to perpetuate pay inequality. For example, in *Hicking* v. *Basford Home Fashions Ltd* (2601155/98), the tribunal rejected the contention that physical effort should be weighted more highly than other aspects of the job because it was a significant feature of the comparator's job as a warehouse operative. The tribunal considered that if that submission were correct it would have the result of perpetuating inequality of pay in any environment where muscle power was a factor.

The frequency with which greater strength may be required may also be relevant here.

9.4   CLAIMING LIKE WORK AND WORK OF EQUAL VALUE IN THE ALTERNATIVE

Where the claimant's job is not identical to the comparator's job, but has similarities, the claimant may claim like work and work of equal value in the alternative. Although the appellate courts have not expressly addressed the point, several cases have come before the EAT involving like work and equal value claims in respect of the same comparator (for example, *Byrne* v. *the Financial Times* [1991] IRLR 417, EAT) and in none of these cases has an objection been taken to the practice.

The advantages to the claimant of including a like work claim are:

(a) a like work claim is usually dealt with at one hearing, no expert evidence is required and there is no reference to an independent expert;

(b) even if the like work claim is unsuccessful, the tribunal has often obtained sufficient information to make an immediate decision on whether to refer the associated equal value claim to an independent expert.

The disadvantages of a like work claim from the claimant's perspective are:

(a) the claimant usually has to give evidence in person, which is less likely in an equal value case, especially where an expert is involved;

(b) a like work hearing may cause delay, for instance, if the issue of equal value is not considered by the tribunal until its reserved decision on the like work question is available.

Note that it is not possible for a woman to succeed in both a like work and an equal value claim in respect of the same comparator.

9.5   EQUAL PAY ACT 1970, S.1(3) DEFENCE

Even if the claimant can show that she does the same sort of work as the man, and that the differences (if any) in the things they do are not so significant as to justify different terms and conditions of employment, it is still open to the employer to establish a defence under s.1(3) (see **Chapter 12**).

9.6   RELATIONSHIP BETWEEN EQUAL PAY ACT 1970, S.1(3) AND S.1(4)

The factors that are relevant to the question of whether there are 'differences of practical importance' under EqPA 1970, s.1(4) will not be relevant to the question of material differences for the purpose of EqPA 1970, s.1(3). So, for example, market forces may be relevant to the EqPA 1970, s.1(3) defence but will not be relevant to the tribunal's consideration of whether there are differences of practical importance under EqPA 1970, s.1(4).

9.7   HOW TO FIND OUT IF THERE IS A LIKE WORK CLAIM

A claimant may use the new questionnaire procedure at EqPA 1970, s.7B to find out the pay of individuals doing the same or a similar job to her. A questionnaire could also be used to obtain information about what a comparator actually does in practice and to find out why he is paid more (see **Chapter 15** for guidance on how to use the questionnaire procedure). It may also be useful for a claimant to keep a diary of the tasks undertaken by herself and her comparator over a certain period, which establish the duties of the two jobs.

Employers will find out if they have a like work problem in their organisation by undertaking a like work check. Guidance on how to conduct a like work check is set out in **Chapter 4**.

It is important to remember that different job titles, job descriptions and contractual obligations do not always reflect what a person does. Employers should look at what people actually do and how often.

CHAPTER 10

Work rated as equivalent

KEY POINTS

- The second way in which a claimant can establish a claim for equal pay
  is if her work has been rated as equal to that of man under a job evaluation study
- The test for work rated as equivalent is defined in Equal Pay Act 1970
  (EqPA 1970), s.1(5)
- A claimant is entitled to equal pay if there is a job evaluation study which:
  - rates the jobs as equivalent; or
  - would have rated the jobs as equivalent but for the fact that sex dis-
    crimination was built into the scheme (that is, the jobs are of equal
    value but the formula for computing the value of the woman's work
    differs from the formula for computing the value of men's work – in
    practice, this type of claim is rare)
- Even if the claimant can show that she does work rated as equivalent, it
  is still open to the employer to establish a defence under EqPA 1970,
  s.1(3).

10.1   JOB EVALUATION

Job evaluation is a technique for comparing the demands of jobs within
a population or organisation, in order to develop a rank order of jobs,
usually as the basis for a grading and pay structure. For details of types
of job evaluation schemes and information about how they are used to
determine pay, see **Chapter 3**.

10.2   BURDEN OF PROOF

Where a claimant bases her claim on an existing job evaluation scheme,
the burden of proving that the scheme meets the requirements of EqPA

1970, s.1(5) is on her: *England* v. *Bromley LB Council* [1978] ICR 1, EAT. The burden also lies with the claimant to show that her job would have been rated as equivalent had the scheme been applied without discrimination.

10.3   REQUIREMENTS OF EQUAL PAY ACT 1970, S.1(5)

Section 1(5) of the EqPA 1970 defines what is a valid job evaluation study for the purpose of claiming work rated as equivalent.

In the first instance, the study must be analytical. This means that each job must have been evaluated in terms of the demands made on the worker under various headings (such as effort, skill, decision). For example, in *Bromley* v. *H&J Quick Ltd* [1988] IRLR 456, CA, the study commissioned by the employers used the paired comparisons method to provide a rank order of benchmark jobs. Jobs not evaluated in this process were then slotted into the rank order on a felt-fair basis, that is, in line with the general level of expectation as to the value of the job. The claimants and comparators were not chosen for the paired comparison exercise but instead were slotted into the rank order on a felt-fair basis. The Court of Appeal held that the method used for the study was not analytical and did not meet the requirements of EqPA 1970, s.1(5).

Second, the scheme must be objective and capable of impartial application. This means the scheme must objectively assess the value to be placed on the work performed. For example, in *Eaton* v. *Nuttall* [1977] IRLR 71, EAT, the job evaluation study used by the employers produced a series of salary grades in respect of which there was a minimum, mid or maximum point. The point at which a particular employee was placed within the range depended on such factors as responsibility. However, it was a matter for management to decide how much responsibility was involved in each job. Thus management made a subjective judgement concerning the nature of the work before the employee could be fitted into the appropriate place in the salary grade. The EAT did not consider the study met the requirements of EqPA 1970, s.1(5). According to the EAT, for a study to be valid, it must be possible by applying the study to arrive at the position of a particular employee at a particular point on a particular salary scale without taking other matters into account, except those unconnected with the nature of the work.

Third, both the woman's job and the man's job must have been analysed under the scheme. It is not enough that benchmark jobs have been evaluated on a factor–demand basis as required by EqPA 1970, s.1(5) if the claimant and comparator jobs have not been. In *Bromley* v.

H&J Quick Ltd, the claimant and comparator jobs were ranked against the benchmark jobs on a whole job or felt-fair basis (sometimes called 'slotting-in'). The Court of Appeal held that this was not good enough for the purposes of EqPA 1970, s.1(5). Likewise, in *Sparks* v. *Department of Environment, Transport and the Regions* (2301739/00), although the claimant and her comparator were in the same employment, their jobs had been evaluated at different times under two different studies that used different methodologies. The tribunal held that the studies fell outside the requirements of EqPA 1970, s.1(5).

Fourth, the woman must have been employed in an undertaking or group of undertakings in respect of which the job evaluation scheme was carried out. Thus a job evaluation scheme undertaken by health boards in Great Britain was held to have no relevance to health board employees in Northern Ireland: *McCauley* v. *Eastern Health and Social Services Board* [1991] IRLR 467, CA (NI).

10.4 ROLE OF BENCHMARK JOBS

It appears that it is not necessary for an employer to have arranged for every single job in an organisation to have been individually evaluated on a factor–demand basis. Most job evaluation studies involve the selection of benchmark jobs that are used as a standard because they are considered to be typical of a grade or group of jobs. In *Bromley* v. *H & J Quick Ltd*, Woolf LJ stated that there will be no objection to using benchmark jobs in this way provided there is no material difference between the benchmark jobs and the other jobs within the group.

10.5 WHEN ARE THE RESULTS OF A JOB EVALUATION STUDY BINDING?

Once a job evaluation study has been undertaken and has resulted in a woman's job being rated as equivalent to a man's, the woman may be able to claim parity with the man even if the employer, for whatever reason, does not implement the study.

For example, in *O'Brien* v. *Sim-Chem Ltd* [1980] IRLR 373, HL, the evaluation of the jobs had been completed but because of government incomes policy the employees could not be paid in accordance with the new job evaluation structure. The employer argued that since the pay structures had not been adjusted at the conclusion of the job evaluation exercise, the claimant could not rely on the study to bring a claim for work rated as equivalent. The House of Lords rejected this argument. It held that once a job evaluation study has been undertaken and has resulted in the conclusion that the job of a woman is of equal value with that of a man, a claim for work rated as equivalent could proceed.

There is conflicting authority on whether the parties must have accepted the results of a study before it is valid. In *Arnold* v. *Beecham Ltd* [1982] IRLR 307, the EAT held that a job evaluation study is not complete unless and until the parties who agreed to carry out the study (namely employer and union) have accepted its validity. According to the EAT, this is because, no matter how carefully a study is undertaken, there is always a risk that the results may offend common sense and be unacceptable to those whose relationship it is designed to regulate. On the facts of the case, the employer and the union had accepted that the study was substantially valid, even though it had not been implemented. In the circumstances, the EAT confirmed that the claimant was entitled to equal pay.

By contrast, in *Dibro Ltd* v. *Hore* [1990] IRLR 129, EAT, the employer was permitted to rely on the results of a job evaluation study carried out after an equal value claim had been brought, even though the claimants and their union had not accepted the results. In the EAT's view, provided the job evaluation study is analytical and valid within the meaning of EqPA 1970, s.1(5) and relevant to the issues between the parties, its results should be admitted in evidence. Any challenge to its validity can be made at that stage.

It should be noted that *O'Brien*, *Arnold* and *Dibro Ltd* seem to be in conflict with Article 1 of the Equal Pay Directive, 75/117/EEC, which refers to the case where 'a job classification system is used for determining pay'.

10.6 CONVERSION OF POINTS INTO A SALARY GRADE

In determining whether two jobs are rated as equivalent, it is appropriate to take into account the conversion of points into a particular salary grade, where this is an integral part of the scheme. In *Springboard Sunderland Trust* v. *Robson* [1992] IRLR 261, EAT, two jobs were assessed as giving 410 and 428 points respectively. Under the rules of the scheme they were placed within the same grade but the employers refused to pay the woman (who had fewer points) the rate for the grade. It was held by the EAT that the two jobs were rated as equivalent within the meaning of EqPA 1970, s.1(5) with the result that the claimant was entitled to equal pay.

10.7   IS THE SCHEME DISCRIMINATORY?

Section 1(5) of the Equal Pay Act 1970 permits the results of a job evaluation study to be challenged on certain limited grounds. Where the
headings under which the work is compared are the same but the formula
for computing the value of the claimant's work differs from the formula
for computing the value of the men's work, then the claimant is entitled
to equal pay if she can show that, had equal treatment been observed, her
job would have been rated as equivalent.

For example, EqPA 1970, s.1(5) would apply where a man and a
woman perform the same under a factor but the man is given more credit
for it. However, it does not permit a challenge to a job evaluation study
on the ground that it undervalues or fails to take account of the types of
skills primarily associated with women, for example, where an undue
number of points is given to strength factors as opposed to manual dexterity. The claimant's option in these circumstances would be to bring a
claim for equal value and rely on the provisions of EqPA 1970, s.2A(2)
to establish that the scheme was discriminatory (assuming the employer
sought to rely on the study as part of its defence).

10.8   PRACTICAL APPLICATION OF EQUAL PAY ACT 1970, S.1(5)

The work rated as equivalent ground for claiming equal pay was introduced into the EqPA 1970 as a result of the way in which sewing
machinists at Ford (see **Chapter 1**), whose job had been evaluated in
grade B, were paid only a proportion of the grade B rate, because they
were women. Following the implementation of the EqPA 1970, a repeat
of this situation is almost inconceivable. In practice, however, EqPA
1970, s.1(5) has been used in a number of quite different circumstances,
for example:

1.   Where claimant and comparator jobs were evaluated under a sin-
     gle job evaluation scheme and paid the same grade, but subse-
     quently the women's rate of pay was reduced in order to win a
     compulsory competitive tendering (CCT) process: *Ratcliffe* v.
     North Yorkshire County Council [1993] IRLR 591, ECJ.
2.   Where claimants, whose jobs had been evaluated under the Health
     Service JES for ancillary workers, were contracted out, during which
     period their weekend premium payments and sick pay provisions
     were removed. The contract failed and they were re-employed by the
     original NHS Trust, but the original weekend working and sick pay

provisions were not restored: *Derbyshire & Ors* v. *St Helens MBC* (2102185/98).

3. Where claimant and comparator jobs have been evaluated under the local government manual worker job evaluation scheme and they received the same basic pay, but the men received productivity supplements in addition. Most such claims have been successful in tribunal, for example, *Ryder and Others* v. *Warwickshire County Council and Others* (1301481/97).

In such claims, the work rated as equivalent issue is not generally in dispute and the question to be decided by the tribunal is whether or not the respondent's genuine material factor defence argument is valid.

10.9 CLAIMING LIKE WORK AND WORK OF EQUAL VALUE IN THE ALTERNATIVE

If the tribunal decides that the claimant's work is not rated as equivalent under EqPA 1970, s.1(5), she will blocked from pursuing an equal value claim by virtue of EqPA 1970, s.2A (see **Chapter 11**). As far as like work is concerned, it is likely that differences of practical importance will have been identified, making such a claim untenable. A claimant's only real option in these circumstances is to choose a different comparator whose job has not been evaluated by the job evaluation study in question.

If, however, the claim failed because the job evaluation study did not meet the requirements of EqPA 1970, s.1(5), for example, because the employer establishes that either the claimant or comparator jobs had not been evaluated under the job evaluation study, or if the JES turned out not to be a valid one (see **10.5** above), it would be appropriate to pursue an equal value claim in the alternative.

Employers who use job evaluation should bear in mind that if the scheme does not cover the whole workforce, or more than one scheme is in use, there is always the possibility of equal value claims between the schemes or outside the schemes altogether.

10.10 EQUAL PAY ACT 1970, S.1(3) DEFENCE

Even if the claimant can show that she does work rated as equivalent, it is still open to the employer to establish a defence under s.1(3) (see **Chapter 12**).

It should be noted that a material factor defence should not succeed if the factor relied upon by the employer is an aspect of the job that was taken into account in the job evaluation study. For example, if the job evaluation study takes into account working conditions, the employer should not be permitted to justify a supplement paid to the comparator for the fact that his working conditions are worse than the claimant's.

10.11   HOW TO FIND OUT IF THERE IS A WORK RATED AS EQUIVALENT CLAIM

A claimant could use the new questionnaire procedure at EqPA 1970, s.7B to find out the pay of individuals on her evaluated grade and to obtain information about the design and implementation of the job evaluation scheme, such as, who is included in the scheme, choice of factors, factor definitions, weighting, choice of grade boundaries, etc. In particular, if proof of evaluation is needed, the claimant should request evidence in relation to the evaluation exercise. A questionnaire could also be used to establish the employer's justification for paying individuals differently despite them being on the same evaluated grade (see **Chapter 15** for guidance on how to use the questionnaire procedure).

Employers will find out if they have a work rated as equivalent problem in their organisation by undertaking a work rated as equivalent check. Guidance on how to conduct a work rated as equivalent check is set out in **Chapter 5**. Regular maintenance of a job evaluation scheme should ensure that any flaws in it are detected. For example, care should be taken when jobs are regraded (owing to changes in job content and the grading of new jobs) to ensure that biased differentials between men's and women's jobs are not restored. The job evaluation scheme can be checked using the Equal Pay Review Toolkit checklist in **Annex 3A**.

CHAPTER 11

Equal value

KEY POINTS

The third way in which a claimant can establish a claim for equal pay under the Equal Pay Act 1970 (EqPA 1970) is by showing that her work is of equal value to that of a man in the same employment.

- The concept of equal value is not formally defined in either EU or domestic legislation
- The question of equal value is determined either by the tribunal itself (usually but not always with the assistance of expert evidence) or with the assistance of the report of an independent expert (from the ACAS panel)
- An equal value claim may be dismissed at a preliminary stage either because it is a 'hopeless' case or because the claimant's job has already been rated as lower than the comparator job(s) on a non-discriminatory analytical job evaluation scheme
- Even if the claimant can prove that she undertakes work of equal value to her comparator, her claim for equal pay will not necessarily succeed if the employer can establish a defence under EqPA 1970, s.1(3)

11.1 BURDEN OF PROOF

Under both domestic and EU law, the burden of proof falls on the claimant to establish that she does work of equal value to that of her comparator and that she receives less pay than him. In *Brunnhofer* v. *Bank der Osterreichischen Postsparkasse AG* [2001] IRLR 571, the ECJ held that if the pay system lacks transparency, so that it is not possible to determine the exact difference in pay between the claimant and her comparator, then the burden of establishing that she receives less pay will be discharged if the claimant establishes, in relation to a relatively large number of employees, that the average pay for women is less than that for men undertaking equal work.

11.2   NO REASONABLE GROUNDS

Equal value cases are subject to special procedures once the case reaches the initial hearing stage. The full procedure is set out in **Chapter 15**. In particular, in EqPA 1970, s.2A the tribunal has the right to dismiss a claim because there are no reasonable grounds for determining that the work is of equal value. Note that this provision is separate from the tribunal's right to strike out proceedings on the basis that they are scandalous, misconceived or vexatious (see **Chapter 15**).

In practice, the no reasonable grounds defence arises in four particular situations:

- where the claim is weak;
- where the issue has already been decided in a substantially similar case;
- where there is an existing job evaluation scheme covering claimant and comparator;
- where a job evaluation scheme has been introduced after proceedings have been commenced.

Weak claims

As originally drafted, EqPA 1970, s.2A was specific about the requirement for tribunals to consider whether there are no reasonable grounds for an equal value claim. Following an amendment to s.2A by the Sex Discrimination and Equal Pay (Miscellaneous Amendments) Regulations 1996, SI 1996/438, it is less clear whether a tribunal must as a matter of course consider whether a claim is too weak to proceed. Section 2A states that a tribunal may choose to determine the question of equal value for itself or 'unless it is satisfied that there are no reasonable grounds for determining that the work is of equal value … ' refer the matter to an independent expert. In practice, tribunals do not usually consider whether there are no reasonable grounds unless the employer specifically raises the point as part of its defence.

If the tribunal holds a hearing to determine whether the case has sufficient merit to proceed, each party will present evidence (oral and documentary) of the claimant and comparator duties and responsibilities for the tribunal to consider. Relevant documentation may include job descriptions, person specifications, organisation charts, etc. The tribunal will consider all the relevant evidence and look at the question in the round. The burden of proof is neutral and it is for the tribunal to judge the issue on all the evidence.

The power to dismiss a claim in these circumstances should be used sparingly since the whole basis of the procedure is that the tribunal needs expert advice before it is in a position to decide the question of equal value. A tribunal should only prevent a case from continuing if it is exceptionally weak (it is worth noting that when the Equal Pay (Amendment) Regulations 1983, SI 1983/1794 were laid before the House of Commons, the minister said that EqPA 1970, s.2A(1) was intended only to apply to a 'hopeless case'). Thus the type of case that ought to be dismissed at this stage is one where it is patently obvious that the claimant is not employed on work of equal value. However, if there is an arguable case, the matter should be allowed to proceed.

The fact that a tribunal has concluded that there is no reasonable prospect of the claimant showing that her work is of equal value to that of her comparator(s) does not thereby put an end to the case. The tribunal must adjourn the hearing to give the claimant an opportunity to adduce expert evidence on the question of equal value, if she so wishes: *Wood* v. *William Ball Ltd* [1999] IRLR 773, EAT. In *Wood*, the EAT envisaged a two-stage process. First, the Tribunal must decide whether an expert's report is to be obtained by the tribunal itself or by the parties. If it is to be obtained by the parties, then the next stage will be for the Tribunal to determine the case on the basis of the evidence presented by the parties.

The issue has already been decided in a substantially similar case

The second situation in which the no reasonable grounds defence arises is where a claimant seeks to pursue an equal value claim after the hearing and rejection of sample cases that have substantially similar facts to her own case: *Ashmore* v. *British Coal Corporation* [1990] IRLR 283, CA (see paragraph **8.2**).

Existing job evaluation scheme

The third situation arises where the employer relies on the existence of a job evaluation study to establish that there are no reasonable grounds. Under EqPA 1970, s.2A(2), where the claimant's work has been given a lower value than the comparator's work under an existing job evaluation study, the tribunal may dismiss the claim. From an employer's perspective, this is the most effective way of blocking an equal value claim.

Burden of proof

The Court of Appeal confirmed in *Bromley* v. *H&J Quick Ltd* [1988] IRLR 456 that an employer who seeks to rely on the existence of a job evaluation study to establish a defence has the burden of establishing in accordance with EqPA 1970, s.2A(2)(a) and s.2A(2)(b), that:

- the existing study meets the requirements of s.1(5); and
- the study is not tainted by sex discrimination.

Requirements of the Equal Pay Act, s.1(5)

To meet the requirements of s.1(5), the scheme must be:

- analytical;
- objective;
- capable of impartial application; and
- have measured both the man's and the woman's jobs.

The requirements of s.1(5) are discussed in **Chapter 10**.

Discriminatory scheme

Section 2A(3) of the EqPA 1970 states that a job evaluation study will be discriminatory if it is made on a system which discriminates on grounds of sex where a difference or coincidence between values set on different demands, under the same or different headings, is not justifiable, irrespective of the sex of the person on whom these demands are made. It is apparent that the test for discrimination under EqPA 1970, s.2A(3) is wider than that laid down in EqPA 1970, s.1(5). Whereas the latter simply prohibits overt discrimination, EqPA 1970, s.2A(3) is drafted to catch indirect forms of discrimination.

It is for the employer to show that the job evaluation scheme in question is not discriminatory. This will involve explanations of the factors taken into account by it and of how the scheme works. Relatively few job evaluation schemes have been tested in the courts. According to the ECJ in *Rummler* v. *Dato-Druck GmbH* [1987] IRLR 32, a scheme is not discriminatory solely because one of its criteria is based on characteristics more commonly found among men provided the choice of factors used in the scheme is representative of the tasks done by both sexes and the criteria in question correspond to the real requirements of the job. A scheme is discriminatory, however, if it fails to include, or properly take into account, a demand (such as caring demands in a job involving looking after sick or elderly people, for example nursing) that is an important element in the woman's job. A study will also be discriminatory if it gives an unjustifiably heavy weighting to factors that are more typical of the man's job.

In *Bromley* v. *H&J Quick*, Dillon LJ observed that every attempt at job evaluation will inevitably involve an element of value judgement, which is inherently subjective to some extent (for example, in measuring how much of a factor or quality is involved in a particular job or in determining what relative weights ought to be attached to different factors or qualities involved). He warned that if the selection of particular factors or factor weightings has a disproportionate impact on women, this would be regarded as discriminatory if not objectively justified. The good intentions of the parties are no guarantee that the scheme will be non-discriminatory.

In the absence of more detailed guidance from the courts on what makes a scheme discriminatory, both the European Commission and the Equal Opportunities Commission (EOC) have developed checklists to assist employers to ensure that their schemes will stand up to legal challenge. A version of the EOC checklist was published as an appendix to the 2002 edition of *Job Evaluation Schemes Free of Sex Bias* (EOC, 2002); and a revised version is incorporated into the Equal Pay Review Toolkit (the checklist can be found in **Annex 3A**). Research and experience indicate that very few job evaluation schemes, especially among those introduced before 1984, meet all the European Commission and EOC checklist criteria.

Examples of job evaluation studies that have failed

To date, a pre-existing job evaluation study has in practice proved a sound defence for employers (which may in part explain its increasing use in the UK) and an intractable obstacle, and thus deterrent, to claimants wishing to pursue equal pay claims in organisations using job evaluation. Only where flaws in the scheme have been very obvious have tribunals rejected the job evaluation study defence. In *Patel* v. *Intarsia International Ltd* (42109/92/LN/B), the respondent's job evaluation study defence to equal pay claims was not accepted by the tribunal because the exercise had been carried out by the firm's production manager with no consultation or involvement of employees, no understanding of bias, using a scheme designed for another company in 1960 and intended in this case only to reduce wages. In *Bateman* v. *Hull & East Riding Community Health NHS Trust* (1807708/00), the tribunal rejected a job evaluation study defence on the grounds that the study had not been objectively carried out. In particular, there was only a half-point difference between male applicant and comparator jobs, which fell above and below a grade boundary, and the original higher score for the male applicant's job had been reduced under pressure from the female head of personnel, while the scores of the female manager of the female comparators had not been challenged. The claim was referred to an independent expert.

Claimants have been rather more successful in demonstrating that their jobs have not been analysed and evaluated under the job evaluation scheme put forward as a defence (the *Bromley* v. *H&J Quick* situation). For instance, in *McCauley* v. *Eastern Health and Social Services Board* [1991] IRLR 467, the Northern Ireland Appeal Court accepted that neither applicant nor comparator jobs had been analysed or evaluated under the NHS scheme for ancillary workers, which had been developed on the basis of jobs in England and Wales only and later transferred for use in Northern Ireland.

Practical considerations for claimants

Since a non-analytical job evaluation study is only binding on classes of workers covered by the study, the claimant should establish:

- exactly who is covered by the study?
- whether the claimant's and the comparator's jobs existed at the time when the study was drawn up;
- if not, have their jobs been evaluated since they were introduced?
- have the claimant's and the comparator's duties and responsibilities changed significantly since the evaluation took place?
- if so, have they been re-evaluated under the scheme?

Note that in order to establish that a job evaluation study is discriminatory, a claimant is likely to require expert evidence from a job evaluation specialist.

Practical considerations for employers

Analytical job evaluation has obvious legal advantages for an employer. Not only do such schemes provide a mechanism for ensuring that the organisation is complying with legislation and has a degree of transparency in pay systems, making equal pay claims less likely, but they also enable the employer to defeat an equal value claim at an early stage.

Employers who use analytical job evaluation will avoid claims being brought against them if they:

- ensure that the scheme has been designed and implemented in a non-discriminatory way;
- ensure that the scheme is reviewed regularly, so that factors used represent all demands made by the jobs and that new or changed jobs are evaluated within a reasonable timescale;
- have one scheme that covers the entire workforce. If the scheme does not cover the whole workforce, or two or more schemes are in use, there is always the possibility of an equal value claim between jobs in different schemes, or between jobs within and outside the scheme.

Introduction of a job evaluation scheme after proceedings have been commenced

The fourth situation arises where the employer seeks to introduce a job evaluation scheme after proceedings have been commenced. The EAT has held that, provided the new scheme relates to the facts and circumstances existing at the time when the proceedings were instituted, it will be admissible in evidence as an EqPA 1970, s.2A(2) defence at any stage up to the final hearing at which the tribunal gives its decision on the whole of the evidence: *Dibro Ltd* v. *Hore* [1990] IRLR 129. The EAT has also held that the tribunal has a discretion to order a stay of the equal value claim pending implementation of a job evaluation scheme: *Avon County Council* v. *Foxall* [1989] IRLR 435. However, for a stay to be ordered, a valid reason for doing so needs to be shown. In *Foxall*, the principal reason relied on by the employer was the risk of the job evaluation scheme being undermined if the results of the independent expert's report were more favourable to the applicants than the results of the scheme. The EAT did not consider that the employer's reason had much force. The EAT held that the loss to the claimants of their statutory right to pursue their claim would significantly outweigh any disadvantages to Avon County Council arising from a refusal to grant the stay.

Amendments to the 'no reasonable grounds' procedure

The government has published draft regulations amending the no reasonable grounds procedure in several respects. Under these regulations, the tribunal will no longer have the power to strike out a hopeless complaint. Moreover, where there is an existing job evaluation scheme, the draft regulations state that the tribunal shall conclude that the work is not of equal value, unless it suspects that the job evaluation scheme itself is discriminatory or otherwise unsuitable to be relied on. In such cases, the tribunal will also have the option of asking an independent expert to prepare a report on whether an existing job evaluation scheme is discriminatory. It is expected the new regulations will be introduced in late 2003.

11.3 WHAT IS EQUAL VALUE?

The concept of equal value is not formally defined in either EU or domestic legislation. Section 1(2)(c) of the EqPA 1970 provides that when a claimant claims equal value, a comparison should be made between the claimant's work and the comparator's work 'under such headings as effort, skill and decision'. This involves a weighing and balancing between the features of the claimant and comparator jobs and thus allows for comparisons between quite different jobs. A description of how the process is carried out is contained in **Chapter 4**.

How does the tribunal determine equal value?

Under EqPA 1970, s.2A(1) it is for the tribunal to determine whether the claimant's work is of equal value to that of the comparator. Usually, the tribunal will commission a report from an independent expert (selected from a panel appointed by ACAS) but the tribunal may in certain circumstances dispense with the services of the independent expert and decide the matter either without any expert evidence or on the basis of expert evidence presented by the parties. The special procedure for equal value claims is set out in **Chapter 15**, together with guidance on working with the independent expert and instructing experts.

At what point in time is the comparison made?

If the claimant is still in the job that forms the subject matter of the claim, the question of equal value will be judged at the date of her application to the tribunal. This may be significant if either the claimant or the comparator have changed jobs or duties in the intervening period. If, on the other hand, the claimant left her post before filing her claim, the tribunal will identify the length of time she was undertaking equal work during the backdating period (see **Chapter 16** for details of the backdating period).

It should be noted that the same principles apply to claims for like work and work rated as equivalent.

What is equal?

The value of the woman's and the man's work need not be precisely equal in order for their work to be adjudged to be of equal value.

In an early equal value case, *Wells & Others* v. *F Smales & Son (Fish Merchants) Ltd* (10701/84–10715/84), the tribunal found the jobs of all claimants to be of equal value to that of the comparator, even though the independent expert had said five were not equal, albeit by small margins. The tribunal said that these claimants 'score so closely that the differences between them and the comparator are not relevant or make real material differences'. In contrast, in *Brown & Royle* v. *Cearns & Brown Ltd* (29411/83) where the independent expert's report found the claimant's work to be worth 95 per cent of that of the male comparator, the tribunal rejected this broad-brush approach and found the jobs to be not of equal value.

In *Worsfold* v. *Southampton & South West Hampshire HA* (18296/87) and *Lawson* v. *South Tees HA* (17931/87) a tribunal again considered what amounts to 'equal'. In the tribunal's view, work is not of equal value where there is 'an overall measurable and significant difference' between the demands of the respective jobs. In this case, the independent expert had found a small points difference between the claimant and comparator jobs of less than 5 per cent. In the circumstances, the tribunal concluded that there was no measurable and significant difference between the jobs under consideration. Their conclusion was supported by the independent expert who conceded under cross-examination that if he, as a manager, had been responsible for grading the jobs the difference between them would not have led to any difference in grading.

It is also clear that equal value can mean greater value: *Murphy* v. *An Bord Telecom Eireann* [1988] IRLR 267, ECJ. However, a woman in such a situation may only claim parity with her male comparator. She does not have the right to be paid more than him.

For the avoidance of doubt, a claimant is not entitled to a proportion of her comparator's pay equivalent to the proportionate value of her job compared to his. For example, a claimant is not entitled to 70 per cent of her comparator's pay on the grounds that her job is shown to be 70 per cent of the value of his job. A failure to establish equal value leaves a woman without any remedy under the EqPA 1970.

Scope of the right to claim equal value

The House of Lords has held that a woman is not debarred from pursuing an equal value claim just because there is a man working alongside her undertaking like work with her: *Pickstone* v. *Freemans* [1988] IRLR 357. In *Pickstone*, the claimant and four other warehouse operatives pursued an equal value claim with checker warehouse operatives. The House of Lords rejected the employer's argument that as there were men employed as warehouse operatives the women were precluded from pursuing a claim. If the House of Lords had come to the opposite conclusion, the presence of a token man doing the same work for the same pay would have precluded a woman from claiming equal pay. The same principle applies to claims for work rated as equivalent.

11.4   EQUAL PAY ACT 1970, S.1(3) DEFENCE

Even if the claimant can show that she does work of equal value, it is still open to the employer to establish a defence under s.1(3) (see **Chapter 12**).

11.5   HOW TO FIND OUT IF THERE IS AN EQUAL VALUE CLAIM

A claimant can find out if she has an equal value claim by using whatever information is available to undertake an equal value assessment. Guidance on how to undertake an equal value assessment is set out in **Chapter 4**. If necessary, a claimant could use the new questionnaire procedure at EqPA 1970, s.7B to obtain information about the comparator's job. At the same time, the claimant could probe the employer about why the comparator is paid more (see **Chapter 15** for guidance on how to use the questionnaire procedure).

Employers who use job evaluation can find out if their scheme(s) will withstand an equal value challenge by utilising the EOC's job evaluation checklists at **Annex 3A**. The checklists aim to identify whether a particular scheme(s) directly or indirectly discriminates on grounds of sex. In the absence of job evaluation, employers should undertake an 'equal value' check (as described in **Chapter 5**) to identify whether they are vulnerable to such claims.

CHAPTER 12

The employer's defence

KEY POINTS

Once a comparison establishes that a woman, who is doing equal work to that of a man, is being treated less favourably than the man, a presumption arises that the equality clause will operate in her favour unless the employer can show that the difference in pay is genuinely explained by something that has nothing to do with sex. If the employer can show a proper reason for the disparity in pay, the claim will fail. In practice, several factors may account for the difference in pay.

The key points under the Equal Pay Act 1970 (EqPA 1970), s.1(3) are:

- What differences are there between the claimant's contract and the comparator's contract?
- To what factor(s) is that difference due?
- Is the difference in treatment 'genuinely due' to the factor?
- Is the factor 'material'?
- Is there evidence of sex discrimination, direct or indirect?
- If there is evidence of indirect sex discrimination, can the discrimination be justified on an objective basis?

This chapter examines the nature of 'material factors'. **Chapter 13** then considers what amounts to evidence of sex discrimination in pay and examines the how tribunals approach the test of discrimination.

12.1 TIMING OF THE DEFENCE

The special procedural rules in equal value cases allow for the employer's EqPA 1970, s.1(3) defence to be taken before the question of equal value (see **Chapter 15**). From the employer's perspective, hearing the defence first potentially saves time and expense. This is because, if the defence succeeds, the claim will be immediately dismissed. From the claimant's point of view, the disadvantage of dealing with the issues in this order is that the quality of the evidence in relation to equal value may deteriorate with the passage of time. Inevitably, individuals' recollections of their duties and responsibilities in years gone by will deteriorate over time. Moreover, if the defence raises issues related to the duties of the posts to be compared (such as the demands of the job), it would be appropriate to deal with the question of equal work first (see paragraph **12.3** below).

The other option, generally now preferred by tribunals, is for the employer's defence to be taken after the issue of equal value. Either way, it is advisable for the employer to plead its defence in the notice of appearance and to raise it at the preliminary hearing because the tribunal may refuse to exercise its discretion to allow an amendment after the independent expert has reported. This also avoids the impression that the defence has been 'thought up' as the action proceeds.

12.2   BURDEN OF PROOF

Once an applicant establishes that she is being treated less favourably than a man with whom she is undertaking equal work, the burden of proof formally passes to the employer to show that there is an explanation for the variation in pay and terms and conditions of employment that has nothing to do with her sex. If the tribunal decides to take the employer's defence first, it will be assumed for this purpose that the woman has established equal work.

The standard of proof on the employer is the ordinary standard in civil proceedings, namely on the balance of probabilities.

12.3   IDENTIFYING THE FACTOR

In practice, one or more factors may account for the difference in treatment between the man and the woman. For convenience, these may be divided into two categories: factors that relate to the individuals concerned and factors that relate to extrinsic matters.

Factors that are personal to the individuals concerned

The difference in treatment may be due to such factors as:

- hours of work;
- overtime payments;
- flexibility;
- training and qualifications;
- experience;

- seniority;
- protected pay, that is, red and green circling;
- location, for example London weighting;
- performance;
- greater potential;
- mistake.

Factors external to the individuals concerned

The difference in treatment may be due to such factors as:

- economic constraints;
- administrative convenience;
- legal requirements;
- different collective bargaining arrangements;
- separate pay structures;
- operation of a grading scheme;
- recruitment and retention (market forces);
- starting salary.

The factor must still exist

For a factor to be valid it must have been known to the employer at the date when the wages were fixed and/or equal work commenced and must still exist at the date of the hearing of the employer's material factor defence. The employer cannot rely on a factor that no longer exists or on a factor that only becomes known after the employees took up their duties: see *Benveniste* v. *University of Southampton* [1989] IRLR 122, CA and *Brunnhofer* v. *Bank der Osterreichischen Postsparkasse AG* [2001] IRLR 571, ECJ respectively at paragraphs **12.4** and **12.6** below.

Factors relevant to the demands of the job

Factors that are relevant to the question whether a claimant and her comparator are employed on like work or work of equal value should not be taken into account when considering the EqPA 1970, s.1(3) defence. This is not because they are irrelevant but because they should already have been taken into account in the determination of equal work. Thus the correct approach is to treat the EqPA 1970, s.1(3) defence as a separate and distinct matter.

Two cases to have addressed this issue are *Waddington* v. *Leicester Council for Voluntary Services* [1977] IRLR 32 and *Davies* v.

McCartneys [1989] IRLR 439. In *Waddington,* the EAT suggested that, in like work cases, any material differences within EqPA 1970, s.1(3) will usually be something other than the differences considered under EqPA 1970, s.1(4). In contrast, in *Davies*, the EAT held that the demands of the job may be relevant not only to the question of whether or not the work is of equal value but also to the explanation for the differences in pay under EqPA 1970, s.1(3). Thus, according to the EAT in *Davies*, it is open to the employer to say that he values one particular job factor so highly that he pays more, provided his reason for doing so is genuine and not attributable to sex. It is suggested that this decision should be treated with caution. It is submitted that the correct approach in an equal value case is for factors relating to the demands of the jobs in question to be referred to the independent expert as part of the question of equal value. For the employer to be permitted to value one job more highly, or prefer a factor found disproportionately or only in the man's work, would be to permit undervaluation of women's work to be a defence.

Multiple factors

In *Davies* v. *McCartneys*, the EAT confirmed that there is no limit to the number of factors on which an employer can rely. Where an employer relies on more than one factor, the claimant has the practical difficulty of identifying the extent to which any particular factor justifies the difference in pay. If the employer does not indicate the precise extent to which each factor is relied upon, it may be appropriate for the claimant to seek an order for further and better particulars so that she is in a position to know the nature of the defence in advance of the hearing. Although in *Byrne* v. *the Financial Times* [1991] IRLR 417 the EAT declined to grant an order for further and better particulars in such circumstances, following the ECJ's decision in *Enderby* v. *Frenchay Health Authority and Secretary of State for Health* [1993] IRLR 591, it is clearly for the employer to apportion more or less precise percentages to each of the factors cited in the defence (see paragraph **13.4**).

Transparency

When more than one factor is relied upon by the employer, the question may arise as to the extent to which the pay system is transparent. In *Handels-og Kontorfunktionaerernes Forbund i Danmark* v. *Dansk Arebejdsgiverforening (acting for Danfoss)* [1989] IRLR 532, the ECJ held that an employer must prove that there is no discrimination behind a pay differential if the pay system lacks transparency. If the employer cannot determine precisely what proportion of the variation in pay is attributable to each factor relied upon, the claimant may argue that the factors concerned cannot be objectively justified (see **Chapter 13** for a discussion of objective justification).

12.4   IS THE FACTOR 'GENUINE' AND 'MATERIAL'?

Under EqPA 1970, s.1(3), the employer must show that the variation in pay between the claimant and comparator is 'genuinely' due to a factor that is 'material'. The requirement of genuineness goes hand in hand with the requirement for the factor to be 'material', by which is meant causally relevant – see below. It follows that a factor that is not relevant and does not sufficiently explain the difference in pay will not satisfy the requirement of genuineness, and vice versa.

The requirement of genuineness is satisfied if the factor put forward by the employer for the variation between the woman's and the man's contract is not a sham or pretence: *Strathclyde Regional Council* v. *Wallace* [1998] IRLR 146, HL. It is a question of fact for the tribunal to decide. Statistical evidence of the employer's overall treatment of women, and of the extent of job segregation in particular, may be probative evidence from which a tribunal can decide whether the explanation put forward by the employer is genuine. In *McKechnie & Ors* v. *Gloucestershire County Council* (12776/96), the tribunal took issue with the time at which the EqPA 1970, s.1(3) defence was introduced into the proceedings and ruled that the employer's market forces defence, raised at a late stage in the proceedings, could not be 'genuine', otherwise it would have been put forward at the outset of the proceedings.

The factor will be 'material' if the employer can show that it is a significant and relevant cause of the difference in pay: *Rainey* v. *Greater Glasgow Health Board* [1987] IRLR 26, HL. Some factors on examination may prove to be not significant and not relevant. For example, once the reason for the variation in pay no longer exists, it will not be possible for the defence to succeed. In *Benveniste* v. *University of Southampton* [1989] IRLR 122, CA, a female lecturer was appointed at a lower point on the relevant salary scale than a male lecturer at a time of financial constraint. The material factor disappeared when the financial constraint ended.

Note that where the employer relies upon more than one factor, it must be established that each factor is genuine and the cause of a difference in pay.

12.5 DOES THE FACTOR AMOUNT TO A MATERIAL DIFFERENCE?

In cases of like work and work rated as equivalent, EqPA 1970, s.1(3) provides that the material factor must amount to a material difference between the woman's case and that of the man. In an equal value case, the employer's defence may be either that the variation amounts to a material difference between the woman's case and that of the man, or that it is a material factor. In other words, in an equal value case the material factor need not necessarily amount to a material difference.

The difference in wording is historic and of little relevance nowadays: *Bower* v. *Schroeder Ltd* (3203104/99). In practice, one question is asked in all three types of cases, namely, is the variation in pay genuinely due to a material factor that is not the difference of sex?

12.6 SPECIFIC MATERIAL FACTORS AND PAY PRACTICES

The following cases illustrate the circumstances in which certain factors and pay practices will provide a material factor defence or themselves be vulnerable to challenge. It must be remembered, however, that the cases are merely examples, and what amounts to a genuine material factor defence depends on the circumstances of each case. In each case the explanation must be examined to see if it passes the tests set out above.

Details of types of pay systems in the UK and how they may discriminate against female employees are considered in **Chapter 2**.

Working time

Hours of work

To the extent that one employee works longer hours than another it is obvious that there will be a difference in pay that can be justified, provided that it is proportional. In *Leverton* v. *Clwyd County Council* [1989] IRLR 28, the House of Lords held that provided men and women are receiving the same notional hourly rate of pay, it is legitimate for them to receive different salaries for longer hours worked.

Time of work

It has been held that the mere time at which work is undertaken may explain and justify a difference in pay. In *Thomas* v. *National Coal Board* [1987] IRLR 451, EAT, 1,500 female canteen assistants compared themselves with a male canteen assistant on permanent night work at a higher rate of pay. It was found that the risk and additional responsibility of unsupervised night work justified the difference in pay.

Part-time work

A series of decisions from the ECJ has confirmed that treating part-timers less favourably than full-timers can amount to unlawful discrimination unless it can be justified. For example, in *Bilka-Kaufhaus GmbH* v. *Weber von Hartz* [1996] IRLR 317, the ECJ held that a pay practice that results in full-timers being paid more than part-timers is prima facie indirectly discriminatory unless it can be objectively justified on factors unrelated to any discrimination on the grounds of sex. In *Bilka*, part-timers had been excluded from joining an occupational pension scheme.

However, certain pay practices have been found to be permissible. For example in *Stadt Lengerich* v. *Helmig* [1995] IRLR 216, the ECJ held that there is no infringement of Article 141 where part-timers are excluded from earning overtime payments, if the total number of hours worked falls within the standard working week for full-timers. In other words, it is lawful to exclude part-timers from overtime payments until they have worked in excess of the standard hours for full-timers.

The converse situation arose in *Rees* v. *NatWest Bank plc* (1200927/97) where a tribunal held that it was unlawful to exclude part-timers who exceeded their contractual hours from receiving the same contractual benefits as the full-timers received for their standard working week. In *Rees*, both the part-timers and the full-timers received the same basic and overtime rates of pay (after working more than seven hours a day). However, the part-timers were excluded from receiving contractual benefits such as pension, holiday pay, profit-related pay, etc. for any extra hours worked that were not classed as overtime. The estimated value of these benefits was 30 per cent of basic salary. The tribunal found that the part-timers were being paid less than the full-timers for these extra hours.

In *Barry* v. *Midland Bank plc* [1999] IRLR 581, the House of Lords held that a severance payment that was calculated on the basis of an employee's current pay at the date of termination was not indirectly discriminatory, even though the scheme made no allowance for employees whose hours of work had fluctuated over the years, thereby disadvantaging part-timers by not taking into account any full-time service that they may have had.

By contrast, in *Hill and Stapleton* v. *Revenue Commission and Department of Finance* [1998] IRLR 466, the ECJ held that it was potentially a breach of Article 141 for the employers to adopt a pay practice that treated job sharing employees who reverted to full-time work less favourably in terms of pay than employees who had always worked full time. Such employees had been placed on a lower point on the pay scale than that which they had occupied while previously working full time. Any such difference in treatment had to be objectively justified and could not be based upon such considerations such as staff motivation, commitment or morale.

Flexibility

Some UK pay structures include elements for flexibility, either in terms of working hours or mobility (see **Chapter 2**). It is not unlawful for men and women undertaking equal work to receive different payments for elements such as flexibility provided the reasons for the differences are transparent and justifiable. This is upheld in EU law. In *Handels-og Kontorfunktionaerernes Forbund i Danmark* v. *Dansk Arebejdsgiverforening (acting for Danfoss)* [1989] IRLR 532, the ECJ held that where flexibility of the employee to work at variable times and at different places is used as a criterion for pay increments and it is found to work systematically to the disadvantage of female employees who have difficulty organising their working time in a flexible manner because of family responsibilities, the employer must justify the use of the criterion by demonstrating that flexibility is important to the performance of the relevant duties.

Personal factors

It is not uncommon for pay structures to reward employees on the basis of criteria such as training, seniority, experience and performance (see **Chapter 2**). An employer who seeks to defend a difference in pay between a claimant and comparator on the basis that it is due to one or more of these factors should bear in the mind the following points.

Training and qualifications

An employer may seek to defend an equal pay claim on the basis that the comparator is more qualified than the claimant. Using training and qualifications as criteria for awarding employees higher pay could systematically disadvantage women in so far as they have generally fewer opportunities to obtain either training or qualifications. For this reason, an employer must justify the use of such a criterion by demonstrating that vocational training is important for the performance of the employees' duties concerned: *Danfoss*.

Seniority and experience

Experience and seniority payments have been common in organisations where employees have been expected to spend their whole career. They can discriminate against women if they are less likely to follow traditional male career patterns. This is particularly so where seniority is made the basis for access to particular benefits or pay increments. Although in *Danfoss* the ECJ held that it was permissible to reward seniority without the need to show its importance for the performance of specific duties, on the basis that seniority goes hand in hand with experience that generally places workers in a better position to carry out their duties. The Court subsequently resiled from this position in the later case of *Nimz* v. *Freie und Hansestadt Hamburg* [1991] IRLR 222, ECJ. *Nimz* involved a promotion rule that disadvantaged employees who worked less than three-quarters time. The rule provided for employees who worked more than three-quarters time to move to a higher scale after six years' service. Those who worked less than three-quarters time (as the applicant did) had to be in post longer to obtain the promotion. The rule was challenged as being discriminatory on the basis that the overwhelming majority of part-time employees were female. The employers argued that the practice was justifiable because, in general, full-timers acquired skills more quickly. The ECJ held that the use of seniority as a pay criterion that has the effect of discriminating predominantly against female employees has to be objectively justified by reference to the experience gained in the job in question. The Court observed that although seniority would appear to go hand in hand with experience, whether this amounts to objective justification will depend on the circumstances of the case.

Performance pay

It is common for organisations to use bonus payments or performance-related pay to encourage and reward performance. An employer may be able to defend an equal pay claim on the ground that the comparator's performance is better than the claimant's provided the difference in pay is transparent and justifiable.

The issue of quality of work was considered in *Danfoss*. The ECJ held that where its application results in systematic unfairness to female workers there can be no scope for justifying it since it is inconceivable that the work carried out by female workers could be generally of lower quality.

If the criterion works systematically to the detriment of female workers, it can only be because the employer has designed or applied the criterion abusively.

See **Chapter 2** for details of how performance-related pay structures may be vulnerable to challenge.

Greater potential

Is it lawful to pay a male employee undertaking equal work to a female employee more because the employer perceives that the male employee has greater potential?

In *Edmunds* v. *Computer Services (South-West) Ltd* [1977] IRLR 359, the EAT held that paying a man more because he has the potential to exercise greater responsibility may be a 'material difference' under EqPA 1970, s.1(3). In contrast, in *Brunnhofer* v. *Bank der Osterreichischen Postsparkasse AG* [2001] IRLR 571, the ECJ held that an employer may not justify a difference in pay on appointment between persons performing work of equal value by reference to performance after appointment.

Pay structures and collective bargaining

Grading schemes

Many pay structures group jobs into pay grades and bands (see **Chapter 2**). The tribunal will want to ensure that, in practice, a grading scheme is not a cloak for sex discrimination. For example, in *Electrolux Ltd* v. *Hutchinson* [1976] IRLR 410, EAT, a man and a woman undertaking like work were graded differently: the man was on one grade (grade 10) and the woman on another (grade 01). It was argued that the wage differential was due to the different grading. However, all 600 women apart from one were on grade 01 and all the men were on grade 10. The EAT found that the grading scheme was a device for implementing sex discrimination.

Traditionally, jobs in the same band are perceived as being of broadly equal value, either because they have been evaluated with similar scores under a job evaluation scheme, or because they are regarded as broadly equivalent within the organisation. Any difference in the average pay of men and women undertaking work rated as equivalent, or within the same pay band or grade, requires explanation (see **Chapter 5**). The reasons for the difference should be transparent and justifiable. Likewise, if jobs of equal worth are graded differently, the basis for doing so must be transparent and justifiable.

Provided a grading scheme is operated on the basis of objective criteria (such as skill, ability and experience) and fairly applied irrespective of sex, it will not infringe the EqPA 1970: *National Vulcan Engineering Insurance* v. *Wade* [1978] IRLR 225, CA. Where such objective criteria are no longer apparent, then the employer may be unable to make out a defence. For instance, in *Crossley* v. *ACAS* (1304744/98), male conciliators undertaking like work to female conciliators were at the top of a broad banded pay structure as the result of a historical assimilation process. The more recently recruited female conciliators were bunched at the bottom. The tribunal held that the pay system indirectly discriminated against the female conciliators (who, on average, had shorter service) and could not be objectively justified on the facts. In *Ruff* v. *Hannant Cleaning Services* (1501271/01), the applicant and the comparator were both cleaning operatives but the applicant was in grade 3 and the comparator in grade 4. The tribunal found that they were doing like work and that the difference in grade was merely a label that could not be justified.

Incremental pay

An incremental pay structure may justify differences in pay between men and women undertaking equal work if the increments are designed to reward demonstrable increased expertise arising from experience in the job. It is unlikely that incremental structures that simply reward loyalty will justify differences in pay: *Nimz* v. *Freie und Hansestadt Hamburg*.

Protected pay

Red circling, or personal protection, is the practice of protecting the pay of individuals whose jobs are downgraded following, for example, an internal reorganisation, a pay/grading review, implementation of a new job evaluation scheme, or a TUPE transfer. Green circling is the practice of phasing-in over a period of time the upgradings that result from a grading review or restructuring. The impact of red and green circling may help to explain differences in pay but will not necessarily justify those differences. In particular, personal protection will not be a valid defence under EqPA 1970, s.1(3) if it is based on sex discrimination. For example, in *Snoxell and Davies* v. *Vauxhall Motors Ltd* [1977] IRLR 123, EAT, the claimants and comparators were quality controllers at Vauxhall. Although they were undertaking like work the women were in a lower grade and paid less. In preparation for the introduction of the EqPA 1970, the job of quality controller was downgraded: the women and new applicants for the job were put on a new 'unisex' rate while the men were allowed to keep their higher rate. The EAT held that because the women had been excluded from the red circle when it was formed, the red circle was itself discriminatory and therefore could not constitute a valid EqPA 1970, s.1(3) defence.

Thus all the circumstances of the particular case, including the situation prior to the formation of the red circle, must be taken into account. For example:

1. If the red circle comprises predominantly or only men, it may raise a suspicion of pre-existing sex discrimination.
2. If the employer lets an outsider into the red circle (by paying the outsider at the higher rate received by those in the red circle) it will destroy the defence, because the women can claim parity with the outsider: *United Biscuits* v. *Young* [1978] IRLR 15, EAT.
3. It is relevant to take into account the length of time that has elapsed since the red circle was introduced, and whether the employer has acted in accordance with good industrial practice in the continuation of the protection: *Outlook Supplies Ltd* v. *Parry* [1978] IRLR 12, EAT.
4. It is desirable that, where possible, arrangements should be phased out. Exactly how soon will depend on the circumstances of the case. In *Parry*, the comparator's pay had been protected for two and a half years following a period of ill health. The EAT thought this was quite short in the circumstances of the case.

In *Parry*, the EAT recognised that the protection of pay, even when done for good reason, gives rise to much misunderstanding and upset and recommended that it should be phased out as soon as possible. For the same reason, the EAT advised employers to consult with the workforce where it is intended to introduce such a practice or, if it has been introduced, to continue it.

In the context of occupational pension schemes, the ECJ has had little tolerance for such practices. For example, in *Van den Akker & Ors* v. *Stichting Shell Pensioenfonds* [1994] IRLR 616, ECJ, the employers sought to maintain a discriminatory pension age policy to enable the women who had elected to retire at 55 to continue to do so after male and female retirement ages were formally equalised at the age of 60. In effect, the employers red circled existing female employees so that they could retire at 60 if they so wished. The employer's policy was declared unlawful. It remains to be seen whether the ECJ would adopt a similar approach in relation to a typical red-circle arrangement.

Separate collective bargaining arrangements and pay structures

Historically, separate collective bargaining arrangements for male-dominated groups and female-dominated groups have been a cause of unequal pay in the UK (see **Chapter 2**). In *Enderby* v. *Frenchay Health Authority and Secretary of State for Health* [1993] IRLR 591, the ECJ held that the fact that the rates of pay for two jobs of equal value, one carried out exclusively by women and the other predominantly by men, had been arrived at by collective bargaining processes that had been conducted separately without any discriminatory effect within each group, is not sufficient objective justification under Article 141. The ECJ pointed out that if an employer could rely on the absence of discrimination within each of the collective bargaining processes as sufficient justification for the differences in pay, it could easily circumvent the principle of equal pay by using separate collective bargaining processes. The ECJ appeared to adopt a different approach in *Specialarbejderforbundet i Danmark* v. *Dansk Industri (acting for Royal Copenhagen A/S)* [1995] IRLR 648, ruling that the national court may take account of the fact that pay rates have been determined by collective bargaining or by negotiation at local level in its assessment of whether differences between the average of two groups of workers are due to objective factors unrelated to discrimination on grounds of sex.

So far as separate pay structures are concerned, in the case of *British Coal Corporation* v. *Smith* [1994] IRLR 342, the Court of Appeal held that the mere existence of separate pay structures is not in itself a defence under EqPA 1970, s.1(3). If one structure is comprised entirely or predominantly of men and the other of woman, there will be prima facie evidence of sex discrimination and it will be for the employer to objectively justify the difference in pay and benefits.

In *Nimz* v. *Freie und Hansestadt Hamburg* (see above), the ECJ confirmed that Article 141 also applies to the provisions in a collective agreement that determines salary in the same way as it applies to individual contracts of employment.

Market forces and economic constraints

Market forces and skill shortages

Perhaps the most common reason an employer is likely to put forward for the difference in pay rates is the need to pay the market rate to recruit and retain staff. Differences in pay may be explained and possibly justified by skill shortages and recruitment and retention difficulties.

The House of Lords decision in *Rainey* v. *Greater Glasgow Health Board* [1987] IRLR 26 confirmed that market forces could amount to a material difference. *Rainey* concerned the establishment of a prosthetic service in the NHS in Scotland. Prosthetists who joined the new service from private practice were paid at a higher rate than those recruited directly into the NHS once the service was established. The House of Lords held that the need to recruit a sufficient number of prosthetists into the service within a short space of time constituted a material factor justifying the comparator's difference in pay.

The availability of market forces as a valid defence was affirmed by the ECJ in *Enderby* v. *Frenchay Health Authority and Secretary of State for Health* [1993] IRLR 591 (see paragraph **13.4** for further details). However, the scope for using market forces as an EqPA 1970, s.1(3) defence is not limitless. The House of Lords decision in *Ratcliffe* v. *North Yorkshire County Council* [1995] IRLR 439 placed an important limit on the use of market forces as a defence in the context of a competitive tendering exercise (see **Chapter 13**). For example, in *Lord & Ors* v. *Knowsley Borough Council* (59559/95), the employer sought to justify the discontinuance of certain benefits to home-care workers in order to secure the economies needed to keep the home-care service in-house. Most of the home-care workers were female while most of their comparators – school caretakers and refuse drivers – were male. The tribunal could find no evidence that there was a shortage of school caretakers or refuse drivers and concluded that the women were paid less than the men in order to compete with other employers elsewhere.

Regional market forces

Different rates of pay based on a geographical distinction, such as London weighting, can constitute a genuine material factor difference within EqPA 1970, s.1(3): *Navy, Army & Air Force Institutes* v. *Varley* [1976] IRLR 408, EAT.

Economic constraints

An employer may seek to defend an equal pay claim on the simple basis that it cannot afford to pay the claimant more, even if she is employed on equal work to her comparator. Unless there are other reasons for the variation in pay, such a defence is unlikely to be successful.

In *Bilka-Kaufhaus GmbH* v. *Weber von Hartz* [1986] IRLR 317, the ECJ stated that economic considerations could constitute a valid defence to an equal pay claim provided the policy could be objectively justified, that is, shown to be 'appropriate' and 'necessary'. However, in the subsequent cases of *Jorgenson* v. *Foreningen af Speciallaeger* [2000] IRLR 726, and *Hill and Stapleton* v. *Revenue Commission and Department of Finance* [1998] IRLR 466, the ECJ has adopted a different approach. In *Jorgenson*, the ECJ held that budgetary constraints could not in themselves justify sex discrimination. The ECJ remarked that if they could do, it would mean that the application of equal treatment might vary according to the state of the public finances of member states. In *Hill*, the ECJ stated that an employer could not justify discrimination solely on the ground that it would involve increased costs.

For the avoidance of doubt, it would also be unlawful to phase in equalisation for economic reasons. It is a fundamental principle of EU law that the application of equal treatment must be immediate and full (*Smith & Ors* v. *Avdel Systems Ltd* [1994] IRLR 602) although, in practice, following a regrading exercise or the like employers often do phase in the resulting new structure with the agreement of the trade union in question.

Miscellaneous factors

Starting salaries

Individuals may receive different starting salaries for very good reasons. Nevertheless, employers can find out if there is a problem with starting salaries in their organisation by looking at the amount paid on recruitment, on change of job, and on promotion for men and women doing equal work over a specified period of time.

Unless the decision reached in each case is transparent and justifiable, a claim defended on this basis will not be successful. For example, in *Compton* v. *St Regis Paper Company Ltd* (1201178/99), the male comparator, a sales representative, had been given a higher salary from the outset of his employment. The tribunal held that the respondent could not claim a material factor defence simply because the comparator had asked for more money.

Administrative efficiency

In *Barry* v. *Midland Bank plc* [1998] IRLR 138, the Court of Appeal held that administrative convenience could be an objective reason unconnected with the difference of sex. *Barry* concerned the administration of the employer's severance scheme. In the Court's view, the scheme had the merit of clarity and simplicity, which was to the benefit of both employer and employees. In *Rainey* v. *Greater Glasgow Health Board* [1987] IRLR 26, the House of Lords also considered that administrative efficiency could amount to a valid defence, provided it could be objectively justified.

Legal requirements

In the public sector it is not uncommon for rates of pay to be regulated by statutory instrument. In *R* v. *Secretary of State for Social Services, ex p. Clarke* [1988] IRLR 22, the Divisional Court held that the fact that the employers were bound by statutory instrument to pay the salaries of the claimant and the comparator at a certain rate was not a material factor defence to an equal pay claim. The real issue is why the particular rates were decided upon and whether there are material factors in this regard.

12.7 WITNESS EVIDENCE

An employer will need to call witness evidence in support of its EqPA 1970, s.1(3) defence. Relevant witnesses will be those responsible for:

(a) devising, implementing and operating the employer's pay policies in general;

(b) setting the claimant's and the comparator's rates of pay in particular; and

(c) conducting any relevant collective bargaining.

The claimant may wish to call evidence from a trade union representative to establish the history of the collective bargaining process or from affected employees to show that the employer's pay structure or policies have inconsistencies that undermine the factual basis of the employer's defence. In some cases, trade union representatives have given evidence to the effect that while they acted in good faith at the time of the relevant negotiations, they now appreciated that the policies had led to pay discrimination: *Lloyds Bank plc.* v. *Fox* [1989] IRLR 103 EAT.

CHAPTER 13

Is there evidence of sex discrimination?

KEY POINTS

The object of the Equal Pay Act 1970 (EqPA 1970) is to prevent discrimination between men and women as regards terms and conditions of employment. The Act is designed so that a presumption of sex discrimination arises once a comparison shows that a woman, who is doing equal work to that of a man, is being paid or treated less favourably than the man. The difference in pay or other contractual terms is presumed to be because of sex discrimination. The burden is then on the employer to show that there is an explanation for the difference in treatment that is not tainted by sex discrimination.

The presence (or absence) of sex discrimination is likely to be vital to the success (or failure) of a claim. This chapter examines what amounts to evidence of sex discrimination in the context of pay and how tribunals approach the test of discrimination.

In practice, three situations may arise:

- The difference in treatment between the man and the woman involves direct discrimination
- The difference in treatment involves indirect discrimination
- There is no evidence of either direct or indirect discrimination

13.1 DEFINITIONS OF DIRECT AND INDIRECT DISCRIMINATION

Direct and indirect discrimination are defined as follows:

1. Direct discrimination is a detriment suffered by a woman that she would not have suffered but for being a woman.
2. Indirect discrimination is a detriment suffered by a class of individuals, men and women alike, but the detriment affects a substantially larger proportion of women than men.

The terms 'direct discrimination' and 'indirect discrimination' are not found in the EqPA 1970. *In Ratcliffe* v. *North Yorkshire County Council*

[1995] IRLR 439, the House of Lords expressed the view obiter that the EqPA 1970 was to be interpreted without introducing the distinction between direct and indirect discrimination. Subsequently in *Strathclyde Regional Council* v. *Wallace* [1998] IRLR 146, the House of Lords clarified this to mean that the EqPA 1970 does not draw the same firm legal demarcation between the two types of discrimination. Nevertheless, it was emphasised that the EqPA 1970 must be construed so as to accord with the Sex Discrimination Act 1975 (SDA 1975) and Article 141. In practice, this means that where an employer establishes some factual basis for the difference in treatment, the tribunal must consider whether there is evidence of either direct or indirect discrimination.

13.2   EVIDENCE OF DIRECT DISCRIMINATION

There will be direct discrimination if a woman is paid less because she is a woman. A classic example would be an assumption that men need higher wages because they are breadwinners. Direct discrimination tends to be prevalent in sectors where there is a predominance of 'women's work', namely where there is a gender-segregated workforce or a gender-segregated labour market.

For instance, in *Ratcliffe*, the jobs of dinner staff had been assessed under the 1987 local government manual workers job evaluation scheme as equivalent to posts such as road sweepers and gardeners (which were traditionally male). Following the introduction of compulsory competitive tendering, the Council decided that if the dinner staff were to remain competitive with commercial organisations bidding for school dinner contracts, they could not continue to be paid on local government rates of pay. Accordingly, they were given notice of dismissal and offered re-employment at lower hourly rates of pay. This gave rise to claims for equal pay. The House of Lords upheld the tribunal's finding that the wages of the dinner staff were reduced by the Council in order to compete with other employers in the private sector who paid their employees less because they were women doing traditionally 'women's work'. Thus the women's pay was reduced precisely because they were women.

Likewise, in *British Coal Corporation* v. *Smith* [1996] IRLR 404, the House of Lords upheld a tribunal's finding that the reason for the different pay and treatment of surface mineworkers, who were traditionally male, and canteen workers, all of whom were female, was due to 'an ingrained approach based on sex'.

Ratcliffe has significant implications for employers involved in competitive tendering in the public sector. In particular, employers who reduce wages in sex-segregated jobs for competitive purposes may be vulnerable to equal pay claims. Any attempt to justify a reduction in wages in these circumstances based on the need to be competitive is likely to be rejected for perpetuating assumptions about the value of so-called women's work. *Ratcliffe* also has implications in both public and private sectors for pay structures based on 'job families', where female job families (for example, a retail sales job family in a voluntary organisation) are placed on lower pay scales than other job families.

13.3 EVIDENCE OF INDIRECT DISCRIMINATION

For the purposes of Article 2 of the Council Directive on the Burden of Proof in Discrimination Cases, 97/80/EC indirect discrimination exists:

> where an apparently neutral provision, criterion or practice disadvantages a substantially higher proportion of the members of one sex unless that provision criterion or practice is necessary and can be justified by objective factors unrelated to sex.

In the context of pay, there will be prima facie evidence of indirect discrimination if it is established that an employer's pay policies or practices have a disproportionately adverse effect on either male or female employees, even though there may be no evidence that the employer intended them to have this effect.

A classic example of an indirectly discriminatory pay practice is one where part-time workers, whether male or female, are paid less per hour than full-time workers. For instance, in *Bilka-Kaufhaus GmbH* v. *Weber von Hartz* [1986] IRLR 317, ECJ, part-time workers were excluded from an occupational pension scheme. Since many more women than men work part time, the exclusion adversely affected significantly more women than men. Thus the ECJ found that the practice of excluding the part-timers from an occupational pension scheme prima facie infringed Article 141.

Other circumstances identified as giving rise to a presumption of indirect sex discrimination are as follows:

(a) where, given sufficiently large numbers, the average pay of women workers is lower than that of men workers doing equal work and the pay system is not transparent: *Handels-og Kontorfunktionaerernes Forbund i Danmark* v. *Dansk Arebejdsgiverforening (acting for Danfoss)* [1989] IRLR 532, ECJ;

(b) where an almost exclusively female group is paid less than a predominantly male group doing work of equal value: *Enderby* v. *Frenchay Health Authority and Secretary of State for Health* [1993] IRLR 591, ECJ;

(c) in *Jamstalldhetsombudsmannen* v. *Orebro Lans Landsting* [2000] IRLR 421, the ECJ refined the test further and held that if there are statistics that show that a group consisting of a substantially higher percentage of women than men is being paid less than other male workers doing work of equal value, that is prima facie evidence of indirect sex discrimination.

It now appears that there is no need to show, as the Court held in *Enderby*, that the higher paid man is part of a mainly male group of employees before the presumption of sex discrimination arises.

What is substantially higher?

There is no rule as to what amounts to a 'substantially higher' proportion. It is a question of fact for the tribunal to determine in the context of each case.

In *Harvest Town Circle Ltd* v. *Rutherford* [2001] IRLR 599, the EAT laid down the proper approach to statistics relating to disparate impact as follows:

1. There will be some cases where, on the statistics, a disparate impact is so obvious that a look at the numbers and proportions alone will suffice to show that members of one sex are substantially or considerably disadvantaged in comparison to the other.
2. In less obvious cases it will be proper for the tribunal to use more than one form of comparison and to look at numbers as well as proportions of both the advantaged and disadvantaged groups.
3. After looking at the figures, the tribunal must stand back and on the basis of all the figures decide whether disparate impact could fairly be described as considerable or substantial.
4. There is no universal yardstick by which to judge what is substantial or considerable. Each case must be judged on its merits.

The EAT added that there is no difference for the purposes of indirect discrimination law between a 'substantial' and 'considerable' disparity (the latter word has been used in SDA 1975, s.1(2)(b) since 12 October 2001).

In *Enderby*, the proportion of women in the applicant's group was 99 per cent and there was no doubt that the test for the applicant's group had been met. *R* v. *Secretary of State, ex p. Seymour-Smith and Perez* [1999]

IRLR 253, ECJ concerned the impact of the two-year qualifying period (as it was then) to bring an unfair dismissal complaint. In 1985, statistics showed that 31.1 per cent of women and 22.6 per cent of men could not meet the two-year qualifying period. In the Court's view, a ratio of 3:2 did not amount to a considerably higher percentage. However, the Court suggested that a lesser statistical disparity may suffice if it is 'persistent and relatively' constant over the years. Applying this alternative test, a majority of the House of Lords thought a ratio of 3:2 over a seven-year period (from 1985 to 1991) while borderline could not be dismissed as insignificant: *R* v. *Secretary of State for Employment, ex p. Seymour-Smith and Perez (No.2)* [2000] IRLR 263, HL. Accordingly, the majority found that the two-year qualifying period to bring an unfair dismissal complaint had an adverse impact on women.

Testing for adverse impact

Following *Jamstalldhetsombudsmannen*, the test for adverse impact will involve the following exercise:

(a) establish the difference in pay between the claimant's group and the comparator's group;

(b) establish the proportion of women and men in the claimant's group; and

(c) determine whether the proportion demonstrates that there is a substantially higher percentage of women than men in the claimant's group.

If the exercise is to be valid it must proceed on the following basis:

(a) the group must comprise all workers in a comparable situation and not be formed in an arbitrary manner;

(b) the statistics must cover enough individuals to be statistically significant;

(c) the statistics must cover several years to ensure that they do not illustrate purely fortuitous or short-term phenomena; and

(d) in general, the statistics must be relevant and sufficient for the purpose of resolving the case.

To ensure that the statistics do not illustrate purely fortuitous or short-term phenomena, the tribunal will want to examine the pattern over several years. Five to ten years is not unusual in these cases. For example, in *Enderby*, statistics showed that men predominated in one of the comparator groups in eight out of ten years, ranging from 54 to 68 per cent. The tribunal was impressed with the persistency and consistency of the figures and held that there was prima facie evidence of sex discrimination.

If necessary, claimants may use a questionnaire or written answers to obtain the information from the employer (see **Chapter 15**).

Expert evidence

Where the level of significance is not immediately obvious and disparate impact is in dispute, it will also be necessary to instruct a statistician to analyse the statistics and give expert evidence as to whether:

(a) the statistics illustrating the gender composition of the claimant's group over the years can (or cannot) be regarded as fortuitous or short-term; and

(b) the statistical difference in the proportions of the women and men in the claimant's group is (not) so small as to be insignificant.

It is not necessary for the claimant to go further and demonstrate that recruitment to the posts was tainted by gender.

13.4 CAN THE DISCRIMINATION BE JUSTIFIED?

Under the SDA 1975 and Article 141, indirect discrimination is not unlawful if it is 'justified'. Likewise, evidence of indirect sex discrimination will not be fatal to an EqPA 1970, s.1(3) defence if it is 'justified'.

It has long been assumed that direct discrimination under the EqPA 1970, like direct discrimination under the SDA 1975, is always unlawful. For example, in the House of Lords decision in *Ratcliffe*, Lord Slynn stated that direct discrimination under the EqPA 1970 could not be justified as a matter of principle. In the recent case of *Strathclyde Regional Council* v. *Wallace* [1998] IRLR 146, however, there is a suggestion that the position under the EqPA 1970 and Article 141 may not be so certain. Even though there have been no cases in which the ECJ has held a directly discriminatory practice to be justified in the *Bilka* sense, the House of Lords refused to rule out such a position.

The test of justification

The correct test for justification under EqPA 1970, s.1(3) was confirmed in *Rainey* v. *Greater Glasgow Health Board* [1987] IRLR 26, HL as the test of objective justification laid down by the ECJ in *Bilka* (for the purposes of Article 141). According to the ECJ, a discriminatory practice can be justified only if the employer can show:

(a) that the discriminatory practice corresponds to a real need on the part of the undertaking;
(b) that the means chosen for attaining those objectives are appropriate; and
(c) that those means are necessary for the purpose.

Note that the standard for justification is objective rather than subjective. In practice, the test of objective justification imposes a substantial burden on the employer. It is a question of fact in every case and the tribunal will want to be satisfied that the justification put forward by the employer stands up to an investigation of the facts on which it is based. According to the House of Lords in *Rainey*, what must be objectively justified is not only the pay differential in terms of the higher pay accorded to the comparator but also the lower pay accorded to the claimant.

The nature of the justification will vary according to the facts of the case and the status of the party who relies on it. For example, the state, seeking to counter an allegation that part-time workers suffered discrimination by reason of the requirements of primary legislation, might invoke considerations of social policy that would not arise in the case of justification put forward by an ordinary employer: *R* v. *Secretary of State for Employment, ex p. Equal Opportunities Commission* [1991] IRLR 493, QBD. In any event, it is not enough for either the state or an employer to rely on general assumptions: the factor relied upon must be shown to be based on valid grounds and pursuant to a genuine need on the part of the employer. It is also important to note that while a pay practice may be justified when it is introduced, it may cease to be with the passage of time and changes of circumstances: *Seymour-Smith*. It is therefore imperative such practices are kept under review.

Principle of proportionality

In all situations where justification has to be shown, the principle of proportionality will apply with the result that the tribunal must strike an objective balance between the discriminatory effects of the employer's pay practice and the reasonable needs of the employer in applying that practice: *Hampson* v. *Department of Education and Science* [1990] IRLR 69, CA. The degree of justification necessary thus becomes proportionate to the degree of disparate impact caused by the employer's pay policy. The greater the degree of discrimination, the greater the burden on the employer to show that the practice corresponds to a real commercial objective and is appropriate for achieving that objective, and vice versa.

Justifying the whole of the differential

Following *Enderby* it is clear that it is not sufficient for the factor(s) relied upon by the employer to account for some but not all of the variation in pay if the factor(s) relied upon by the employer is (are) to defeat the claim. In *Enderby* the ECJ was concerned with the question whether a pay differential could be justified by market forces. The ECJ stated that:

> if the national court has been able to determine precisely what proportion of the increase is attributable to market forces, it must necessarily accept that the pay differential is objectively justified to the extent of the proportion.

The Court went on to say that:

> if that is not the case, it is for the national court to assess whether the role of market forces in determining the rate of pay was sufficiently significant to provide objective justification for part or all of the difference.

Thus the ECJ envisages a two-stage approach. In the first instance, the tribunal is required to consider whether all of the difference in pay is objectively justified by the material factor advanced by the employer. If not, the tribunal is required to consider what proportion of the differential is objectively justified. For example, in *Enderby*, the evidence indicated that market forces accounted for 10 per cent of the difference in pay between the applicant speech therapists and their pharmacist comparators with the result that the speech therapists received 90 per cent of the difference in pay.

It should be remembered that this approach is not confined to market forces and may apply to all situations where there are multiple or partial factors.

13.5   WHERE THERE IS NO EVIDENCE OF DISCRIMINATION

It appears there is no consistent position between UK courts and the ECJ about the standard of evidence required to justify unequal pay in the absence of indirect discrimination.

The House of Lords has held that where there is no evidence of sex discrimination, there is no question of the employer having to justify (in the *Bilka* sense) all disparities in pay: *Glasgow City Council* v. *Marshall* [2000] IRLR 272, HL. Provided there is no element of sex discrimination, the employer establishes an EqPA 1970, s.1(3) defence by:

(a)   identifying the factor that he alleges caused the disparity in pay;
(b)   proving that the factor is genuine and not a sham;

(c) proving that the factor is 'material', namely that it caused the disparity in pay;

(d) in the case of like work and work rated as equivalent, that the factor is a 'material difference' between the woman's case and the man's, namely that it is the significant and relevant cause of the difference in pay.

The burden on the employer in these circumstances is much lighter. For example, in *Marshall*, where there was no evidence of sex discrimination, the House of Lords held that the employer was under no obligation to prove a 'good' reason for the pay disparity.

A purely historical explanation of the pay difference between the sexes would be insufficient to establish objective justification but, provided the explanation is genuine, may well suffice in establishing an EqPA 1970, s.1(3) defence under *Marshall*. Similarly, a careless mistake (for example, mistakenly placing the comparator on a higher salary point), in the absence of sex discrimination, can amount to a defence provided the tribunal is satisfied that the mistake was of sufficient influence to be significant and relevant: *Tyldesley* v. *TML Plastics Ltd* [1996] IRLR 395, EAT. According to the EAT in *Tyldesley*, if a genuine mistake suffices so too does a genuine perception, whether reasonable or not, about what it is necessary to pay. In this case the employers offered the comparator a higher rate of pay because they perceived him to be better qualified.

In contrast, in *Brunnhofer* v. *Bank der Osterreichischen Postsparkasse AG* [2001] IRLR 571, ECJ, there was no suggestion that the requirement to have an objectively justified and proportionate reason is restricted to cases of indirect discrimination. The claimant and the comparator were in the same job category under a collective agreement but the comparator received an individual supplement higher than the supplement received by the claimant. There was no evidence of what might be characterised as direct or indirect discrimination, yet the ECJ held that the employer must have objectively justified and proportionate reasons to explain the difference in pay between a woman and a man undertaking equal work. This appears to cast doubt on the approach of the House of Lords in *Marshall*.

CHAPTER 14

Claims under other provisions

KEY POINTS

The key UK and EU provisions relevant to equal pay are the Equal Pay Act 1970 (EqPA 1970) and Article 141 of the Treaty of Rome. Depending on the particular circumstances, a number of other provisions may be relevant including:

- The Sex Discrimination Act 1975 (SDA 1975) covers non-contractual benefits
- The Race Relations Act 1976 (RRA 1976) covers discrimination in terms and conditions of employment and the provision of non-contractual benefits
- The Part-time Workers (Prevention of Less Favourable Treatment) Regulations 2000, SI 2000/1551 (PTW Regs) deal with discrimination against part-time workers on the grounds that they work part time
- The Fixed-term Employees (Prevention of Less Favourable Treatment) Regulations 2002, SI 2002/2034 (FTE Regs) deal with discrimination against fixed-term employees on the grounds that they are employed for a fixed term

From the claimant's perspective, where there is an overlap between the various provisions, consideration should be given to bringing a claim under more than one provision.

14.1   SEX DISCRIMINATION ACT 1975

Who is protected?

The definition of employee under the SDA 1975 is the same as under the EqPA 1970. It includes those working under a contract of service or apprenticeship, or a contract personally to execute any work or labour. There is no qualifying period or hours requirement.

Direct discrimination

There is direct discrimination under the SDA 1975 if an employer treats a woman less favourably than it treats or would treat a man for the reason that she is a woman: s.1(2)(a). The comparison is between a man and a woman in the same or similar circumstances: s.5(3).

In *King* v. *Great Britain-China Centre* [1991] IRLR 513 the Court of Appeal laid down guidance for proving direct discrimination. According to the Court of Appeal, it is a two-stage process. First, the tribunal must make findings of primary fact and determine whether these show less favourable treatment and a difference of gender. The test of less favourable treatment is not whether there was less favourable treatment than would have been accorded by a reasonable employer in the same circumstances but whether the employer treated the woman less favourably than he treated or would have treated a male employee: *Zafar* v. *Glasgow City Council* [1998] IRLR 36, HL. Second, the tribunal must consider whether it is appropriate to draw an inference that the less favourable treatment was on the grounds of gender, that it would not have occurred 'but for' the fact that the applicant was a woman: *James* v. *Eastleigh Borough Council* [1990] IRLR 288, HL. At this stage the tribunal looks to the employer for a credible, non-discriminatory explanation for the difference in treatment, namely an explanation that is genuine, whether or not it was correct or reasonable. Unless the employer proves such an explanation, the tribunal must draw the inference of unlawful discrimination: SDA 1975, s.63A.

Non-contractual benefits, such as bonuses and performance-related pay, often depend on performance assessments and appraisals. In *Martins* v. *Marks & Spencer Plc* [1998] IRLR 326, the Court of Appeal held that the role of the tribunal in these circumstances is to consider whether the assessment is so obviously wrong or flawed that it could not have been made honestly and genuinely. In order to establish less favourable treatment, the claimant must satisfy the tribunal that she was significantly, or very clearly, or obviously unreasonably undervalued or under-assessed. It is important to bear in mind that weak and incompetent management does not, of itself, constitute unlawful discrimination.

Indirect discrimination

There is indirect discrimination under SDA 1975, s.1(2)(b) where an employer applies a provision, criterion or practice to a woman that it applies or would apply to a man, but:

(a) which is such that it would be to the detriment of a considerably larger proportion of women than of men; and

(b) which it cannot show to be justifiable irrespective of the sex of the person to whom it applies; and

(c) which is to her detriment.

For example, a 'provision, criterion or practice' may include the criteria adopted by an employer for awarding discretionary benefits.

In order to establish a prima facie case, a woman must show that the criteria are such that they would be to the detriment of a considerably larger proportion of women than men. In the context of discretionary benefits, this may be established by statistics showing that a considerably larger proportion of women receive on average lower benefits than their male colleagues (see **Chapter 13** for guidance on what amounts to 'considerably larger').

If the applicant can establish a prima facie case, it is open to the employer to objectively justify the use of the criteria (see **Chapter 13** for the test of justification).

Victimisation

It is unlawful (under SDA 1975, s.4) to treat a woman less favourably because she has:

(a) brought proceedings under the EqPA 1970;

(b) given evidence or information in connection with proceedings under the EqPA 1970;

(c) done anything else under or by reference to the EqPA 1970;

(d) alleged that the employer or any other person has committed an act that would amount to a contravention of the EqPA 1970.

The woman must prove that she was treated less favourably than the employer treated or would treat other employees who have not done the protected act: *Chief Constable of Yorkshire* v. *Khan* [2001] IRLR 830, HL. An example of less favourable treatment in this context would be to make a woman redundant for the reason that she has made an allegation of unequal pay. The woman does not have to prove that the employer was consciously motivated to victimise her because she made the allegation. However, it will be necessary to prove some link in the mind of the discriminator between the doing of the 'protected act' and the less favourable treatment: *Nagarajan* v. *London Regional Transport* [1999] IRLR 572, HL.

Striking out discriminatory terms of a contract

The EqPA 1970 provides a remedy only in individual cases. In contrast, SDA 1975, s.77 gives trade unions and other interested parties the right to apply to a county court to have a discriminatory provision in a contract of employment removed or modified, including provisions relating to pay.

In practice, this provision is little used even though it has the potential to address systemic discrimination. In *Meade-Hill and NUCPS* v. *British Council* [1995] IRLR 478, CA, SDA 1975, s.77 was used to disapply a mobility clause requiring that employees must work in any location in the UK required by the employer on the basis that it had a disproportionate impact on female employees.

Differences between the Sex Discrimination Act and Equal Pay Act

There are a number of important differences between the SDA 1975 and the EqPA 1970. For example, under the SDA 1975:

(a) it is possible to use a hypothetical comparator;
(b) there is no cap on arrears of compensation;
(c) the tribunal has the power to award compensation for injury to feel-ings, aggravated and exemplary damages;
(d) it is possible to use the SDA 1975 to strike out discriminatory terms of a contract.

Note also that the SDA 1975 does not cover contractual terms and has different time limits to the EqPA 1970 (see **Chapter 15**).

14.2 RACE RELATIONS ACT 1976

Who is protected?

The RRA 1976 protects the same categories of workers as the SDA 1975 (see paragraph **14.1** above). As in the SDA 1975, there is no qualifying period or hours requirement.

Direct discrimination under the Race Relations Act

The scheme of the RRA 1976 closely mirrors that of the SDA 1975. Direct discrimination under the RRA 1976 is treating an employee on racial grounds less favourably than you treat or would treat others: RRA 1976, s.1(1)(a). Thus there are two elements: less favourable treatment and racial grounds.

The correct approach is to ask whether the claimant was treated less favourably than the employer treated or would have treated someone of a different racial group in the same or relatively similar circumstances: RRA 1976, s.3(4). It does not matter that the employer did not act solely on the grounds of race as long as racial grounds were a substantial cause for what occurred. Where other factors play a part, the tribunal must decide whether the racial element was an operative cause: *Owen & Briggs* v. *James* [1982] IRLR 502, CA.

Racial grounds are defined in RRA 1976, s.3(1) as meaning colour, race, nationality or ethnic or national origins. A person can be a member of several racial groups at the same time.

The guidance laid down by the Court of Appeal in *King* v. *Great Britain-China Centre* for proving direct discrimination applies (see paragraph **14.1** above) although, until the implementation of the Race Discrimination Directive, 2000/43/EC in July 2003 (see below), the burden of proof remains with the claimant at all times. So, for example, to pay a black employee less than a white one would be prima facie evidence of discrimination on racial grounds. However, it may be that the differential is due to red circling, for example, or some other factor apart from race or colour, so that it is not racial discrimination.

Indirect discrimination

There is indirect discrimination under RRA 1976, s.1(1)(b) where an employer applies a requirement or condition that on the face of it applies irrespective of race and where:

- the proportion of persons from one racial group who can comply with it is considerably smaller than the proportion of persons not of that racial group who can comply;
- it cannot be justified irrespective of the racial origins of the person concerned;
- it is to the person's detriment because they cannot comply.

A requirement or condition is absolutely essential. A preference, not being an absolute requirement, is not a basis for indirect discrimination. A requirement does not have to be express. It can arise from the employer's practices; for example, an employer's standard procedures for awarding discretionary bonuses.

Claimants must show that a considerably smaller proportion of persons from their racial group can comply with the requirement or condition. For example, if the results of a regrading exercise in an NHS Trust show that nurses on the night shift tend to be graded lower than those undertaking the same work on the day shift and there are more black nurses on the night shift than on the day shift, it could be argued that the employer has imposed a requirement or condition that to achieve the higher grade nurses must work on the day shift.

To establish that a considerably smaller proportion of black nurses than white nurses can comply with the requirement, the following exercise should be undertaken:

(a) take the total number of white nurses in the pool (say 100); and
(b) take the number of white nurses in the pool who can comply with the requirement to work on the day shift (say 90);
(c) divide (b) by (a) to give the proportion of white nurses in the pool who can satisfy the requirement;
(d) take the number of black nurses undertaking like work (say 100); and
(e) take the number of black nurses in the group who can comply with the requirement to work on the day shift (say 60);
(f) divide (e) by (d) to give the proportion of black nurses in the pool who can satisfy the requirement to work on the day shift.

The proportion of white nurses who can comply (90 per cent) is compared to the proportion of black nurses who can comply (60 per cent) and if 60 per cent is accepted by the tribunal as being considerably smaller than 90 per cent, disproportionate impact has been proved. There is no rule as to what amounts to considerably smaller. In *London Underground* v. *Edwards (No.2)* [1998] IRLR 364, the Court of Appeal stated that it is not appropriate to lay down a rule of thumb defining what amounts to a proportion that is considerably smaller. According to the Court of Appeal, the concept has a degree of flexibility, which will vary from case to case. Nevertheless, the Court was of the view that there must be a substantial and not merely marginal discriminatory effect. In *R* v. *Secretary of State for Employment, ex p. Seymour-Smith and Perez (No.2)* [2000] IRLR 263, the House of Lords held that a persistent and constant disparity of the order of 10:9 was sufficient (see **Chapter 13**).

The black nurses in the example must then show that they cannot comply with the requirement in practice. If the nurses work at night out of choice, this would not be sufficient. If they can establish that they cannot comply, possibly because of child care responsibilities, it is open to the employer to objectively justify its pay practice (see **Chapter 13** for the test of justification).

Race Discrimination Directive

Implementation of the Race Discrimination Directive, 2000/43/EC in July 2003 will amend the RRA 1976 in a number of respects. Direct discrimination is defined under the Directive as 'where one person is treated less favourably than another is, has been or would be treated in a comparable situation on the grounds of racial and ethnic origin'. Once the claimant proves facts from which the tribunal could draw an inference of discrimination, the burden of proof will formally shift to the employer to establish an adequate explanation for the less favourable treatment.

The Directive defines indirect discrimination as occurring:

> where an apparently neutral provision, criterion or practice would put persons of a racial or ethnic origin at a particular disadvantage compared with other persons, unless that provision, criterion or practice is objectively justified by a legitimate aim and the means of achieving that aim are appropriate and necessary.

Thus the definition of indirect discrimination will be brought closer into line with the definition in the SDA 1975.

Statutory duty on public authorities

Under RRA 1976, s.71, public authorities are under a general duty to have due regard to the need to eliminate unlawful race discrimination and to promote equality of opportunity in everything they do. In particular, public authorities are required to assess and monitor the impact of proposed policies on racial equality. Arguably, this provision requires public authorities to monitor the effect of pay policies, including for example, job evaluation schemes and performance-related pay systems, on ethnic minority employees through pay audits and other means.

Pension rights

It is important to note that the equal treatment provisions in the Pensions Act 1995 (PA 1995) only relate to claims based on sex discrimination. Claims based on race discrimination continue to be governed by the Race Relations Act 1976: *Barclays Bank* v. *Kapur* [1991] 136, HL. In *Kapur,* employees who had originally worked for Barclays Bank in Africa brought a claim under the RRA 1976 alleging that the Bank's refusal to credit them with their previous service for pension purposes was discriminatory in comparison to the treatment of employees of European origin.

Striking out discriminatory terms

RRA 1976, s.72 mirrors SDA 1975, s.77 and gives trade unions and other interested parties the right to apply to a county court to have a discriminatory provision in a contract of employment removed or modified, including provisions relating to pay (see paragraph **14.1** above).

Relationship with the Equal Pay Act 1970

If the applicant is a black woman and her comparator is a white man, or vice versa, it may be appropriate to bring the claim under the RRA 1976 as well as the EqPA 1970. If the applicant and the comparator are the same sex, the claim should be brought under the RRA 1976 only. Note that there are different time limits under the RRA 1976 (see **Chapter 16**).

14.3 PART-TIME WORKERS (PREVENTION OF LESS FAVOURABLE TREATMENT) REGULATIONS 2000

The PTW Regs, SI 2000/1551 give part-time workers the right not to be treated less favourably than comparable full-time employees, unless the less favourable treatment is justified on objective grounds.

Who is protected?

The Regulations cover the following:

- employees working under a contract of employment;
- self-employed;
- contract and casual workers;
- trainees and apprentices.

There is no qualifying period or hours requirement.

Meaning of full-time worker and part-time worker

There is no general definition of full-time and part-time workers in terms of the numbers of hours worked. Who is a full-time worker and who is a part-time worker is determined by the custom and practice of the employer: PTW Regs, reg.2(1). A full-time worker is one who is paid and identifiable as a full-time worker. A part-time worker is one who is not identifiable as a full-time worker.

The relevant comparison

In order to bring a complaint the worker must be:

- employed by the same employer as the comparator;
- under the same type of contract;
- on the same or broadly similar work.

In contrast to the position under the EqPA 1970 and the SDA 1975, the comparator does not have to be of the opposite sex.

Same employer

Under PTW Regs, reg.2(4), the claimant and the comparator must be employed by the same employer at the time the discrimination takes place. Thus there is no scope for an applicant to use a hypothetical comparator, a comparator from an associated employer, or a comparator from another employment.

Same type of contract

The comparison, for the purpose of determining whether there has been less favourable treatment, is limited to those on the same type of contract. Four categories are set out in PTW Regs, reg.2(3):

(a) employees who are employed under a contract that is not a contract of apprenticeship;
(b) employees who are employed on a contract of apprenticeship;
(c) workers who are not employees;
(d) any other description of worker that it is reasonable for the employer to treat differently from other workers on the ground that they have a different type of contract.

Note that there are no such restrictions on claims brought under EU and domestic equal pay and sex discrimination provisions.

Same or broadly similar work

Under PTW Regs, reg.2(4)(a)(ii) a comparison can only be made with a full-time worker:

> engaged in the same or broadly similar work having regard, where relevant, to whether they have a similar level of qualification, skills and experience.

The test is similar but not identical to the test of like work under the EqPA 1970. The burden is on the part-time worker to establish the similarity (in contrast to the EqPA 1970 where it is for the employer to show relevant differences once work of a broadly similar nature has been established).

Pro rata principle

Under PTW Regs, reg.5 a part-time worker is entitled to equal rates of pay and other benefits to a full-time worker in proportion to the hours per week worked unless:

- the employer can justify different treatment on objective grounds; or
- it is inappropriate.

For example, the provision of a company car is likely to be one instance of where it would be inappropriate to use the pro rata principle. Arguably, it would be appropriate to give a pro rata cash allowance instead.

Establishing objective grounds

What constitutes objective grounds is not defined by the Regulations but the guidance notes issued by the DTI state that less favourable treatment will only be justified on objective grounds if it:

- is to achieve a legitimate objective;
- is necessary to achieve that objective; and
- is an appropriate way to achieve that objective.

Although not legally binding, the DTI guidance notes give some indication of how the PTW Regs should be interpreted. A key question is whether the cost of providing a benefit for a part-time worker will be regarded as an objective justification.

The PTW Regs contain a specific limitation in respect of overtime. Regulation 5(4) provides that part-time workers do not have the right to claim overtime until they exceed the normal working hours for full-timers. Note also that the Regulations allow for direct discrimination to be justified.

If a woman wishes to compare herself with a full-time worker (of the opposite sex) working for an associated employer or another employer, the claim must be brought under the EqPA 1970.

Workers who become part time after an absence

Under PTW Regs, reg.4, where a worker changes from working full time to working part time following an absence of less than 12 months, s/he is entitled to retain her/his pay and benefits on a pro rata basis. The provision covers those returning from maternity and parental leave, as well as those returning to work part time after an illness, career-break or sabbatical. For the provision to apply, the worker must return to a part-time post that is either the same job or a job at the same level under the contract, even though it does not need to be the same type. Essentially, the worker makes a self-comparison with how they would have been treated if they were still working full time in the post in which they were previously employed. This includes changes that have occurred during their absence period.

Workers who change from full time to part time

Under PTW Regs, reg.3, a full-time worker who ceases to work full time and starts working fewer hours, either as a result of a variation to their contract, or after a termination and re-engagement, is entitled to the same pay and benefits on a pro rata basis as s/he enjoyed previously immediately before the termination or variation. As with a worker who becomes part time after an absence, the part-time worker essentially makes a self-comparison.

Practical application of the Regulations

According to the guidance notes issued by the DTI, pay for these purposes includes (but is not limited to) shift allowances, unsocial hours payments, bonuses, profit sharing, share options, contractual sick and maternity pay, occupational pensions and holiday entitlement. Where a benefit such as health insurance cannot be applied pro rata, the guidance notes state that this is not of itself a justification for denying it to part-timers. If the cost to the organisation of providing the benefit to part-timers is disproportionate, this may be a justification although, arguably, the part-timers concerned could be given a pro rata cash payment instead.

Relationship with the EqPA 1970

The overlap between the PTW Regs and the EqPA 1970 is discussed in **Chapter 6**. If a claim is brought under both provisions, it is important to note that different time limits may apply (see **Chapter 15**).

157

14.4   THE FIXED-TERM EMPLOYEES (PREVENTION OF LESS FAVOURABLE TREATMENT) REGULATIONS 2002

The FTE Regs, SI 2002/2034 give fixed-term employees the right not to be treated less favourably than comparable permanent employees unless the less favourable treatment is justified on objective grounds.

Who is protected?

The Regulations protect those with a contract of employment that is due to end when a specified date is reached, a specified event does or does not happen, or a specified task has been completed. For example:

(a) employees doing seasonal or casual work;
(b) employees covering for maternity, parental or paternity or sick leave;
(c) employees employed to undertake a specific task (such as painting a house).

There is no hours requirement or qualifying period but note that the Regulations do not cover the self-employed, agency workers, apprentices, members of the armed forces and employees on certain training contracts.

Meaning of permanent employee

The FTE Regs, reg.1 defines permanent employee as an employee who is not on a fixed-term contract.

The relevant comparison

The FTE Regs, reg.2 defines the scope of permissible comparisons. In order to bring a complaint the employee must be :

(a) employed by the same employer as the comparator; and
(b) on the same or broadly similar work, having regard, where relevant, to qualifications and skills.

The first point of reference should be an employee in the same establishment with similar skills and qualifications to the fixed-term employee. If there is no comparator in the establishment, a comparison can be made with a similar permanent employee working for the same employer in a different establishment.

The scope for comparison is very similar to that permitted under the PTW Regs (see paragraph **14.3** above). A comparison with a permanent employee employed by an associated employer or a hypothetical comparator is not permitted. The FTE Regs, reg.2(2) states, in particular, that a comparison cannot be made with a permanent employee whose employment has ceased.

The pro rata principle

Under FTE Regs, reg.3, a fixed-term employee is entitled to receive equal rates of pay and other benefits (contractual and non-contractual) to a comparable permanent employee in such proportion as is reasonable in the circumstances having regard to the length of the employee's contract of employment and the particular benefit concerned unless the employer can justify different treatment on objective grounds or it is inappropriate.

In the case of benefits offered on an annual basis, such as season ticket loans or health insurance, it may be appropriate to offer them in proportion to the duration of the contract. The guidance notes issued by the DTI state that where it is not possible to offer a benefit on a proportionate basis, employers may be able to objectively justify not giving it to fixed-term employees if the cost of doing so would be disproportionate to the benefit. Each case must be considered on its merits.

The FTE Regs specifically provide that service qualifications for particular benefits must be the same for fixed-term employees as for permanent employees: FTE Regs, reg.3(2). So, for example, if permanent employees get extra holiday after two years' service, fixed-term employees should also get the same increase, unless there are objective reasons why they should not.

So far as occupational pensions are concerned, employers are required to offer fixed-term employees access to occupational pension schemes on the same basis as for permanent ones, unless different treatment is objectively justified. For example, where the term of the contract for the fixed-term employee is shorter than the vesting period of the pension scheme, the employer may be able to justify excluding that employee from the scheme. The DTI guidance notes state that the employer will not be required to provide alternative compensation in these circumstances.

Establishing objective grounds

What constitutes objective grounds is not defined by the FTE Regs but the DTI guidance notes state that less favourable treatment will only be justified on objective grounds if it is:

(a) to achieve a legitimate objective;

(b) necessary to achieve that objective; and

(c) an appropriate way to achieve that objective.

As under the PTW Regs, a key question is whether the cost of providing a benefit is disproportionate when compared to the benefit the employee would receive.

Under FTE Regs, reg.4, objective justification can be established in one of two ways by:

(a) showing that there is objective justification for not giving the fixed-term employee a particular benefit or for giving a benefit on less good terms; or

(b) showing that the value of the total package is at least equal to the value of the comparable permanent employee's total package of terms and conditions.

In contrast to the position under the EqPA 1970, employers are able to balance a less favourable term against a more favourable one, provided the overall value of the package, judged on its objective monetary worth, is not less favourable than that of a comparable permanent employee. This may not be a straightforward exercise in respect of certain benefits on which it may be difficult to place a monetary value.

Relationship with the Equal Pay Act

The overlap between the FTE Regs and the EqPA 1970 is discussed in **Chapter 6**. If a claim is brought under both provisions, it is important to note that different time limits may apply (see **Chapter 15**).

CHAPTER 15

Procedure

KEY POINTS

- The Employment Act 2002 (EA 2002) requires claimants to raise a grievance under the employer's grievance procedure before making a claim to a tribunal
- A questionnaire may be served prior to the commencement of proceedings seeking information that will help a claimant to decide whether she has a claim, and to frame her claim in the most effective way
- Employers should consider whether they are in a position to provide information on what people are paid, and why
- It is essential to have regard to the different time limits if a claim is brought under more than one legislative provision
- A directions hearing should be requested in order to plan the course of the proceedings
- Special procedures apply in equal value cases

15.1 JURISDICTION

Jurisdiction of the tribunal

An equal pay claim must be brought before an employment tribunal. There are five ways in which this may occur:

1. The employee can present a complaint: EA 2002, s.2(1).
2. The employer can apply to the tribunal for a declaration as to the true effect of an equality clause. This provision can only be used where a dispute actually exists. It cannot be used to test a hypothetical case: EA 2002, s.2(1A).
3. The Secretary of State can initiate proceedings if it appears that an employer may be in breach of an equality clause and it is not reasonable to expect the women concerned to pursue the matter them-

selves. The matter is treated as a claim by the women themselves: EA 2002, s.2(2).

4. The High Court or county court can refer to a tribunal any question that has arisen in the course of proceedings about the operation of an equality clause, or it may direct a party to refer such a question to a tribunal: EA 2002, s.2(3).

5. The Equal Opportunities Commission may refer certain issues to a tribunal for determination.

In practice, nearly all equal pay claims are presented to the tribunal by the employee.

Jurisdiction of the High Court and county court

The Equal Pay Act 1970 (EqPA 1970) does not exclude the jurisdiction of the ordinary civil courts. It does however give them discretion to decline to exercise jurisdiction. When presented with an equal pay issue, the court has two options: if it considers a tribunal could more conveniently deal with the issue, it may strike out the claim. If, however, the equal pay claim cannot be severed from the rest of the proceedings, the court may adjourn the proceedings pending a reference to a tribunal: EA 2002, s.2(3).

15.2 STEPS TO TAKE BEFORE BRINGING A CLAIM

Internal grievance

In due course, EA 2002, s.32 will preclude a claimant from commencing equal pay proceedings without first taking steps to resolve the matter through the employer's internal grievance machinery. It is expected the provisions will be introduced in late 2003.

The grievance must be submitted to the employer in writing: EA 2002, s.32(2). The employer must then be given 28 days in which to respond: EA 2002, s.32(3). Once 28 days have elapsed, proceedings may be commenced.

Employment Act 2002, s.32(4) deals with the situation in which a complaint cannot be accepted by the tribunal because the claimant did not first submit a written grievance to the employer or wait 28 days. The provisions say that where the statutory procedure was not complied with, a complaint can still be brought up until one month after the original time limit for making the tribunal complaint.

Questionnaire procedure

The Employment Act 2002 has also introduced a new questionnaire procedure for equal pay claims. An individual who believes she is the subject of gender pay discrimination may use the procedure to ask her employer for information that will help her to decide whether she has a claim, and to frame the claim in the most effective way. The procedure is included at EqPA 1970, s.7B and is almost identical to the procedures available in disputes over matters of race, sex and disability. Regulations implementing the provision are expected in early 2003.

The questions and replies are admissible in evidence. Although employers are not obliged to answer a questionnaire, if they do not do so within a prescribed time, or if their reply is evasive or equivocal, then it is open to the tribunal to draw any inference that it considers just and equitable, including the inference that the employer has been guilty of unlawful discrimination: EA 2002, s.7B(6).

Using the questionnaire procedure

Standard forms are to be printed for this purpose, although it does not matter if the standard form is not used. A form can be obtained from the Equal Opportunities Commission (EOC).

Questions generally fall into four areas:

(a) why the employer has treated the employee in a particular way;
(b) the identity of appropriate comparators, their relevant salary details, and information about their jobs;
(c) the employer's pay policies and practices, which could include information about a job evaluation scheme or performance-related pay system, if not readily available to employees; and
(d) general statistical evidence about the workforce.

The procedure can be used in such a way that it leads to the disclosure of documents, even though it is not intended for this purpose. While it is possible to ask for documents once the proceedings have commenced, sometimes it is not possible to assess the merits of a claim and thus to commence proceedings without certain key documents (for example, job descriptions).

A claimant trying to identify a suitable comparator and to establish historical differences could ask her employer to:

(a) identify the individuals in certain posts or on certain grades by name and gender;
(b) provide details of the claimant's and the comparator's remuneration

packages from the date of recruitment (for a full list of possible payments and benefits see the checklist in **Chapter 7**);

(c) provide details of relevant salary scales during the relevant period; and

(d) provide information about their jobs.

See paragraph **8.5** for the practicalities of identifying a suitable comparator generally.

The questionnaire may be used to explore the steps the employer has taken generally to address the issue of equal pay within his organisation. For example:

1. Does your organisation have a stated policy on equal pay?
2. If so, how and when was the policy communicated to employees?
3. Have you carried out an equal pay review to establish whether you have a gender pay gap, in line with the EOC's Code of Practice (see **Chapter 5**)? If so, please provide details.

Questions could also be asked about the employer's pay practices generally and his reasons for paying the man and the woman differently in particular. For example:

1. What is your justification for paying the claimant and the comparator differently?
2. Do you have any documents relating to the design and implementation of the incremental pay structure/grading structure and grading criteria/bonus scheme/performance-related pay scheme? Are you prepared to provide copies? If not, why not?
3. Have there been any grading reviews? If so, please provide details.
4. Is the performance pay scheme monitored? If so, with what result?
5. On what basis are payments made to a specific section of the workforce for criteria such as seniority, flexibility, training, etc. and how do they relate to the specific duties concerned?
6. How have the rates of pay for the claimant, the comparator and their respective groups been arrived at historically? Are you prepared to disclose any relevant collective agreements, collective bargaining minutes, and employee pay claims? If not, why not?

If the employer is likely to rely on market forces/financial constraints/red or green circling as a defence, it could be asked for:

(a) evidence of unfilled vacancies, turnover of staff, recent recruitment exercises and the going rate for the job during the relevant time;

(b) information that demonstrates the extent of any financial problems throughout the relevant time and how these impacted on the employer's pay policies;

(c) details of those affected by the red or green circling, broken down by gender, and information about why the circling was introduced in the first place and the length of time it is expected to last.

Written statement of reasons for less favourable treatment

Where a part-time worker or a fixed-term employee believes that she has been treated less favourably than a comparable full-time worker/permanent employee, she can ask her employer for a written explanation as to the reasons for her treatment. The right to ask for this written explanation is contained in the Part-time Workers (Prevention of Less Favourable Treatment) Regulations 2000, SI 2000/1551 (PTW Regs), reg.6 and the Fixed-term Employees (Prevention of Less Favourable Treatment) Regulations 2002, SI 2002/2034 (FTE Regs), reg.5. The request must be made in writing and the employer must respond within 21 days of receipt.

A written statement is admissible in evidence in any proceedings under the respective regulations. If the employer deliberately, and without reasonable excuse, fails to provide a statement, or the employer's answer is evasive or equivocal, the tribunal may draw any inference that it considers it just and equitable to draw, including one that the employer has infringed the right in question.

This right combines elements of the questionnaire procedure in the Sex Discrimination Act 1975 (SDA 1975), Race Relations Act (RRA 1976) and Disability Discrimination Act (DDA 1995) and the right to a written statements of reasons for dismissal under the Employment Rights Act 1996 (s.92). From a claimant's point of view, it offers a simple and straightforward means of establishing the reasons for the treatment she has received. When answering the request, it would be advisable for the employer to set out its objective justification for the particular pay practice that is being challenged.

Practical implications for employers

Given the availability of these procedures to a claimant, employers need to consider whether they are in a position to provide information on what people are paid, and why. To be able to respond to a questionnaire, or a request for a written list of reasons for less favourable treatment, employers will need to hold comprehensive information on the operation of their pay and benefit systems. In particular, they may need to confirm whether or not a particular pay practice has a disproportionate impact on women and, if it does, how it is objectively justified.

15.3 TIME LIMITS FOR BRINGING A CLAIM

Equal Pay Act 1970

There is no time limit for an existing employee bringing proceedings under the EqPA 1970. However, a claim must be lodged with the tribunal within six months of the termination of employment: EqPA 1970, s.2(4). When notice of termination is given, the six-month limitation period runs from the date of expiry of the notice, even if the claimant has been paid in lieu: *HQ Service Children's Education (MOD)* v. *Davitt* [1999] ICR 978, EAT. There is no provision for the period to be extended to allow for late claims.

Change of job within the same employment

A distinction is drawn between the termination of a contract and the end of the particular job on which the claimant bases her claim. The six-month time limit begins when the employee's contract of employment terminates regardless of when she ceased performing the type of work on which her claim is based: *National Power Plc* v. *Young* [2001] IRLR 32, CA. In this case, the claimant's claim related to a job she had undertaken some years before she left the company. The six-month time limit did not begin to run until she left the company.

Employees on a series of short-term contracts

In *Preston* v. *Wolverhampton Healthcare NHS Trust (No.2)* [2001] IRLR 237, the House of Lords considered the application of the six-month time limit to employees on a series of short-term contracts. Provided the employees can show that they are on regular contracts, in respect of the same employment and in a stable employment relationship, then the six-month time limit should apply only once at the end of the series of contracts, that is, when the sequence of contracts is interrupted in some way, for example by a break between contracts.

Armed service personnel

A claim cannot be presented to a tribunal by armed service personnel unless a complaint has already been made under the Service Redress Procedure (and has not been withdrawn): EqPA 1970, s.7A(5). In the case of a claimant who has left the service, the complaint must be presented to the tribunal within nine months from the end of her period of service. The Service Redress Procedure may continue after the complaint has been presented to the tribunal: EqPA 1970, s.7A(7).

Amendment to the time limit provisions

The government has issued draft regulations amending the rules relating to the time limits in EqPA 1970 claims. The proposed regulations do not change the general principle that proceedings must be brought within six months of the end of the employment, but allow for the time limit to be extended in certain circumstances. The first applies where the employer deliberately concealed from the woman any fact relevant to the claim, and the woman did not discover it (or could not reasonably have discovered it) during the employment. In such a case the six-month period does not start to run until the woman has either discovered the fact, or could with reasonable diligence have discovered it. The second exception applies if the woman was under a disability at any time during the six months following the end of the employment. The new regulations will also introduce a new rule to make it clear that a woman who has been employed under a stable employment relationship consisting of two or more contracts can bring a claim within six months of the end of that relationship.

It is expected the new regulations will be introduced in late 2003.

Article 141

UK domestic law time limits apply to a claim relying on Article 141, unless it can be shown that they are less favourable than those relating to similar actions of a domestic nature or are such as to make it impossible in practice to exercise the rights under Article 141: *Biggs* v. *Somerset County Council* [1996] IRLR 203, CA.

Pensions Act 1995 and Occupational Pension Schemes (Equal Treatment) Regulations 1995

The provisions under the EqPA 1970 apply: Pensions Act 1995, s.63(4).

Sex Discrimination Act and Race Relations Act

Under SDA 1975, s.76 and RRA 1976, s.68 claims must be lodged with the tribunal within three months of the act of discrimination unless the act of discrimination extends over a period, in which case the three-month time limit runs from the end of that period. A discriminatory pay practice may be treated as a continuing act of discrimination for limitation purposes. Thus the three-month time limit may not begin to run until the pay practice or the contract of employment comes to an end, whichever is the sooner. For example, in *Barclays Bank plc* v. *Kapur* [1991] IRLR 136, HL, the employer's refusal to allow an employee's previous service to count towards a pension was considered by the House of Lords to be a continuing act of discrimination. Likewise, in *Calder* v. *James Finlay Corporation Ltd* [1989] IRLR 55, the EAT held that the employer's refusal to allow the claimant access to a mortgage subsidy scheme was a continuing act of discrimination against her for as long as she remained in the employment. In contrast, it is likely that a one-off grading exercise (of the type described at paragraph **14.2**) would be regarded as a single act of discrimination, even though it had continuing consequences (namely a lower rate of pay). Thus the time limit would run from the date on which the claimant was awarded her grading. If there is any doubt about whether the act of discrimination is one-off or continuing, it is advisable to submit the application as soon as possible.

For members of the armed forces, the time period is six months beginning with the act complained of. However, they must first make a complaint under the service redress procedure: SDA 1975, s.85(9) and RRA 1976, s.75(9).

A tribunal has a discretion to hear a claim under the SDA 1975 and the RRA 1976 out of time if 'in all the circumstances of the case, it is just and equitable to do so'. Thus the tribunal has a wide discretion to allow a claim to be heard out of time. The tribunal will have regard to (among other things):

(a) any prejudice that might be caused to the respondent;
(b) the merits of the case;
(c) the extent of and the reasons for the delay (for example, the health of the claimant, the circumstances of any postal delays, pursuit of an internal grievance, mistaken understanding of the law, mistaken legal advice).

Provided the claimant considers she has a good reason for the delay, she has nothing to lose by making the claim.

Part-time Workers Regulations and Fixed-term Employees Regulations

The provisions are almost identical in both sets of Regulations (PTW Regs, reg.8 and FTE Regs, reg.7) and include the following:

1. The claim must be lodged with the tribunal within three months of the date of the less favourable treatment or detriment.

2. Where the act is part of a series of acts, the three-month time limit runs from the last act complained of.
3. Where the complaint relates to a term of the contract, it is treated as continuing for as long as the contract continues.
4. A claim may be brought out of time where it is just and equitable to do so.

In respect of the PTW Regs, members of the armed services must first make a complaint under the Service Redress Procedure.

15.4 INITIAL STEPS IN A CLAIM

The rules referred to in this section are in Schedule 1 to the Employment Tribunals (Constitution and Rules of Procedure) Regulations 2001, SI 2001/1171 (ET Regs).

Making a claim

A claim is brought by lodging an originating application (ET1 form) with the employment tribunal office specified on the form for the postal district concerned. In order to be a valid complaint, the application must contain sufficient information to:

(a) identify who is making the complaint (give the name and address of the claimant);
(b) identify against whom the complaint is made (give the name and address of the respondent); and
(c) show what sort of complaint it is.

The EAT has held that the other requirements on the ET1 are directory, not mandatory: *Dodd* v. *British Telecom plc* [1988] IRLR 16, EAT. Application forms are available from the Employment Tribunals Service and on their website (see **Appendix E** for details).

The contents of the claim

It is important to set out the nature of the claim (for example, whether it is a claim for like work, work rated as equivalent or work of equal value, or some combination of these provisions) and all relevant facts in support. If the comparator cannot be named at this stage, he should at least be identified in terms of his post or grade (it may not be possible to name a comparator until after the employer has answered a questionnaire or disclosed relevant documentation).

It is also desirable (although not essential) to identify the statutory provisions on which it is intended to rely (see the checklist of statutory provisions in **Chapter 6**). Best practice is to plead Article 141 in addition to the EqPA 1970 in case the claim does not fall within the EqPA 1970. Note that it is not possible to plead Article 141 on its own. If a claim is made relying directly on EU law, the claim must be made through the relevant UK statute as there is no freestanding right to rely on EU law. So, for example, if a claim is made under Article 141, the corresponding domestic provision is the EqPA 1970 'as interpreted in accordance with Article 141'.

It is always advisable to take and retain a copy of the application and to have some proof of dispatch or hand delivery. If the application is being submitted close to the limitation period, it is also wise to telephone the tribunal to ensure that the application has been received.

Claimants in group claims

The Rules provide for one originating application to be filed in a group claim provided all the cases arise out of the same set of facts: ET Regs, r.1(2).

The employer's response

Employers have 21 days in which to submit their response, that is, the ET3 form. The notice of appearance should set out:

(a) the employer's full name and address;
(b) whether or not the employer intends to resist the application; and
(c) the grounds on which the application is to be resisted.

Unlike out-of-time originating applications, late appearances do not affect the jurisdiction of a tribunal. Thus the 21-day time limit can be and often is extended.

Employers should set out the grounds on which they intend to resist the application. In particular, they should set out any jurisdictional points on which they intend to rely (for example, no reasonable grounds) and any relevant EqPA 1970, s.1(3) defences. Late identification of a defence may be taken to imply that it is not a genuine reason for the difference in pay (see paragraph **12.4**). The tribunal may also refuse to exercise its discretion to allow an amendment after the independent expert has reported.

Further and better particulars

A claimant may wish to serve a request for further and better particulars to explore the nature of the employer's defence. For example, if the employers' notice of appearance identifies more than one factor to account for the difference in treatment, it may be appropriate to serve a request for further particulars asking the employer to identify the proportion of difference attributable to each individual factor. A respondent may wish to serve a request for further and better particulars where, for example, the claimant has failed to name her comparator(s) in the ET1.

Directions hearing

Given the complex nature of equal pay claims, it is likely the tribunal will decide to hold an interlocutory (directions) hearing to give directions at the outset of the proceedings. The purpose of a directions hearing is to clarify the issues and to lay down a timetable for the conduct of the proceedings. Either party or both may suggest to the tribunal that a directions hearing should be held. A directions hearing is usually before a chairman sitting alone.

The kinds of matters on which directions are commonly given are:

(a) defining the issues;
(b) identification of comparators;
(c) discovery and inspection of documents;
(d) requests for further and better particulars;
(e) requests for written answers;
(f) exchange of witness statements;
(g) exchange of expert evidence, if relevant;
(h) preparation of the trial bundle;
(i) witness orders;
(j) the order of the proceedings where more than one claim is involved. For example, if the claimant is claiming like work and work of equal value, the tribunal will want to make arrangements for the like work claim to be heard first (if the like work claim is successful, it will necessarily dispose of the equal value claim);
(k) combining proceedings in group cases and multi-party actions;
(l) whether it is necessary to hold a preliminary hearing (a preliminary hearing may be necessary to consider any issue relating to the tribunal's jurisdiction to hear the claim or to determine any issue of law; preliminary hearings are commonly held in equal value cases – see paragraph **15.5**); and
(m) the length and date of the hearing.

15.5 SPECIAL PROCEDURE IN AN EQUAL VALUE CASE

Equal value cases are subject to special procedures once they reach the initial hearing stage. The relevant rules are set out in Schedule 1 as modified by Schedule 3 to the ET Regs.

In an equal value case, the tribunal may hold one or more preliminary hearings for the purpose of:

(a) inviting the parties to adjourn;
(b) considering any no reasonable grounds defence;
(c) considering any EqPA 1970, s.1(3) defences before the question of equal value;
(d) considering whether to appoint an independent expert to advise the tribunal on the question of equal value;
(e) considering whether the tribunal has jurisdiction to hear the claim, for example, where the claim may be out of time.

Preliminary hearings are before a full tribunal.

Invitation to adjourn

At the outset of equal value proceedings, the tribunal must enquire whether the parties want an adjournment for the purpose of negotiating a settlement of the claim. If both parties wish to avail themselves of this opportunity, an adjournment must be granted for this purpose: ET Regs, r.15(6A). In practice, the invitation is rarely accepted in equal value claims.

No reasonable grounds defence

The right of a tribunal to dismiss a claim because there are no reasonable grounds for determining that the work is of equal value is laid down in EqPA 1970, s.2A. Note that this is separate and additional to the tribunal's right to strike out proceedings on the basis that they are scandalous, misconceived or vexatious: ET Regs, r.15(2)(c).

The no reasonable grounds defence arises where:

(a) the merits of the claim are weak;
(b) a claimant seeks to pursue a claim after the hearing and rejection of sample cases that have substantially similar facts;
(c) the employer relies on the existence of a job evaluation scheme to establish that there are no reasonable grounds;
(d) the employer seeks to introduce a job evaluation scheme after proceedings have been commenced.

The circumstances where the no reasonable grounds defence arises are discussed in **Chapter 11**.

Should the Equal Pay Act 1970, s.1(3) defence be heard first?

The tribunal has a discretion to hear the employer's EqPA 1970, s.1(3) defence at a preliminary hearing before deciding whether to appoint an expert to prepare a report on the question of equal value: ET Regs, r.11(2E). Usually, it will be the employer who makes such a request, because it may spare the time and expense of dealing with the question of equal value. Until recently, it was relatively common for tribunals to accede to such requests but, as a result of delays caused by appeals on EqPA 1970, s.1(3) issues, tribunals nowadays are less inclined to hear the issues out of order (see paragraph **12.1** for further details).

The independent expert (IE)

Appointment of an IE

There are three ways in which the tribunal may approach the question of equal value:

(a) by seeking the advice of an expert on the ACAS panel of independent experts; or
(b) by dispensing with the services of an IE and determining the question of equal value on the basis of expert and other evidence submitted by the parties; or
(c) by determining the issue on the basis of the evidence of the parties (without the benefit of expert evidence).

Once the tribunal is satisfied that the claimant has a prima facie case, it has to decide whether to seek the advice of an expert on the ACAS panel of independent experts: ET Regs, r.10A(1).

Before coming to a decision, the tribunal must give the parties an opportunity to make representations: ET Regs, r.10A(2). Usually, this takes place at a preliminary hearing at which all three members of the tribunal are present.

It is unusual for a tribunal to determine the question of equal value without the report of an IE, and even rarer for the tribunal to proceed without the benefit of any expert evidence at all, unless the case is entirely straightforward on the issues. Even where the parties instruct their own job evaluation experts, there are still benefits to having an IE appointed to the case. Although it may be quicker to proceed without an

IE, the IE's involvement can be beneficial precisely because s/he is seen as independent. The fact that an IE's report favours one party commonly persuades the other to settle or withdraw the claim.

The tribunal may be more inclined to appoint an IE if only one party has instructed an expert, for the reason that it may leave the other party at a disadvantage. In these circumstances, the tribunal should have regard to its overriding duty to deal with cases justly and that includes ensuring that the parties are on an equal footing: ET Regs, reg.10.

If the tribunal decides to appoint an IE, it must issue a written 'requirement'. The requirement must stipulate (among other things):

(a) details of the parties and the establishments at which the claimant and the comparator are employed;
(b) the date by which the IE is required to submit the report to the tribunal;
(c) the intervals at which the IE must submit progress reports to the tribunal.

The requirement is sent to the parties with a warning that if they unreasonably delay the preparation of the IE's report they may be penalised in costs or have the originating application or notice of appearance struck out: ET Regs, r.10A(4). With increasing emphasis on case management, it is expected that tribunals will make more use of this power than they have in the past.

Having decided to appoint an IE to prepare a report, the tribunal will then adjourn the hearing, pending the receipt of the expert's report: ET Regs, r.10A(6).

The role of the independent expert

The role of the IE is to prepare a report on the question of equal value for submission to the tribunal. The IE must:

(a) take account of all information supplied and all representations made by the parties: ET Regs, r.10A(5)(a);
(b) before drawing up the report, produce and send to the parties a written summary of all information and representations and invite representations of the parties on the material contained therein: ET Regs, r.10A(5)(b);
(c) submit progress reports to the tribunal as required, stating whether the report will be submitted on time and, if not, giving reasons for the delay: ET Regs, r.10A(8);
(d) notify the tribunal if s/he is unable to submit the report on time, giving reasons for the delay: ET Regs, r.10A(9);

(e) notify the tribunal if the conduct of one of the parties is causing a delay: ET Regs, r.10A(10).

If the IE notifies the tribunal that the report will not be submitted on time, the tribunal must consult the parties and then do one of the following:

(a) give notice that the report is still required on time;
(b) substitute a later date for the submission of the report;
(c) replace the IE, if it is in the interests of justice to do so: ET Regs, r.10A(11).

Tribunals are very reluctant to replace an IE because of the delay it causes to the proceedings. Nevertheless, tribunals have been known to do so where the time taken by the IE to produce a report is particularly excessive, as it did in relation to one of the speech therapist test cases, where the tribunal was working to a timetable agreed with the parties.

The tribunal's powers in relation to the work of the independent expert

If the IE considers that any person has any information or documentation that may be relevant to the question of equal value, the IE may apply to the tribunal for an order for the information to be furnished in writing and for the documentation to be disclosed: ET Regs, r.4(5A).

Usually, the comparator works for the employer, so his cooperation in the assessment process is assured. However, if the comparator does not work for the employer, the tribunal has limited powers to require his cooperation. The tribunal may order him to disclose any relevant documentation, such as a job description and person specification, or order him to furnish relevant information in writing, or both: ET Regs, r.4(5A). If the comparator's failure to cooperate results in the IE being unable to reach a conclusion on the question of equal value, either party may seek a witness order to compel his attendance at the resumed hearing: ET Regs, r.11(2D)(b). In one of a series of claims against electricity supply companies, the IE sought information from an uncooperative comparator's colleague and supervisor and considered this sufficient as the basis for the report. It should be noted that the tribunal has no power to order the comparator to cooperate with the parties' experts: *Lloyds Bank plc* v. *Fox* [1989] IRLR 103, EAT.

Although the tribunal does not have the power to order the employer to provide the IE with access to his premises, if the employer refuses to cooperate, and the completion of the report is delayed as a result, the tribunal can exercise the sanctions contained in ET Regs, r.10A(14) (see above).

175

Working with the independent expert

The IE will usually initiate contact with the parties direct, or via their legal representatives, through the addresses set out in the requirement, and request submissions. The IE may arrange early separate meetings with the parties to explain how s/he will proceed and in order to draw up the schedule required by the tribunal.

It is worth bearing in mind that the IE is unlikely to have been supplied with any previous documentation by the tribunal, so initial submissions might usefully include information compiled for any previous 'no reasonable grounds' argument. Apart from that, the IE needs any existing information about the claimant and comparator jobs, for example, job descriptions or specifications, organisation charts. Strictly speaking, the IE is not interested in the 'history' of the case, but may request some background information, in order to set the jobs and issues in context.

The IE will arrange a programme of interviews with each of the claimant(s) (or the agreed representative cases – see **Chapter 8**), comparator(s) and their line managers, to obtain detailed information about the work in question. Depending on the nature of the work, s/he may wish to observe the claimant(s) and comparator(s) undertaking typical duties.

The parties will each need to decide who, in addition to the interviewee, will be present at these meetings. Claimants, and possibly comparators, may wish to be accompanied by a trade union representative and this is generally acceptable to IEs. Respondents may wish to have a manager or personal representative present.

Once the IE has obtained all the relevant information, including that supplied by the parties, the IE will prepare a written summary and invite the parties to make representations upon it: ET Regs, r.10A(5). The IE's summary of representations forms a crucial stage in the procedure. The summary, and the responses to it, forms the basis on which the IE determines whether the jobs are of equal value or not. So this is the point at which to correct any misunderstandings or inaccuracies and to ensure that the IE has all the information each party considers necessary. Practice on whether or not IEs should produce their own job descriptions, especially where the parties have already supplied written job information, has varied in the past. However, the independent experts appointed to the speech therapist claims, *Evesham* v. *North West Hertfordshire HA* (17844/87), *Worsfold* v. *Southampton & South West Hampshire HA* (18296/87) and *Lawson* v. *South Tees HA* (17931/87), were criticised by the tribunal for not having produced their own job descriptions, on the grounds that it was then difficult to know on what factual basis they had actually made their assessments. So it is to be expected that IEs will normally produce job descriptions as part of the summary in the future. The parties should check carefully that these job descriptions are accurate and include all significant features of the jobs under consideration.

Independent expert's methodology and the content of the report

No particular method of evaluation is required by the rules and so the IE has considerable freedom in deciding how to make the assessment, provided the method of assessment is analytical. Usually, IEs will include in their report an explanation of their methodology. **Chapter 4** looks at the methodologies adopted by experts in a number of cases to date.

The IE's report is required to reproduce the summary that was sent to the parties during the course of the assessment (see above) and to include a brief account of any representations received from the parties in response. It must also set out a reasoned conclusion on the question of equal value: ET Regs, r.10A(5)(c). The ACAS guide, *Equal Pay for Work of Equal Value: A Guide to Good Practice for Independent Experts* (1990) suggests the following format for the IE's report:

1. A table of contents with paragraph and page references.
2. A notice of requirement (unless included in the summary).
3. A short general background to the case.
4. The method of enquiry.
5. A comparison of the methods of evaluation used by the parties and the IE, including choice of factors.
6. The system of assessment adopted, with reasons for choice.
7. The assessments and allied argument.
8. Findings and conclusions.
9. Appendices are to include:
   (a) the summary of representations and information issued to the parties;
   (b) brief accounts of the parties' representations on the summary;
   (c) schedule or timetable of the progress of the enquiry;
   (d) definitions of factors/sub-factors and demand levels; and
   (e) copies of any reference documents not included in the summary.

Proceeding without an independent expert

If an IE is not appointed, the tribunal must adjourn to enable the parties to produce expert evidence on the issue of equal value: *Wood* v. *William Ball Ltd* [1999] IRLR 773, EAT (see paragraph **11.2**). It should be noted that there is nothing to prevent the tribunal changing its mind and appointing an IE at a later stage, if appropriate, after further consultations with the parties: ET Regs, r.10A(3).

Role of the parties' experts

Experts may be used by either or both of the parties to an equal pay claim for one or more purposes, for example:

(a) to make a preliminary assessment of the merits of the claim (and in the claimant's case, to recommend additional or alternative comparators);

(b) to provide a report in relation to a 'no reasonable grounds' argument;

(c) to provide a report on a job evaluation study defence;

(d) to provide a report for a claim under EqPA 1970, s.1(5), namely, work rated as equivalent (for example, where the claimant may need proof of evaluation or the employer may want to establish that the job evaluation scheme in question does not meet the requirements of EqPA 1970, s.1(5));

(e) to provide a report as the basis for the substantive hearing on the question of equal value (where no IE is appointed);

(f) to assist a party in respect of an IE, for example, by coordinating or providing comments in response to the IE's summary of representations;

(g) to give evidence in relation to the IE's final report at the substantive hearing, where there is an IE.

Each party is at liberty to call one expert to give evidence to support or contradict the opinion of the IE: ET Regs, r.11(2B). This can result in the tribunal having to consider three separate 'expert' reports, possibly using three sets of job descriptions, three different methodologies and coming to different conclusions. Perhaps not surprisingly, tribunals do not like this situation and sometimes ask the parties' experts to use a common approach, or to identify areas of agreement and disagreement before the hearing.

The parties' experts have no enforceable right of access to witnesses and premises. Nevertheless, it is in the parties' interests to cooperate with one another. From the claimant's point of view, if access is likely to be a problem, it underlines the advantage of choosing a comparator who will be cooperative so that initial interviews can take place off-site.

Occasionally, access is granted on terms, for example, that another party sits in on the interviews, or that the interviews are taped, or that job observation by both parties' experts should be conducted together. On balance, it is preferable not to have 'sitters in' at interviews because it may disturb the witness who is being interviewed, although comparators sometimes find it supportive to have their own line manager or a personnel or human resources manager present. There is no reason why the interview cannot be taped, although the practice is rare (indeed, it may prove to be a useful record of the interview). Joint interviews or observation are also rare unless jobs need to be reconstructed, or a plant is closing, or time pressures on jobholders are so great that two or three interviews with the various experts will be regarded as an excessive burden.

The equal value hearing

The procedure adopted by the tribunal at the main hearing will depend on whether an independent expert is appointed to the case and, if not, whether the tribunal intends to determine the issue of equal value by itself or on the basis of expert evidence presented by the parties.

Cases involving an independent expert

On receipt of the expert's report, the tribunal must send a copy to each party and fix a date for the resumed hearing: ET Regs, r.10A(16). If either party wishes the IE to attend the resumed hearing, they should notify the tribunal accordingly although, usually, the tribunal will arrange for the IE to attend as a matter of course.

At the resumed hearing, the tribunal first decides (after hearing evidence and/or submissions) whether to admit the report in evidence. The tribunal may not reject the report as unsatisfactory simply because it does not agree with its conclusions. The report may be rejected as unsatisfactory under ET Regs, r.10A(18) if:

(a) the IE has failed to comply with the requirement in ET Regs, r.10A(5); or
(b) the report's conclusions are perverse; or
(c) for some other material reason (other than disagreement with the conclusion or the reasoning), the report is unsatisfactory.

If either party wishes to challenge the factual basis of the IE's report, they must do so at this stage before the IE's report is admitted in evidence. A challenge on this basis may involve calling the claimant, the comparator, their line managers and the parties' experts to give evidence. Possible bases for a challenge may be that the IE:

(a) has failed to take into account the submissions (documentary and otherwise) of either or both parties;

(b) has failed to provide a reasoned exposition on which the conclusions of the report are justified, such as why the particular factors and weightings were chosen, why the particular evaluation system was used; and give reasons for the conclusion of equal value;

(c) has used an unsatisfactory method, for example, used a non-analytical method; failed to compile job descriptions; failed to take into account relevant factors, employed unbalanced or inconsistent weighting patterns; misdirected him/herself by taking into account something which s/he should not, or by not taking something relevant into account.

In coming to a decision, the tribunal must take account of the evidence of the IE, the parties' experts and any other witnesses. Where a tribunal declines to admit an IE's report, it has no choice but to appoint another IE to the case. Since this is likely to cause significant delay to the proceedings, it is rare for a tribunal to take such a step. The usual course is for the tribunal to admit the report and then give it such weight as it deems fit in the final weighing of the evidence. If the report is unsatisfactory, the weight to be attributed to the report is likely to be small.

Examples of cases in which the IE's report has been rejected include the following:

1. In *Allsopp & Others* v. *Derbyshire Police Authority* (13509–516/87), the tribunal declined to admit the independent expert's report because of his refusal to answer questions and be cross-examined on the parties' experts' reports.

2. In *Davies* v. *Francis Shaw & Co* (22420/85), the tribunal determined that the report of the independent expert 'shall not be admitted in evidence', because the IE had failed to take full account of the parties' submissions, had not reproduced the summary in the final report and, most important, had not provided full reasons for the report's conclusions.

3. In *Thompson* v. *John Blackburn Ltd* (15650/92), the tribunal decided not to admit the report, on the grounds that the independent expert had not made findings of fact in relation to significant features of the claimant's job.

Report admitted in evidence

Once the report has been admitted in evidence, either party may present arguments to the tribunal on the question of equal value (for example, where there is more than one comparator and the IE finds that the claimant undertakes work of equal value to one but not others). The IE will be cross-examined by one or both parties and may also be questioned by the tribunal. The parties in turn will call their own experts (if they have them), who will give evidence about their own reports and those of the other experts and the IE. Note that once the IE's report has been admitted in evidence, the parties are not allowed to reopen a question of fact upon which the expert's report is based (ET Regs, r.11(2C)) save in two circumstances:

(a) where the evidence is relevant to the EqPA 1970, s.1(3) defence; or
(b) where the IE has been unable to reach a conclusion on the question of equal value because s/he has been unable to obtain all the information s/he needed: ET Regs, r.11(2D).

In *O'Connor* v. *The Perry Group* (103392/94), the employers sought to challenge the IE's report without commissioning their own expert's report. The tribunal observed that their efforts merely constituted an attempt to pressurise the expert into reconsidering her conclusions. In the tribunal's view, it was unreasonable, given that they had not obtained an expert's report to support their stance, for the employers not to have conceded the issue of equal value in the light of the expert's findings of fact. This amounted to unreasonable conduct and the tribunal therefore ordered the employers to pay the claimant's costs and to reimburse ACAS any costs and expenses incurred by the expert as a result of her attendance at the tribunal. The lesson of the case is that, in the absence of an alternative expert's report, challenges to the IE's report are best raised at the earlier stage when the tribunal is considering whether or not to admit the report in evidence.

Either party may seek to modify the IE's conclusions. For example, in *Evesham* v. *North West Hertfordshire Health Authority* (17844/87), where the IE had found the claimant's job to be of equal value to that of the comparator, the respondents adduced expert evidence to try to persuade the tribunal that the jobs were not of equal value, while the claimant's expert broadly supported the independent expert. In *Worsfold* v. *Southampton & South West Hampshire HA* (18296/87) and *Lawson* v. *South Tees HA* (17931/87) where the IE (and the respondents' expert) had found the claimants' jobs not to be of equal value to the relevant comparators, the claimants sought to demonstrate that small modifications to the IE assessments would give a conclusion of equal value. As a result, the claimants were successful.

In another NHS case, *Hayes and Quinn* v. *Mancunian Community Health NHS Trust & South Manchester Health Authority* (16977/93) and

(16981/93), the IE found the jobs of the claimant dental surgery assistants of equal value to one of their comparators, a technical instructor in the occupational therapy department, but not to others, including a senior dental technician and a mortuary assistant. Faced with a respondents' expert arguing that the IE report should be modified to find the claimants' jobs of equal value to none of the comparators, and a claimants' expert arguing that their jobs were of equal value to all of the comparators, the tribunal, perhaps not surprisingly in the circumstances, followed the conclusions of the IE's report.

It is important to note that the IE's report is not conclusive of the question of equal value and does not attract any special status. The tribunal must make the final determination based on the whole of the evidence, of which the IE's report is only a part: *Tennants Textile Colours Ltd* v. *Todd* [1989] IRLR 3, CA (NI). For example, in *Worsfold*, the tribunal rejected the IE's conclusion that the claimant was not employed on work of equal value in view of the fact that she had scored 55 points under the evaluation exercise whereas the comparator had scored 56.5 points. The tribunal concluded that there was no measurable and significant difference between the jobs under consideration. In coming to a view, the tribunal will also take account of the evidence of expert witnesses, documentary evidence, oral evidence from the IE in cross-examination (which may cause a change to the original report) and the representations of the parties.

If the tribunal finds against the claimant, that will be the end of the matter. If the finding is favourable, it is likely there could be other stages to the proceedings (such as a hearing on the EqPA 1970, s.1(3) defence or a remedies hearing).

Cases where there is no independent expert but the parties call expert evidence

In cases where there is no independent expert but the parties call expert evidence, the appropriate procedure will be for the parties in turn to call their expert to give evidence about their own reports and those of the other experts. The claimant, the comparator and their line managers may also be called to give evidence. The tribunal will come to a view on the question of equal value on the basis of the evidence and the parties' closing submissions.

In *McKechnie & Others* v. *Gloucestershire County Council* (12776/96), the tribunal made its own comparative assessments in determining that the jobs of the claimant nursery nurses were of equal value to the higher graded of two comparators, an architectural technician. The respondent's expert had conceded in evidence that the claimants' jobs were of equal value to that of the lower graded comparator, a waste technician. The tribunal undertook its own assessment on the basis of the evidence heard from some of the claimants and the claimants' expert as well as the respondent's expert, using the respondent's expert's methodology. In *Prince & Others* v. *National Union of Teachers* (1501573/97), another tribunal took a similar approach. They heard evidence from some of the claimants (regional solicitors comparing themselves with regional officers) and the parties' experts only, and found against the claimants.

In *William Ball Ltd* v. *Wood* 89/01 EAT, the tribunal had before it two experts reports (one for each party). The claimants' expert used an evaluation system called *PayCheck* (see paragraph **4.4** and **Appendix F**) to determine the relative values of the two jobs whereas the employer's expert did not adopt any form of evaluation system at all, instead basing his report on a critique of the claimants' expert's methodology. The tribunal decided that it had no option but to rely on the only effective report before it (the claimants' expert's report). The EAT declined to interfere on appeal. The lesson of the case is that a party whose expert does not carry out a proper evaluation exercise should not be surprised if the tribunal prefers the other party's expert report.

Cases where there is no expert evidence

In cases where there is no expert evidence, it is likely the tribunal will hear oral evidence about the content of the claimant's and the comparator's jobs from such witnesses as the parties wish to call and then take submissions. It will then be for the tribunal to undertake an analytical evaluation of the jobs in question. In these circumstances it will doubtless assist the tribunal if the parties in their submissions:

(a) indicate the factors and sub-factors that each wishes the tribunal to select;
(b) clarify what falls within each (what defines it);
(c) identify the features of the jobs that are relevant to each factor and sub-factor;
(d) make submissions about marking systems, weighting and so on.

At the end of this process the tribunal must reach its own conclusion on the question of equal value.

Hearing of Equal Pay Act 1970, s.1(3) defence

If the tribunal did not hear the employer's EqPA 1970, s.1(3) defence before determining the question of equal value, the tribunal must now make arrangements to do so (and to address the question of remedies, if the defence is defeated).

15.6   REVIEW AND APPEAL

Rule 13 (of Schedule 1 to the ET Regs) provides that a tribunal may, either of its own motion or on the application of either party, review its decision, confirm it, vary it or revoke it. The grounds on which a tribunal may conduct a review are strictly limited but include circumstances where the tribunal has made a procedural mistake, for example, in the calculation of a claimant's compensation or some other aspect of the case. An application for a review must be made within 14 days from the date when the decision is sent to the parties. If the application is late, the chairman has a discretion under ET Regs, r.17(1) to extend the time limit.

An appeal lies to the EAT on a point of law only. An appeal must be lodged with the EAT within 42 days of the date on which the full (extended) reasons are sent to the parties. The EAT will decide at a preliminary hearing whether the appeal has any prospects of success. If not, it will not be allowed to proceed.

15.7   REFERENCE TO THE ECJ

Many of the most significant developments in equal pay law in recent years have been made as a result of references to the European Court of Justice. Thus recourse to the ECJ is a valuable option to employees who seek to establish that domestic law fails to implement in full the provisions enshrined in European Treaties and Directives or is incompatible with EU requirements.

The ECJ has the power under Article 117 to make a preliminary ruling on the proper interpretation of EU law. Although a tribunal has a discretion under Article 234 to make a reference to the ECJ for an interpretation of EU law, the general policy of tribunals appears to be that the decision to refer is best left to the higher courts when the full facts of the case have been established.

CHAPTER 16

Remedies

KEY POINTS

Under the Equal Pay Act 1970 (EqPA 1970), the tribunal has the power to:

- Make a declaration
- Equalise contractual terms for the future (if the claimant is still in the relevant employment)
- Award compensation consisting of arrears of pay (if the claim is about pay) and/or
- Award damages (if the complaint is about some other contractual term), if appropriate

Under the Sex Discrimination Act 1975 (SDA 1975) and the Race Relations Act 1976 (RRA 1976), the tribunal has the power to:

- Make a declaration
- Award compensation for loss of arrears of pay and/or damages
- Award damages for injury to feelings, aggravated damages and personal injury, if appropriate
- Make a recommendation that the employer take action likely to reduce the effect of the discrimination on the claimant

Under the Part-time Workers (Prevention of Less Favourable Treatment) Regulations 2000, SI 2000/1551 (PTW Regs) and the Fixed-term Employees (Prevention of Less Favourable Treatment) Regulations 2002, SI 2002/2034 (FTE Regs), in addition to making a declaration, the tribunal has the power to:

- Award compensation for loss of arrears of pay and/or damages
- Award compensation for any future losses
- Make a recommendation

The tribunal also has the power to award interest on an award of compensation.

16.1 REMEDIES UNDER THE EQUAL PAY ACT

Declaration

A claimant is entitled to an order declaring her rights. Once the order has been made she has a contractual right to the increased pay and/or improved contractual terms.

Operation of the equality clause

The effect of a declaration is to operate the equality clause, the device used by the EqPA 1970 to achieve equality in pay and terms and conditions.

Principles of equalisation

The general principles of equalisation are as follows (the equalisation of pension rights is dealt with separately below):

1. Modification of the claimant's contract takes place on a term-by-term basis, if necessary by inserting a corresponding term in the contract where none existed before.
2. Particular terms that are unfavourable may not be counterbalanced by others that are in the claimant's favour.
3. The equality clause operates to bring the lower standard up to the higher and cannot be used to bring the higher down to the lower.
4. Equalisation must be immediate and full: *Smith & Ors* v. *Avdel Systems Ltd* [1994] IRLR 602.
5. Differences in working conditions must not be taken into account in the equalisation process: *Jamstalldhetsombudsmannen* v. *Orebro Lans Landsting* [2000] IRLR 421, ECJ.
6. Additional payments for night and unsocial hours may be disregarded in the equalisation process if the claimant's work is not undertaken at similar times.
7. A claimant who undertakes work of greater value to that of her male comparator is entitled to parity and no more.

So, for example, in *Hayward* v. *Cammell Laird Shipbuilders Ltd (No.2)* [1988] IRLR 257, HL, the claimant received lower basic and overtime rates of pay than her male comparators but benefited from superior sickness benefit, paid meal breaks and extra holidays. The employers argued that the claimant was entitled to equality on a broad basis and that equal pay meant ensuring that the claimant's contract as a whole was no less favourable than that of her male comparators. The House of Lords rejected this approach.

The ECJ adopted the same approach in *Jamstalldhetsombudsmannen* v. *Orebro Lans Landsting* [2000] IRLR 421, ECJ. While the claimants' basic pay was lower than that of their comparator they worked fewer hours and received a supplement for working inconvenient hours. The employers argued that the women were not paid less than the technician once the inconvenient hours supplement and the value of the reduced working time was considered.

The ECJ disagreed, holding that the principle of equal pay under Article 141 applies to each of the elements of remuneration and that neither the shift supplement nor the value of the reduced working hours should be taken into consideration. The Court considered it would make the practical implementation of equal pay very difficult and result in a lack of transparency if national courts had to make a comparison of all the various elements of the contract.

The Court added that any differences that might exist could constitute objective reasons justifying a difference in pay.

In practice, equalising contractual terms is not always a straightforward exercise, as the case of *Evesham* v. *North Hertfordshire Health Authority* [2000] IRLR 257, CA illustrates. The claimant and her comparator were employed on different pay scales that contained automatic annual pay increments based on years in post. The claimant had many years' service with the result that she occupied the highest point on her scale, whereas at the date of claim the comparator had only recently joined the employer's service and therefore occupied a lower point on his scale. The claimant contended that she ought to be placed on her comparator's pay scale but at the point on the scale that her length of service warranted, in other words the highest point. The Court of Appeal was of the opinion that the claimant's entitlement was to be placed on her comparator's pay scale at the point occupied by him. The Court reasoned that the claimant's greater length of service and experience had played a significant part in establishing that she was doing work of equal value to that of her comparator. Were she to enter the comparator's pay scale at an incremental point higher than her comparator, the effect would be that she would receive pay at a level in excess of that of her comparator and commensurate with the pay scale of someone with whom she had not established equal value.

From a claimant's perspective, *Evesham* underlines the importance of the selection of an appropriate comparator at the outset of the claim.

How long does equalisation last?

The variation of the claimant's contract of employment takes effect in the same way as any other variation of contract agreed between an employer and employee. The contract as varied remains in force until varied by further agreement or by operation of law. In particular, the claimant does not lose the benefits derived from the equality clause if her male comparator leaves his employment or moves to a different post. However, the claimant may lose the benefits she has achieved if she accepts another post with the same employer depending on whether such a move amounts to a variation of her contract of employment.

If the claimant moves to a new employer or takes up a new post with the same employer during the course of the proceedings, there may be grounds for pursuing a fresh claim. This is particularly relevant where the claimant works in the public sector, where pay structures in organisations providing the same or similar services to the public are very similar, for example in the NHS.

Arrears of compensation

Section 2(5) of the EqPA 1970 enables the tribunal to award arrears of pay and compensation arising out of the employer's failure to comply with the equality clause for a period of up to two years immediately preceding the commencement of proceedings. No power is given to the tribunal under the EqPA 1970 to extend this period.

In *Levez* v. *T H Jennings (Harlow Pools) Ltd* [1999] IRLR 36, ECJ, it was argued that EqPA 1970, s.2(5) complied neither with the EU principle of equivalence nor with the principle that compensation for failure to apply the principle of equal pay must be full and effective enabling the loss actually sustained to be made good. The principle of equivalence in EU law requires that procedural rules giving effect to EU rights under EU law are no less favourable than those governing similar domestic actions. Mrs Levez argued that a claim in respect of any breach of contract of employment apart from breach of the equality clause implied by the EqPA 1970 is subject to a time limit of six years. The ECJ held that it was for the national court, in this case the EAT, to decide whether the limit on back pay infringed the principle of equivalence in EU law. However, the ECJ stated that an employer whose deceit had caused the delay in bringing proceedings could not be permitted to rely on the time limit, however long it may be. Applying the principles laid down by the ECJ, the EAT subsequently held in *Levez* v. *T H Jennings (Harlow Pools) Ltd (No.2)* [1999] IRLR 764 that the two-year limitation on arrears of compensation in EqPA 1970, s.2(5) is in breach of the principle of equivalence in EU law because it is less favourable than equivalent provisions governing similar claims such as unlawful deduction from wages and unlawful discrimination on grounds or race or disability, which contain no restriction on compensation that can be awarded. The EAT decided that a six-year time limit should be applied.

Amendment to the backdating provisions

The government has issued draft regulations amending EqPA 1970, s.2(5), which will mean that arrears or damages for unequal pay could be awarded for up to six years before the date when the proceedings were instituted. However, the period may be longer if the employer deliberately concealed facts relevant to the claim from the claimant. It is expected the regulations will be introduced in late 2003.

In the meantime, as a result of the overriding effect of Article 141, claimants can take advantage of the extended backdating period of six years (or longer if there has been any deception on the part of the employer), or for as long as they have been engaged on the relevant work (if this is less than six years).

Factors affecting compensation

The claimant will be entitled to equal pay during the six-year backdating period only if she can establish that she was performing equal work to her comparator throughout the period.

If the claimant has already left the employment, her claim will be limited to arrears of compensation. From the claimant's perspective, it is vital that the claim is submitted to the tribunal as soon as possible to prevent its value diminishing. The longer the delay in commencing proceedings, the shorter the backdating period will be.

Calculating the claim

The concept of 'pay' is very broad and can include any of the items listed in **Chapter 7**.

The general principles to be applied when calculating arrears of compensation (excluding pension rights) in an equal pay claim are as follows:

1. Begin by conducting an item-by-item comparison of the claimant's and the comparator's remuneration packages during the relevant period.
2. Calculate the gross difference between what the claimant and the comparator earned during the backdating period.
3. Evidence may be needed of the value of some benefits, such as share options and the use of a car, to enable the tribunal to place a value on the claim. The value of the use of a car may be estimated from tables produced by the AA and RAC.

4. Deduct tax, national insurance and pension contributions from the gross sum at the appropriate rate. The claim may need to be calculated on a year-by-year basis to reflect the changes in taxation rates.
5. If part or all of the compensation will be taxable in the hands of the claimant, compensation must be 'grossed up' at the appropriate rate: see paragraph **16.4** below.

Pension rights

The ECJ has drawn a sharp distinction between claims concerning access to a pension scheme (including access to a particular benefit under the scheme) and claims for retrospective benefits. The retrospective claims are limited in time by the ECJ's decision in *Barber* v. *Guardian Royal Exchange Assurance Group* [1990] IRLR 240 whereas the access claims are governed by the principles established in *Bilka-Kaufhaus GmbH* v. *Weber von Hartz* [1986] IRLR 317, ECJ. In *Barber*, the ECJ imposed a temporal limit on retrospective claims with the result that only occupational pension benefits that relate to years of service after 17 May 1990, the date of the *Barber* decision, have to be calculated by reference to the principle of equal pay. The decision in *Bilka* included no such limit and consequently a claimant who has been denied access to an occupational pension scheme, or to a particular benefit under a scheme, is entitled to have all periods of service since 8 April 1976 – the date on which the ECJ ruled in *Defrenne* v. *Sabena (No.2)* [1976] ECR 455 that Article 141 had direct effect – taken into account.

The ECJ has also considered the validity of EqPA 1970, s.2(5) (as amended by regulation 12(1) of the Occupational Pension Schemes (Equal Access to Membership) Regulations 1976, SI 1976/142) in the context of claims to secure membership of an occupational pension scheme: *Magorrian* v. *Eastern Health and Social Services Board* [1998] IRLR 86, ECJ and *Preston* v. *Wolverhampton Healthcare NHS Trust* [2000] IRLR 506, ECJ. The claimants in *Magorrian* began employment as full-time workers but transferred to part-time work when they had children. When they retired, they were not entitled to the more favourable pension benefits available to full-time workers. In *Preston,* some 60,000 part-time workers complained that they were unlawfully excluded from occupational pension schemes because membership was dependent upon an employee working a minimum number of hours each week. In both cases, the ECJ upheld the part-timers' claim that the two-year time limit imposed on retrospective membership of an occupational pension scheme by EqPA 1970, s.2(5) was contrary to EU law. The Court considered that EqPA 1970, s.2(5) breached the principle of effectiveness in that it prevented an employee's entire record of service being taken into account for the purposes of calculating pension benefits.

Principles of equalisation

According to the ECJ, it is for the national court to ensure correct implementation of Article 141. The court may use its powers in a number of ways, for example, to order an employer to pay additional sums into the pension scheme or to determine whether any sum to be paid out comes out of surplus funds or the scheme's assets. If there are insufficient funds to equalise benefits, the matter must be resolved in accordance with the principles of equal pay: *Coloroll Pension Trustees Ltd* v. *Russell* [1994] IRLR 586, ECJ.

The general principles of equalisation in relation to pensions are:

(a) disadvantaged employees should be granted the same benefits as those previously enjoyed by other employees as regards periods of service completed before the entry into force of measures designed to eliminate discrimination: *Coloroll*;

(b) in relation to periods of service thereafter, equal treatment may be achieved by reducing the benefits of the scheme: *Coloroll*;

(c) retroactive reduction of benefits is not permitted: *Coloroll*;

(d) if a pension scheme requires contributions from both employer and employee, a claimant who has previously been excluded from access is likely to have to pay a sum equal to the contributions she would have had to pay over the relevant years in order to gain the right to equal benefits;

(e) claims for retrospective benefits (as opposed to claims for access to a pension scheme) will be limited by the six-year backdating period.

Calculating the claim

If the claimant is or was a member of the employer's occupational pension scheme, the tribunal should make a declaration of the claimant's right to equal treatment during the relevant period and an order that the employer make additional resources available, if necessary, to secure equal treatment and the payment of any arrears of benefit.

If the claimant had her own personal pension, it will be necessary to calculate the value of her lost rights. Guidelines for calculating a claim for pension rights are set out in a booklet entitled *Industrial Tribunals – Compensation for Loss of Pension Rights* (2nd edition, HMSO, 1991)

prepared by the Committee of Chairmen of Employment Tribunals in consultation with the government actuary's department. Under the guidelines,
which have been widely adopted by tribunals, a claim for retrospective
pension rights in respect of all types of pension claims (money purchase
and final salary) is calculated by the contribution method (the claim is
treated as the employer's notional contributions for the requisite period).
The guidelines state that in the absence of any specific evidence the claim
should be treated as 10 per cent of salary for a contributory scheme and
15 per cent of salary for a non-contributory scheme.

Although the EAT has approved the use of the guidelines (in *Ministry
of Defence* v. *Cannock & Ors* [1994] IRLR, 509), tribunals are not required
to follow them. In particular, the approach adopted in the guidelines may
not accurately assess the value of the claim in every case. So, for example,
in *Clancy* v. *Cannock Chase Technical College* [2001] IRLR 331, the EAT
said that it was necessary to look at the guidelines to see if they could still
be relied upon as providing a fair computation of losses. In practice, actuarial assistance may be required to calculate accurately the value of the
claim. With many schemes, the value to the claimant of being a member of
the employer's pension scheme during the backdating period will not bear
a direct relationship to the employer's (and employee's) contributions.

Enforcing an award

The usual contractual remedies are available to the claimant to enforce
an award in the High Court and county court. Depending on the circumstances, it may also be possible to bring a claim in the employment tribunal under the Employment Rights Act 1996, ss.13–27.

16.2   REMEDIES UNDER THE SEX DISCRIMINATION ACT AND RACE RELATIONS ACT

The following remedies are available under the SDA 1975 and RRA
1976:

(a) a declaration stating that discrimination has taken place: SDA 1975,
s.65(1)(a) and RRA 1976, s.56(1)(a);
(b) compensation, including an award for injury to feelings, aggravated
damages, exemplary damages, personal injury and interest: SDA
1975, s.65(1)(b) and RRA 1976, s.56(1)(b);
(c) a recommendation that the employer take action likely to reduce the
effect of the discrimination on the claimant.

Overlap with the Equal Pay Act

If a claim is successful under the SDA 1975 and/or RRA 1976 as well as the EqPA 1970, in addition to awarding compensation under the EqPA 1970, the tribunal has the power to make recommendations and awards for injury to feelings, aggravated damages, exemplary damages and personal injury, if appropriate.

Compensation under the Sex Discrimination Act and Race Relations Act

The principles on which compensation is awarded are as follows:

1. Compensation is assessed on the basis that the claimant must be put in the position she would have been in had the discrimination not been committed (subject to the principles of causation and mitigation of loss).
2. There is no upper limit on the amount of compensation that can be awarded.
3. A claimant can claim for any financial loss that is properly attributable to the unlawful act of discrimination. In a claim under the SDA 1975, this will be for loss of actual and future non-contractual benefits. In a claim under the RRA 1976, this will be for loss of actual and future contractual and non-contractual earnings and benefits. If the financial loss is for a lengthy period into the future, it may be appropriate to make a percentage reduction to take account of the benefit of receiving the money early. The tribunal may make use of the Ogden tables for this purpose.
4. Where the claim is for indirect discrimination under the RRA 1976, the tribunal cannot award any money compensation unless the employer intended to discriminate on racial grounds: RRA 1976, s.56(1)(b).
5. The claimant is under a duty to mitigate her loss.

Injury to feelings

Damages in respect of an unlawful act of discrimination may include compensation for injury to feelings, subject to causation being established: SDA 1975, s.66(4) and RRA 1976, s.57(4). The relevant principles for assessing awards for injury to feelings were set out by the EAT in *Armitage, Marsden & HM Prison Service* v. *Johnson* [1997] IRLR 162.

- awards for injury to feelings are compensatory. They should be just to both parties. They should compensate fully without punishing the tortfeasor. Feelings of indignation at the tortfeasor's conduct should not be allowed to inflate the award;
- awards should not be too low as that would diminish the respect for the policy of the anti-discrimination legislation. On the other hand, awards should also be restrained;
- they should bear some broad similarity to the range of awards in personal injury cases. This should be done by reference to the whole range of such awards, rather than any particular type of award (for example, awards for psychiatric injury);
- the tribunal should remind itself of the value in everyday life of the sum they have in mind;
- they should also bear in mind the need for public respect for the level of awards made.

Further guidance was given in *Tchoula* v. *ICTS (UK) Ltd* [2000] ICR 1191. In *Tchoula*, the EAT suggested that awards for injury to feelings could be grouped into two categories – a lower category of £7,000 to £13,000 and a higher category from £13,000 with compensation reaching £20–28,000 for severe cases. In deciding whether to make an award in the lower or higher category, the tribunal will be concerned to know whether the discrimination took place over a long period of time, and the extent of the injury suffered.

The categories defined in *Tchoula* were not intended to be exhaustive. Logically, there must be a middle bracket, where the extent of the effect suffered by the claimant falls between the higher and the lower category.

In *Doshoi* v. *Draeger* Ltd (939/01), the EAT increased an award from £750 to £4,000. The EAT described the award of £750 as being at the very bottom or very close to the bottom of the entire scale of awards for injury to feelings.

According to *Equal Opportunites Review* No.108 survey of awards in 2001, the average and median awards for injury to feelings relating to terms and conditions of employment (in sex discrimination cases) were £3,096 and £1,250 respectively.

Aggravated damages

Tribunals may award aggravated damages where they consider the sense of injury has been heightened by the manner in which, or the motive for which, discrimination has been carried out. In *Alexander* v. *Home Office* [1988] IRLR 190, the Court of Appeal said that compensation in some cases should include an element of aggravated damages where, for example, the defendant may have behaved in a high handed, malicious, insulting or oppressive manner in committing the act of discrimination.

In *McConnell* v. *Police Authority for Northern Ireland* [1977] IRLR 625, the CA (NI) held that aggravated damages should not be treated as an extra award of compensation. According to the CA (NI), any element of aggravation should be taken into account in reckoning the extent of the injury to feelings, for it is part of the cause of the injury. Thus a tribunal should weigh the evidence and form a view as to the level of distress caused by the discrimination, including any features that may have had the effect of aggravating the sense of injury by the claimant. The final result will be a single award, reflecting the totality of the injury to feelings.

Exemplary damages

Until recently, it was generally considered that exemplary damages could not be awarded in discrimination claims. However, in *Kuddus* v. *The Chief Constable of Leicestershire* [2001] 3 All ER 193, all five Law Lords asserted that exemplary damages could be awarded where:

(a) there are oppressive, arbitrary or unconstitutional acts by servants of the government; or

(b) the defendant's conduct has been calculated by him to make a profit for himself, which may well exceed the compensation payable to the claimant.

Although two of their Lordships (Lord MacKay and Lord Scott) expressed the view obiter that exemplary damages should not be awarded in respect of statutory torts unless the statute expressly says so (which the SDA 1975 and RRA 1976 do not), following *Kuddus*, one tribunal has decided that it has the power to award exemplary damages although it declined to make an award on the facts: *Bower* v. *Schroder Securities Ltd* (3202104/99). *Bower* concerned a claim for sex discrimination in the provision of discretionary bonuses. Similar reasoning would apply to awards in race discrimination cases.

Personal injury

The Court of Appeal held in *Sheriff* v. *Klyne Tugs (Lowestoft) Ltd* [1999] IRLR 481 that tribunals have jurisdiction to award compensation by way of damages for personal injury, including both physical and psychiatric injury, caused by the statutory tort of unlawful discrimination. Stuart-Smith LJ noted that the advantage of bringing the claim under the RRA

1976 and SDA 1975 is that foreseeability does not need to be established; all that needs to be established is the causal link.

In assessing the value of the claim, the tribunal will have regard to the current *Judicial Studies Guidelines for the Assessment of General Damages in Personal Injury Cases* (5th edition, OUP, 2002), which sets out bands of general damages (with definitions) for different degrees of injury, and also to *Kemp and Kemp: The Quantum of Damages* (Sweet & Maxwell, 1975) and like publications. It is worth bearing in mind that these publications may not be available at the tribunal.

Recommendations

Under the SDA 1975 and the RRA 1976, the tribunal has a wide discretion to make recommendations that the employer take within a specified period action appearing to the tribunal to be practicable for the purpose of obviating or reducing the adverse effect on the complainant of any act of discrimination to which the complaint relates: SDA 1975, s.65(1)(c) and RRA 1976, s.56(1)(c). For example, the tribunal may be invited in appropriate circumstances to recommend that the employer carry out a pay audit. If the employer fails, without reasonable justification, to comply with a recommendation, the tribunal may increase the amount of compensation or, if no award of compensation has been made, make an award of compensation.

16.3 REMEDIES UNDER THE PTW REGS AND THE FTE REGS

Where a complaint is upheld under the PTW Regs and the FTE Regs, the tribunal can take such of the following steps as it considers just and equitable in the circumstances:

(a) make a declaration as to the rights of the parties;
(b) order the employer to pay compensation;
(c) make a recommendation(s) that the employer take action likely to reduce the effect of the discrimination on the claimant: PTW Regs, reg.8(7) and FTE Regs, reg.7(7).

Compensation

The amount of compensation awarded is what the tribunal considers to be just and equitable having regard to:

(a) the infringement to which the complaint relates;
(b) any loss to which the infringement relates;
(c) the pro rata principle: PTW Regs, reg.8(9) and FTE Regs, reg.7(8).

Losses include any expenses reasonably incurred in consequence of the infringement and any benefits the claimant might reasonably have expected to receive but for the infringement: PTW Regs, reg.8(10) and FTE Regs, reg.7(9).

Compensation may be reduced where:

(a) the claimant fails to mitigate her loss;
(b) the claimant caused or contributed to the employer's action: PTW Regs, reg.8(12) and (13) and FTE Regs, reg.7(11) and (12); and
(c) no compensation may be awarded for injury to feelings: PTW Regs, reg.8(11) and FTE Regs, reg.7(10).

If the employer fails, without reasonable justification, to comply with a recommendation, the tribunal may increase the amount of compensation or, if no award of compensation has been made, make an award for compensation: PTW Regs, reg.8(14) and FTE Regs, reg.7(13).

16.4   TAXATION OF AWARDS AND SETTLEMENTS

Part or all of an award or settlement may be taxable in the hands of the claimant. It is necessary therefore for the parties to consider the potential impact of tax on an award or settlement.

The tax position on awards and settlements is complex. No general guidance is available from the Inland Revenue and the practice of tax inspectors has been known to vary. As it is likely that awards of compensation for unequal pay will be taxable (even if paid net of tax), the best option may be for the parties to consult their local tax inspector for specific advice.

The general principles are that:

1. Tax is payable under Schedule E on 'emoluments' from an employment: Income and Corporation Taxes Act 1988 (ICTA 1988), s.19. Emoluments include wages, bonuses and taxable benefits.
2. The first £30,000 of a payment in connection with the termination of employment is tax free: ICTA 1988, s.148.
3. An award made in relation to a sum or benefit expressly provided for in the employment contract will be taxable: ICTA 1988, s.131.
4. Payments made directly into a pension fund are generally not taxable.
5. It is arguable that payments for injury to feelings should not be taxable by analogy with damages paid to an employee on account of personal injury, which are not taxable: ICTA 1988, s.188.

6. Interest awarded on compensation will be subject to tax.
7. Legal fees payable directly to a claimant's solicitor are not taxable.
8. Liability to tax arises in the year in which payment is received.

Grossing up

If an award is taxable, the net amount of compensation must be grossed up at the rate at which the individual will pay tax. The standard and higher rates are currently (2002–3) 22 per cent and 40 per cent respectively.

Practical steps

If the tax position is uncertain, there are a number of practical steps a claimant can take to protect her position. In the context of a tribunal award, it would be advisable to ask the employer or tribunal to pay the award grossed up or ask the tribunal to give liberty to apply to return to the tribunal for an additional amount if there is an unexpected tax liability. Logically, this should extend for seven years from the date of payment.

In the context of a settlement, a claimant could:

(a) ask the employer for an indemnity in respect of any payments due to the Inland Revenue (to include tax on any additional sum); or
(b) ask her tax inspector for a ruling in advance of what the tax position on the award will be.

16.5 INTEREST

Interest on compensation

The Industrial Tribunals (Interest on Awards in Discrimination Cases) Regulations 1996, SI 1996/2803 (IT Regs) give a tribunal discretion to award interest on awards of compensation in equal pay and discrimination cases. The principles on which interest is awarded are as follows:

1. The tribunal must consider whether to award interest even if the claimant does not specifically apply for it: IT Regs, reg.2(1).
2. In general, interest is calculated as simple interest, which accrues on a day-to-day basis: IT Regs, reg.3(1).
3. If the rate of interest has varied over the period of the calculation, the tribunal has the discretion to apply a median or average of the rates as appropriate: IT Regs, reg.3(3).

4. For the purposes of calculating interest on arrears of remuneration, interest is awarded from the midpoint between the 'date of the act of contravention' to the date of the hearing at which compensation is determined: IT Regs, reg.6(1)(b). In the context of an equal pay claim, the date of the act of contravention will be the first day of the backdating period.

5. No interest can be awarded in relation to a loss or matter that will arise after the day of calculation: IT Regs, reg.5. This means that no interest can be awarded on claims for any future loss or in respect of pension rights: *Ministry of Defence* v. *Cannock & Ors* [1994] IRLR 509.

6. The tribunal may calculate interest for periods other than those specified in IT Regs, reg.6(1) where there would be 'serious injustice' if these dates were used: IT Regs, reg.6(3). In *Cannock* the EAT held that payment over a longer period may be appropriate where the whole of the loss was incurred many years previously.

7. The tribunal's decision must contain a statement of total interest awarded and, where interest has not been agreed between the parties, a table setting out how it has been calculated or an explanation of the method used: IT Regs, reg.7.

8. If no award of interest is made, the tribunal must set out its reasons for this: IT Regs, reg.7(2).

Rate of interest

In England and Wales, the rate of interest is the rate from time to time prescribed for the special investment account under rule 27(1) of the Court Funds Rules 1987, SI 1987/821 (L3). In Scotland, the rate is fixed by the Act of Sederunt (Interest in Sheriff Court Decrees or Extracts) 1975, SI 1975/948, reg.3(2).

The special investment account rates over the last 10 years have been:

- 1 February 1993 to 31 July 1999 – 8 per cent;
- 1 August 1999 to 31 January 2002 – 7 per cent;
- 1 February 2002 to date – 6 per cent.

Interest on a late payment of compensation

If an employer pays the full amount awarded by the tribunal within 14 days, no further interest will be payable: IT Regs, reg.8(2).

Under the Employment Tribunals (Interest) Order 1990, SI 1990/479 if all or part of the award is outstanding after 14 days, interest accrues on the sum outstanding from the day after the award was made to the date of payment. The rate of interest is specified in the Judgments Act 1838, s.17. The current rate is 6 per cent.

16.6   COSTS

It may be possible to recover some of the costs of the proceedings if the conduct of the other party gives rise to an entitlement to costs. A tribunal's power to order a party to meet in whole or in part costs incurred by the opposing party is set out in rule 14 of the Employment Tribunals (Constitution and Rules of Procedure) Regulations 2001, SI 2001/1171 (ET Regs). Where a party's conduct falls within one of the situations described below, the tribunal has a duty to consider making a costs order:

(a)   where a party has in bringing the proceedings, or a party or a party's representative has in conducting the proceedings acted vexatiously, disruptively or otherwise unreasonably;

(b)   where the bringing or conducting of the proceedings by a party has been misconceived. Under ET Regs, reg.2(2) misconceived includes having no reasonable prospects of success; or

(c)   where the proceedings have been postponed or adjourned on the application of a party. Costs may be awarded either for or against the party requesting the adjournment or postponement, depending on the circumstances giving rise to the request.

It is not necessary for a tribunal to have issued a costs warning to a party before making an order. A tribunal has the power to award from £500 to £10,000. If it is necessary for costs to be assessed by way of a detailed assessment this takes place in the county court in accordance with the Civil Procedure Rules 1998, SI 1998/3132 (L7).

Relevant factors

Circumstances that commonly give rise to an application for a costs order include:

(a)   the late withdrawal by a party;

(b)   where there has been an offer in settlement during the course of proceedings expressed to be without prejudice to costs (a Calderbank offer) and the claimant ultimately recovers less than was originally offered;

(c)   where a party has no reasonable prospects of success (which includes in respect of the defence).

The tribunal will consider a wide range of factors in reaching its decision to make an award of costs, including the extent of the evidence available to the parties and whether they were acting under legal advice. In particular, there is a new power contained in the Employment Act 2002, s.22(1), enabling the Secretary of State to make regulations authorising tribunals to have regard to a person's ability to pay when deciding whether or not to make an award of costs. At present, when deciding whether to make an award of costs, a tribunal should not take into account the ability of a party to pay: *Kovacs* v. *Queen Mary & Westfield College* [2002] IRLR 414, CA.

Section 22(1) also gives the Secretary of State the power to make regulations authorising tribunals to make a 'wasted costs' order against a party's representative because of the way the representative has conducted the proceedings (save in respect of non-profit making representatives such as trade unions, law centres, CABs, etc.). The circumstances in which an award will be made include:

(a) where the party's representative has in bringing or conducting the proceedings acted vexatiously, abusively or otherwise unreasonably; or
(b) the bringing or conducting of the proceedings by a party has been misconceived.

Costs in equal value cases

Note that the special rules for equal value cases set out in Schedule 1 as modified by Schedule 3 to the ET Regs detail specific situations in which a party may be liable for costs. Where a party has unreasonably delayed the preparation of the independent expert's report, a tribunal is empowered to make an award of costs in favour of the innocent party and/or an award in respect of the expert's fees: ET Regs, r.10A(14). But no such order can be made without giving the party an opportunity to make representations.

16.7 CONCILIATION AND SETTLEMENT

Agreeing a settlement may be advantageous to both parties. A settlement that is reached under the auspices of the Advisory, Conciliation and Arbitration Service (ACAS) or that fulfils the conditions regulating compromise agreements under the Employment Rights Act 1996 binds an employee so that she cannot subsequently present a complaint to a tribunal on the same subject matter or continue to pursue her claim if proceedings have already been commenced.

Advisory, Conciliation and Arbitration Service

Where an application has been presented to a tribunal under the EqPA 1970 a copy will be sent to an ACAS conciliation officer. ACAS has a duty to try to promote a settlement of the dispute if requested to do so by both parties to the dispute or where ACAS considers there is a reasonable prospect of achieving a settlement. ACAS also has the power to conciliate if asked to do so by either party in dispute even where no complaint has been lodged with a tribunal.

The role of the ACAS conciliator is to assist the parties to reach a voluntary resolution of the complaint without the need for a tribunal hearing. ACAS describes the service as impartial, voluntary, confidential, independent and free of charge.

Once a settlement has been reached, the terms are normally recorded on a COT3 form that is signed by both parties. The settlement will be binding on both parties and may be expressed to be in full and final settlement of all claims arising out of the claimant's employment. A claimant should be particularly careful about entering into an agreement expressed in these terms where employment is continuing.

Unlike in other employment disputes, the services of ACAS are rarely used in equal value cases. If negotiations take place, they generally do so between the parties without any outside involvement.

Compromise agreements

To be valid, a compromise agreement must comply with the Employment Rights Act 1996, s.203(1). In order to be binding the agreement must:

(a) be in writing;
(b) relate to a particular complaint;
(c) only be made where the claimant has received independent legal advice from a qualified lawyer or an independent legal adviser (including a trade union adviser) who is insured to give such advice as to the terms and effects of the agreement and its effect on the claimant's ability to pursue her rights before the tribunal;
(d) identify the adviser; and
(e) confirm that the conditions regulating compromise agreements have been complied with.

A failure to comply with any of these requirements may render the agreement void. As with agreements conciliated by ACAS, a claimant should be particularly careful about entering into an agreement expressed to be in full and final settlement of all claims arising out of her employment where employment is continuing.

Mediation may occasionally be an appropriate way of settling an equal pay case, for example, where the claimant wishes to continue in employment, but neither claimant nor employer can see how to arrive at a settlement acceptable to both sides.

However achieved, a settlement may include terms that would not have been awarded by the tribunal in the event of the claim being successful, for example, agreement to carry out an equal pay review or undertake a job evaluation exercise, or to provide specialist training to the claimant to facilitate promotion.

DIX A

Sections of the Equal Pay Act 1970 (incorporating amendments as at 31 August 2001)

1. Requirement of equal treatment for men and women in same employment

1(1)   If the terms of a contract under which a woman is employed at an establishment in Great Britain do not include (directly or by reference to a collective agreement or otherwise) an equality clause they shall be deemed to include one.

1(2)   An equality clause is a provision which relates to terms (whether concerned with pay or not) of a contract under which a woman is employed (the 'woman's contract'), and has the effect that –

1(2)(a)   where the woman is employed on like work with a man in the same employment –

1(2)(a)(i)   if (apart from the equality clause) any term of the woman's contract is or becomes less favourable to the woman than a term of a similar kind in the contract under which that man is employed, that term of the woman's contract shall be treated as so modified as not to be less favourable, and

1(2)(a)(ii)   if (apart from the equality clause) at any time the woman's contract does not include a term corresponding to a term benefiting that man included in the contract under which he is employed, the woman's contract shall be treated as including such a term;

1(2)(b)   where the woman is employed on work rated as equivalent with that of a man in the same employment –

1(2)(b)(i)   if (apart from the equality clause) any term of the woman's contract determined by the rating of the work is or becomes less favourable to the woman than a term of a similar kind in the contract under which that man is employed, that term of the woman's contract shall be treated as so modified as not to be less favourable, and

1(2)(b)(ii) if (apart from the equality clause) at any time the woman's contract does not include a term corresponding to a term benefiting that man included in the contract under which he is employed and determined by the rating of the work, the woman's contract shall be treated as including such a term;

1(2)(c) where a woman is employed on work which, not being work in relation to which paragraph (a) or (b) above applies, is, in terms of the demands made on her (for instance under such headings as effort, skill and decision), of equal value to that of a man in the same employment –

1(2)(c)(i) if (apart from the equality clause) any term of the woman's contract is or becomes less favourable to the woman than a term of a similar kind in the contract under which that man is employed, that term of the woman's contract shall be treated as so modified as not to be less favourable, and

1(2)(c)(ii) if (apart from the equality clause) at any time the woman's contract does not include a term corresponding to a term benefiting that man included in the contract under which he is employed, the woman's contract shall be treated as including such a term.

1(3) An equality clause shall not operate in relation to a variation between the woman's contract and the man's contract if the employer proves that the variation is genuinely due to a material factor which is not the difference of sex and that factor –

1(3)(a) in the case of an equality clause falling within subsection (2)(a) or (b) above, must be a material difference between the woman's case and the man's; and

1(3)(b) in the case of an equality clause falling within subsection (2)(c) above, may be such a material difference.

1(4) A woman is to be regarded as employed on like work with men if, but only if, her work and theirs is of the same or a broadly similar nature, and the differences (if any) between the things she does and the things they do are not of practical importance in relation to terms and conditions of employment; and accordingly in comparing her work with theirs regard shall be had to the frequency or otherwise with which any such differences occur in practice as well as to the nature and extent of the differences.

1(5) A woman is to be regarded as employed on work rated as equivalent with that of any men if, but only if, her job and their job have been given an equal value, in terms of the demand made on a worker under various headings (for instance effort, skill, decision), on a study undertaken with a view to evaluating in those terms the jobs to be done by all or any of the employees in an undertaking or group of undertakings, or would have been given an equal value but for the evaluation being made on a system setting different values for men and women on the same demand under any heading.

1(6)   Subject to the following subsections, for purposes of this section –

        1(6)(a)   'employed' means employed under a contract of service or of apprenticeship or a contract personally to execute any work or labour, and related expressions shall be construed accordingly;

        1(6)(b)   [*Repealed.*]

        1(6)(c)   two employers are to be treated as associated if one is a company of which the other (directly or indirectly) has control or if both are companies of which a third person (directly or indirectly) has control,

and men shall be treated as in the same employment with a woman if they are men employed by her employer or any associated employer at the same establishment or at establishments in Great Britain which include that one and at which common terms and conditions of employment are observed either generally or for employees of the relevant classes.

1(7) – 1(13) [...]

2.   Disputes as to, and enforcement of, requirement of equal treatment

2(1)   Any claim in respect of the contravention of a term modified or included by virtue of an equality clause, including a claim for arrears of remuneration or damages in respect of the contravention, may be presented by way of a complaint to an employment tribunal.

2(1A)   Where a dispute arises in relation to the effect of an equality clause the employer may apply to an employment tribunal for an order declaring the rights of the employer and the employee in relation to the matter in question.

2(2)   Where it appears to the Secretary of State that there may be a question whether the employer of any women is or has been contravening a term modified or included by virtue of their equality clauses, but that it is not reasonable to expect them to take steps to have the question determined, the question may be referred by him as respects all or any of them to an employment tribunal and shall be dealt with as if the reference were of a claim by the women or woman against the employer.

2(3)   Where it appears to the court in which any proceedings are pending that a claim or counter-claim in respect of the operation of an equality clause could more conveniently be disposed of separately by an employment tribunal, the court may direct that the claim or counter-claim shall be struck out; and (without prejudice to the foregoing) where in proceedings before any court a question arises as to the operation of an equality clause, the court may on the application of any party to the proceedings or otherwise refer that question, or direct it to be referred by a party to the proceedings, to an employment tribunal for determination by the tribunal, and may stay or sist the proceedings in the meantime.

2(4)   No claim in respect of the operation of an equality clause relating to a woman's employment shall be referred to an employment tribunal otherwise than by virtue of subsection (3) above, if she has not been employed in the employment within the six months preceding the date of the reference.

2(5)   A woman shall not be entitled, in proceedings brought in respect of a failure to comply with an equality clause (including proceedings before an employment tribunal), to be awarded any payment by way of arrears of remuneration or damages in respect of a time earlier than two years before the date on which the proceedings were instituted.

2(6)–(7) [*Repealed.*]

2A.   Procedure before tribunal in certain cases

2A(1)   Where on a compliant or reference made to an employment tribunal under section 2 above, a dispute arises as to whether any work is of equal value as mentioned in section 1(2)(c) above the tribunal may either –

2A(1)(a) proceed to determine that question; or

2A(1)(b) unless it is satisfied that there are no reasonable grounds for determining that the work is of equal value as so mentioned, require a member of the panel of independent experts to prepare a report with respect to that question;

and, if it requires the preparation of a report under paragraph (b) of this subsection, it shall not determine that question unless it has received the report.

2A(2)   Without prejudice to the generality of subsection (1) above there shall be taken, for the purpose of that subsection, to be no reasonable grounds for determining that the work of a woman is of equal value as mentioned in section 1(2)(c) above if –

2A(2)(a) that work and the work of the man in question have been given different values on a study such as is mentioned in section 1(5) above; and

2A(2)(b) there are no reasonable grounds for determining that the evaluation contained in the study was (within the meaning of subsection (3) below) made on a system which discriminates on grounds of sex.

2A(3)   An evaluation contained in a study such as is mentioned in section 1(5) above is made on a system which discriminates on grounds of sex where a difference, or coincidence, between values set by that system on different demands under the same or different headings is not justifiable irrespective of the sex of the person on whom those demands are made.

2A(4)   In paragraph (b) of subsection (1) above the reference to a member of the panel of independent experts is a reference to a person who is for the time being designated by the Advisory, Conciliation and Arbitration Service for the purposes of that paragraph as such a member, being neither a member of the Council of that Service nor one of its officers or servants.

3–4   Collective agreements and pay structures
[*Repealed.*]

5.   [...]

6.   Exclusion from ss.1 to 5 of pensions, etc.

6(1)   An equality clause shall not operate in relation to terms –

      6(1)(a)   affected by compliance with the laws regulating the employment of women, or

      6(1)(b)   affording special treatment to women in connection with pregnancy or childbirth.

6(1A)   [*Superseded by ss.(1B) and (1C).*]

6(1B)   An equality clause shall not operate in relation to terms relating to a person's membership of, or rights under, an occupational pension scheme, being terms in relation to which, by reason only of any provision made by or under sections 62 to 64 of the Pensions Act 1995 (equal treatment), an equal treatment rule would not operate if the terms were included in the scheme.

6(1C)   In subsection (1B), 'occupational pension scheme' has the same meaning as in the Pensions Schemes Act 1993 and 'equal treatment rule' has the meaning given by section 62 of the Pensions Act 1995.

6(2)   [*Superseded by ss.(1B) and (1C).*]

7A–11 [...]

Treaty of Rome – Article 141

[*Article 141 (ex Article 119)*]

1. Each Member State shall ensure that the principle of equal pay for male and female workers for equal work or work of equal value is applied.

2. For the purpose of this Article, 'pay' means the ordinary basic or minimum wage or salary and any other consideration, whether in cash or in kind, which the worker receives directly or indirectly, in respect of his employment, from his employer.

    Equal pay without discrimination based on sex means:

    (a) that pay for the same work at piece rates shall be calculated on the basis of the same unit of measurement;
    (b) that pay for work at time rates shall be the same as for the same job.

3. The Council, acting in accordance with the procedure referred to in Article 251, and after consulting the Economic and Social Committee, shall adopt measures to ensure the application of the principle of equal opportunities and equal treatment of men and women in matters of employment and occupation, including the principle of equal pay for equal work or work of equal value.

4. With a view to ensuring full equality in practice between men and women in working life, the principle of equal treatment shall not prevent any Member State from maintaining or adopting measures providing for specific advantages in order to make it easier for the under-represented sex to pursue a vocational activity or to prevent or compensate for disadvantages in professional careers.

APPENDIX C

Council Directive 75/117/EEC (10 February 1975)

ON THE APPROXIMATION OF THE LAWS OF THE MEMBER STATES RELATING TO THE APPLICATION OF THE PRINCIPLE OF EQUAL PAY FOR MEN AND WOMEN

The Council of the European Communities,

Having regard to the Treaty establishing the European Economic Community, and in particular Article 100 thereof;

Having regard to the proposal from the Commission;

Having regard to the Opinion of the European Parliament;

Having regard to the Opinion of the Economic and Social Committee;

Whereas implementation of the principle that men and women should receive equal pay contained in Article 119 of the Treaty is an integral part of the establishment and functioning of the common market;

Whereas it is primarily the responsibility of the Member States to ensure the application of this principle by means of appropriate laws, regulations and administrative provisions;

Whereas the Council resolution of 21 January 1974 concerning a social action programme, aimed at making it possible to harmonize living and working conditions while the improvement is being maintained and at achieving a balanced social and economic development of the Community, recognized that priority should be given to action taken on behalf of women as regards access to employment and vocational training and advancement, and as regards working conditions, including pay;

Whereas it is desirable to reinforce the basic laws by standards aimed at facilitating the practical application of the principle of equality in such a way that all employees in the Community can be protected in these matters;

Whereas differences continue to exist in the various Member States despite the efforts made to apply the resolution of the conference of the Member States of 30 December 1961 on equal pay for men and women and whereas, therefore, the national provisions should be approximated as regards application of the principle of equal pay

Has Adopted This Directive:

Article 1

The principle of equal pay for men and women outlined in Article 119 of the Treaty, hereinafter called 'principle of equal pay', means, for the same work or for work to which equal value is attributed, the elimination of all discrimination on grounds of sex with regard to all aspects and conditions of remuneration. In particular, where a job classification system is used for determining pay, it must be based on the same criteria for both men and women and so drawn up as to exclude any discrimination on grounds of sex.

Article 2

Member States shall introduce into their national legal systems such measures as are necessary to enable all employees who consider themselves wronged by failure to apply the principle of equal pay to pursue their claims by judicial process after possible recourse to other competent authorities.

Article 3

Member States shall abolish all discrimination between men and women arising from laws, regulations or administrative provisions which is contrary to the principle of equal pay.

Article 4

Member States shall take the necessary measures to ensure that provisions appearing in collective agreements, wage scales, wage agreements or individual contracts of employment which are contrary to the principle of equal pay shall be, or may be declared, null and void or may be amended.

Article 5

Member States shall take the necessary measures to protect employees against dismissal by the employer as a reaction to a complaint within the undertaking or to any legal proceedings aimed at enforcing compliance with the principle of equal pay.

Article 6

Member States shall, in accordance with their national circumstances and legal systems, take the measures necessary to ensure that the principle of equal pay is applied. They shall see that effective means are available to take care that this principle is observed.

Article 7

Member States shall take care that the provisions adopted pursuant to this Directive, together with the relevant provisions already in force, are brought to the attention of employees by all appropriate means, for example at their place of employment.

Article 8

1. Member States shall put into force the laws, regulations and administrative provisions necessary in order to comply with this Directive within one year of its notification and shall immediately inform the Commission thereof.
2. Member States shall communicate to the Commission the texts of the laws, regulations and administrative provisions which they adopt in the field covered by this Directive.

Article 9

Within two years of the expiry of the one-year period referred to in Article 8, Member States shall forward all necessary information to the Commission to enable it to draw up a report on the application of this Directive for submission to the Council.

Article 10

This Directive is addressed to the Member States.

Done at Brussels, 10 February 1975.
For the Council
The President
G. FITZGERALD

The EOC Equal Pay Review Model

The Equal Pay Review Model is reproduced with the kind permission of the Equal Opportunities Commission.

The equal pay review model recommended by the EOC is in five steps:

STEP 1: Deciding the scope of the review and identifying the data required
STEP 2: Identifying where men and women are doing equal work
STEP 3: Collecting and comparing pay data to identify any significant equal pay gaps
STEP 4: Establishing the causes of any significant pay gaps and assessing the justifications for these
STEP 5: Developing an Equal Pay Action Plan or reviewing and monitoring

In the following pages a brief description of each step (*what* you need to do) is given in the left hand column. The right hand column contains an explanation of *why* you need to do this, and some preliminary guidance on *how* to do it. Further details on how to carry out the various aspects of the review will be set out in supporting guidance notes. Together the model and guidance notes comprise the equal pay review kit.

STEP 1 Deciding the scope of the review and identifying the information required

What will be the scope of the review?

The equal pay review kit deals with the gap between men's pay and women's pay, but you may also want to look at ethnicity, disability and age. Before deciding to do so it can be helpful to consider the quality of the information available about the ethnicity, disability status and age of the workforce and whether this is good enough to enable these dimensions to be included in the review.

Scoping the review watch points

The only way in which you can be sure that black and ethnic minority women are receiving equal pay is to include both race and gender in the equal pay review.

Organisations that are obliged by the Race Relations (Amendment) Act 2000 to adopt a Race Equality Plan should ensure that the review deals with any gaps between men's and women's pay and between the pay of different ethnic groups. Organisations that use the Local

Government Equality Standard will find that the kit helps them work through the Standard.

In scoping the review it may be helpful to bear in mind the principle of transparency. Carrying out an equal pay review will help to ensure employees understand how their pay is made up.

You need to decide which employees are going to be included.

It is advisable to include all those employees who are in the same employment.

For practical reasons you may decide to carry out the review in stages, but you need to be aware that this increases the risk of an equal pay claim being made.

Scoping the review watch point
Deciding to exclude certain groups of employees will result in only a partial exercise and will increase the risk of an equal pay claim being taken.

Who should be involved?
● **The project team**

In larger organisations an equal pay review can be a substantial exercise. You may need to set up a project team. It is also advisable to agree on a timetable and set targets for progress.

An equal pay review requires different types of input from people with different perspectives. You will need knowledge and understanding of the pay and grading arrangements; of any job evaluation schemes; of the payroll and personnel systems and of how to get information from these. It is also useful to have some insight into how all of these have developed over time. Sensitivity to equality issues such as men and women being segregated into different types of work is also helpful.

● **The workforce**

You need to consider when you are going to involve trade unions or other employee representatives. Involving the workforce is important for several reasons:
● Employees and their representatives may be able to contribute valuable information, which managers could be unaware of, about the operation of the existing system and the likely effect of a new one.
● Time, trouble and expense can be saved, especially by reducing the risk of any disagreement at a later stage, particularly if the outcome of the review is likely to affect existing pay differentials.

214

- Employees will have more opportunity to understand the new system and the reasons for any changes. This will help to ensure that pay systems are transparent and easy to understand.

In organisations where an independent trade union is recognised, the employer is required to disclose to that union any information necessary for collective bargaining, and this is likely to include information about pay systems.

• **Experts**	You may also wish to consider whether to bring in expertise from outside of the organisation. The Advisory, Conciliation and Arbitration Service (ACAS), the employment relations experts, offer practical, independent and impartial help to help bring pay systems up to date.
What information will be needed?	Employers will need to collect and compare two broad types of information about each employee included in the review: • All the various elements of their pay. • The personal characteristics of each employee i.e. whether male or female; what qualifications they have; their grade or pay band, what hours they work and when they work these; their length of service and so on. The information required will vary depending upon the type of organisation and on the particular pay and grading system. **Information watch point** If you have difficulty in getting the necessary information together then this may be an indication that your pay systems do not meet the requirement for transparency.

STEP 2 Determining where men and women are doing equal work

You will need to carry out one or more of the following checks: *Like work; Work rated as equivalent; Work of equal value.*	These checks determine where men and women are doing equal work. *This is the foundation of an equal pay review.*

Step 2 Check 1: Like work	**Like work watch points**
Like work is where men and women are doing work which is the same or broadly similar.	

Men and women are likely to be doing like work where they have the same job title, or where, even if their job titles differ, they do the same, or broadly similar work.

Job titles can be misleading. You need to look at what the employees actually do. Minor differences can be ignored.

Step 2 Check 2: Work rated as equivalent	Work rated as equivalent watch points
Work rated as equivalent is where men and women have had their jobs rated as equivalent under an analytical job evaluation scheme.	Employers who use analytical job evaluation schemes need to check that their scheme has been designed and implemented in such a way that it does not discriminate on grounds of sex. Employers who use bought in job evaluation schemes should ask their supplier if the scheme meets this standard.
Men and women are likely to be doing work rated as equivalent where they have similar, but not necessarily the same, job evaluation scores and are in the same grade.	Look carefully at jobs just above and below grade boundaries as these could easily be regarded as rated as equivalent, even though they are in different grades.

Step 2 Check 3: Equal value	Equal value watch points
Work of *equal value* is work that is different but which is of equal value in terms of the demands of the job. 'Demands' mean the skills, knowledge mental and physical effort and responsibilities that the job requires.	The most reliable way of assessing whether jobs are of equal value is to use an analytical job evaluation scheme specifically designed and introduced to take account of equal value considerations and of the types of jobs being done by your workforce. Ideally the scheme should cover all employees.
	Employers who do not use analytical job evaluation need to find an alternative means of checking whether men and women are doing work of equal value. It is important to recognise that these alternative estimates of equal value are not as reliable as analytical job evaluation, and that the organisation is therefore still vulnerable to equal pay claims.

Which checks apply to your organisation?	Organisations with no job evaluation scheme should check:
	• Like work
	• Equal value:
	Organisations with one or more job evaluation schemes should check:
	• Whether the scheme has been designed with equal value in mind
	• Like work
	• Work rated as equivalent
	• Equal value.

Organisations with a single job evaluation scheme covering all employees should check:
- Whether the scheme has been designed with equal value in mind
- Work rated as equivalent
- Like work.

STEP 3 Collecting and comparing pay data to identify any significant equal pay gaps

Once you have determined where women and men are doing equal work, you need to collect and compare pay information to identify any significant gaps between men's pay and women's pay. This is done by:
1. Calculating average basic pay and total average earnings.
2. Comparing access to and amounts received of each element of pay.

Unless there is a genuine reason for the difference in pay, that has nothing to do with the sex of the jobholder, women and men doing equal work are entitled to equal pay.

1: Calculating and comparing average basic pay and average total earnings	Comparing pay watch points

To ensure comparisons are consistent, when calculating average basic pay and average total earnings for men and women separately, you should do so either on an hourly basis or on a full-time salary basis (grossing up, or down, for those who work fewer, or more, hours – excluding overtime – per week than the norm).

Averages are a useful step in identifying gaps between men's and women's pay, but averages can conceal important differences between individuals.

You should review the pay comparisons to establish any gender pay gaps, and decide if any pay gaps are significant and need further investigation.

As a general guide, any differences of 5% or more, or patterns of differences of 3% or more will require exploration and explanation.

If any of the checks reveal either:
- *Significant differences between* the basic pay or total earnings of men and women performing equal work (differences of 5% or more), or
- *Patterns of basic pay difference* e.g. women consistently earning less than men for equal work at most, or all, grades or levels in the organisation (differences of 3% or more) then further investigation is needed.

It is advisable to record all the significant or patterned pay differences that have been identified. Step 4 explores the reasons for those differences and whether they can be explained on grounds other than sex.

2: Comparing access to and amounts received of each element of pay for men and women doing equal work

For each element of pay received by men or women doing equal work employers should calculate:

1. The proportion of men and women who receive this element.
2. The average amount of each pay element received by men and women.

This analysis will show:

If men and women have differential access to the various pay elements

If the **Step 3** analysis has shown significant gaps between the pay of men and women doing equal work then it will be necessary to work through **Step 4**.

If the analysis does not show significant gaps, it is still good practice to examine the payment system in detail.

STEP 4 Establishing the causes of any significant pay gaps and assessing the justifications for them

1. Find out which aspects of the pay system are contributing to the gaps between men's and women's pay and why.
2. Find out if there is a genuine reason for the difference in pay that has nothing to do with the sex of the jobholder.

Once this has been done you will be able to decide whether a particular pay policy, practice or pay element is discriminatory and whether the resultant pay gaps need to be closed. The process will also help build an Equal Pay Action Plan.

What should be checked
All aspects of the pay system – policies, practices and pay elements.

These need to be checked from a variety of standpoints: design; implementation; impact. It is how pay policies and practices actually affect pay that matters – not the intention behind them.

Assessing the reasons
Once it has been established where gaps between men's and women's pay are occurring, you need to assess whether the reasons for them are satisfactory.

Assessing the reasons watch point
The question of what amounts to a satisfactory explanation of the pay gap is a complex area dependent on the detailed and individual circumstances of each organisation, as well as on equal pay case law. If there is any doubt, you should seek legal advice.

The next step
You can now decide whether:

- the pay policies and practices are operating free of sex bias
- the pay policies and practices are causing sex based pay inequalities and need changing
- there is a need to close any pay gaps.

STEP 5 Developing an Equal Pay Action Plan *or* Reviewing and Monitoring

Developing an Equal Pay Action Plan
The Plan should include arrangements to:

Provide equal pay.	*If there are gaps between men's and women's pay for which there is no genuine reason employers will need to provide equal pay for current and future employees*
Change the pay policies and practices that contribute to unequal pay.	There is no legal guidance on what amounts to a reasonable period of time within which to phase in equal pay, yet for practical reasons it may not be possible to introduce equal pay for equal work immediately. Employers need to be aware that in the interim they are vulnerable to equal pay claims. The action plan should make clear what timescale the organisation has in mind, and how it is going to compensate employees who may be entitled to equal pay. The organisation should stick to the timescale set out in the action plan. In working out the timing you will need to consider the impact on employee relations. You may need to manage factors such as costs and the possible dissatisfaction of employees who perceive a loss of status, or the erosion of differentials whilst equal pay is being provided.
Introduce an Equal Pay Policy.	It can be helpful to produce a policy that commits the organisation to providing equal pay with clear accountabilities, regular monitoring and adequate resources for Equal Pay Reviews.
Introduce ongoing monitoring of pay outcomes by gender.	There is a need to decide how you are going to involve employees in the ongoing equal pay review process. Pay systems need to be reviewed regularly, to check existing and, in particular, any proposed changes to pay systems *before* they are implemented. You may also wish to examine other employment practices identified during the review. These might include gender segregation by job type and seniority, approaches to training and development.

Reviewing and Monitoring
Carrying out 3 and 4, as set out above, will help ensure your pay system is, and remains, free from sex bias.

APPENDIX E

Useful addresses

Advisory, Conciliation and Arbitration Service (ACAS)
Brandon House
180 Borough High Street
London
SE1 1LW

Tel: 020 7210 3613
www.acas.org.uk

ACAS public enquiry points are listed in local phone books

Chartered Institute of Personnel and Development
CIPD House
35 Camp Road
London
SW19 4UX

Tel: 020 8971 9000
E-mail: cipd@cipd.co.uk
www.cipd.co.uk

Commission for Racial Equality
St Dunstan's House
201–211 Borough High Street
London
SE1 1GZ

Tel: 020 7939 0000
E-mail: info@cre.gov.uk
www.cre.gov.uk

Confederation of British Industry
Centrepoint
103 New Oxford Street
London
WC1A 1DU

Tel: 020 7379 7400
www.cbi.org.uk

Department for Trade and Industry
1 Victoria Street
London
SW1H 0ET

Tel: 020 7215 5000
www.dti.gov.uk

Disability Alliance
Universal House
88–94 Wentworth Street
London
E1 7SA

Tel: 020 7247 8776
E-mail: office-da@dial.pipex.com
www.disabilityalliance.org

Disability Rights Commission
2nd floor Arndale House
The Arndale Centre
Manchester M4 3AQ

Tel: 08457 622633
Textphone: 08457 622644
E-mail: enquiry@drc-gb.org
www.drc-gb.org

Discrimination Law Association
PO Box 36054
London
SW16 1WF

Tel: 020 7450 3663
E-mail: info@discrimination-
law.org.uk
www.discrimination-law.org.uk

Employment Tribunals Service
19–20 Woburn Place
London
WC1H 0LU

Tel: 020 7273 8512
Enquiry helpline: 0845 795 9775
*Regional ETS offices can be found in
the telephone directory
Application forms can be downloaded
from* www.employmenttribunals.gov.uk

Equal Opportunities Commission
Arndale House
Arndale Centre
Manchester
M4 3EQ

Telephone helpline: 0845 601 5901
E-mail: info@eoc.org.uk
www.eoc.org.uk

Incomes Data Services Ltd
77 Bastwick Street
London
EC1V 3TT

Tel: 020 7250 3434
E-mail: ids@incomesdata.co.uk
www.incomesdata.co.uk

Industrial Relations Service
Eclipse Group Ltd
18–20 Highbury Place
London
N5 1QP

Tel: 020 7354 5858
www.irseclipse.co.uk

Investors in People UK
7–10 Chandos Street
London
W1G 9DQ

Tel: 020 7467 1900
E-mail: information@iipuk.co.uk
www.investorsinpeople.co.uk

Labour Research Department
78 Blackfriars Road
London
SE1 8HF

Tel: 020 7928 3649
E-mail: info@lrd.org.uk
www.lrd.org.uk

Law Centres Federation
Duchess House
18–19 Warren Street
London
W1T 5DB

Tel: 020 7387 8570
E-mail: info@lawcentres.org.uk
www.lawcentres.org.uk

Law Society
113 Chancery Lane
London
WC2A 1PL

Tel: 020 7242 1222
www.lawsociety.org.uk

Trades Union Congress
Congress House
Great Russell Street
London
WC1B 3LS

Tel: 020 7636 4030
Rights helpline: 0870 600 4882
E-mail: info@tuc.org.uk
www.tuc.org.uk

Women and Equality Unit
DTI
10 Great George Street
London
SW1 3AE

Tel: 020 7273 8880
www.womenandequalityunit.gov.uk

Work Foundation
Peter Runge House
3 Carlton House Terrace
London
SW1Y 5DG

Tel: 020 7479 2000
www.theworkfoundation.co.uk

APPENDIX F

Useful Resources

Publications

Armstrong, M. and Baron, A., *The Job Evaluation Handbook*, IPD, 1995

Armstrong, M. and Murlis, H., *Reward Management: A Handbook of Remuneration Strategy and Practice*, 4th edition, Kogan Page in association with Hay Management, 1998

Chartered Institute of Personnel and Development, *Equal Pay Guide*, IPD, 2001

IDS, 'The equal pay challenge', *IDS report 856,* May 2002

IDS, 'The gender pay gap', *IDS report 838*, August 2001

IDS, *Problems of Equal Pay*, IDS, 2001

IRS, 'The new reward agenda', *IRS Management Review* 22, July 2001

TMS Equality and Diversity Consultants, *PayCheck: Auditing Pay Systems for Sex Bias, a Practical Guide*, TMS Equality and Diversity Consultants, 1998

Internet resources

www.kingsmillreview.gov.uk
The Kingsmill Review of Women's Employment and Pay, Women and Equality Unit

www.eoc.org.uk
Useful downloads including: Equal Pay Review Kit 2002, Practical Tips on Equal Pay 2002, *Just Pay* (Equal Pay Task Group, 2001), *The Gender Pay Gap: A Research Review* 2001

Courses

TUC Equal Pay Training Course *Close the Gap*, 2001

Index